Walt Disney World Dining Guide 2020

Andrea McGann Keech

Theme Park Press
The Happiest Books on Earth
www.ThemeParkPress.com

Although every precaution has been taken to verify the accuracy of the information contained herein, no responsibility is assumed for any errors or omissions, and no liability is assumed for damages that may result from the use of this information.

Theme Park Press is not associated with the Walt Disney Company.

The views expressed in this book are those of the author and do not necessarily reflect the views of Theme Park Press.

Theme Park Press publishes its books in a variety of print and electronic formats. Some content that appears in one format may not appear in another.

Editor: Bob McLain
Layout: Artisanal Text

ISBN 978-1-68390-216-4
Printed in the United States of America

Theme Park Press | www.ThemeParkPress.com
Address queries to bob@themeparkpress.com

For
Katherine, Drew, Will, and Lucy

Contents

Introduction

To those who haven't yet read the Walt Disney World Dining Guide, *welcome. To those who've read an earlier edition, welcome back. In this latest addition, any new full service, casual, or quick service restaurants, as well as new carts and kiosks, will be reviewed; price and menu changes will be updated; and alterations to the Disney Dining Plan will be noted (for example, this is the first year alcoholic beverages and specialty drinks have been included as part of the dining plans). Pull up a seat, dig in, and don't forget to bring your appetite...*

Why in the Walt Disney World would you need to spend any of your valuable leisure time preparing six months (or more!) ahead of your vacation for exactly where, when, and what you plan to eat on your much-anticipated visit to the Most Magical Place on Earth? The fact that you'd even ask means you desperately need help—and fast! Without doing your homework many months before the first day of your trip, you'll miss out on some of the best experiences that can make a vacation at Walt Disney World so memorable.

If you have never visited Walt Disney World, or if it's been awhile since your last visit, you'll be surprised to discover how important it is these days to make Advance Dining Reservations. That's right, the phrase is capitalized and even has its own acronym: ADRs. Securing ADRs has become almost an art form. People across the country, and indeed the world, have their eager fingers poised above their keyboards ready to hit the "submit" button at the stroke of 6:00 a.m. Orlando time on the first day they are allowed to book those critical reservations. Don't be left out! This guide will ensure that *you* have the best chance to dine when and wherever you want.

Sampling entirely new flavors and cuisines, participating in one-of-a-kind themed dining experiences, and enjoying some of those unique Disney snacks only available at Walt Disney

World will add significantly to how much you and your family enjoy yourselves. It's surprising how much a character meal, dinner show, or a memorable dinner will add to the pleasure and enjoyment of your vacation.

Some dining guides jump back and forth like a pinball between the four theme parks (Magic Kingdom, Epcot, Animal Kingdom, Disney's Hollywood Studios), the Disney resort hotels, the BoardWalk, and Disney Springs. You're left spinning and overwhelmed. These guides are often divided into sections like "best kids meals" or "great snacks." You need to flip back and forth a thousand times comparing offerings among the various venues. As far as I'm concerned, that's not the easiest nor most useful way to get a good sense of where you'll want to eat on any given day of your vacation. As a Disneyland Tour Guide and VIP Hostess throughout college, I learned the importance of organizing any visit one area at a time. You'll be in *one* place at a time, not twenty, and that's exactly how this simple, informative guide is organized.

I won't often tell you what I like to eat because maybe, *probably*, you and I differ on our preferences. When a member of the wait staff says, "I'd suggest the scallops tonight—they're excellent," that doesn't help me because scallops are never my choice. Likewise, when a reviewer advises trying the fresh sashimi (raw fish) at Morimoto Asia, count me out. Honestly, I don't care what someone *else* likes; I want to know what a particular place has on its menu that *I* might like. A guide that gives you just one or two ideas from a menu, usually what the writer ate, simply isn't enough information to inform my decision.

While I won't list entire menus (you can see those online easily), I *will* tell you the types of foods, preparation styles, and special experiences you can expect at any given place. Food critics who detail just one meal at a restaurant miss the other fifty things I'd be willing to try before I'd ever choose the charred octopus or goat cheese ravioli. Therefore, I'll give you a very good idea of what you'll find at the many Walt Disney World places to dine. You decide which places have menu selections that are likely to please most members of *your* party.

Not only that, I've found some guides to be so extensive that unless you're *only* going to Disney World to eat, and you're not, they're too unwieldy to navigate and contain more information than you could use in two lifetimes. There's a limit to how many hundreds of pages you can wade through and how many hundreds of hours you're prepared to spend searching for relevant bits and pieces of information online. How much time are you willing to devote to sifting through the scattered entries of individual restaurants and evaluating the confusing array of websites?

It would take months to uncover for yourself all of the information I've put right here at your fingertips. I'd like to make your search for great food *easy*. It simply shouldn't require you to spend days, weeks, or months figuring out your vacation meals. Those of us who live in the real world are too busy with work and family to devote that kind of time to meal planning!

Whether your trip is an adults-only romantic getaway or a kid-friendly romp with an emphasis on the toddlers, tadpoles, tweens, or teens in the family, you *will* need to do some background research and make those key dining reservations six months in advance. Yes, you heard that last bit right: *six months* ahead of time. A full 180 days (and make that 180+10—see chapter 18, Getting Hard-to-Get ADRs) before your vacation starts, you need to have your fingers poised above the screen on your iPhone, iPad, or computer. Be ready to go the second you are allowed to do so because every other savvy guest you'll be rubbing shoulders with during your upcoming vacation will be doing the exact same thing *and* doing it at the exact same moment.

Planning matters (more than you ever thought possible) when it comes to dining at Disney World, but it *can* be done with a reasonable effort. That's where this guide will help you. It will group the many choices into manageable sections you can skim quickly. It will highlight the best places to dine that will satisfy all members of your party.

You are on vacation to enjoy the attractions and the ambience, true, but without some sustenance, it's going to be a very rocky—and hungry—road, my friends. If you've ever been desperate to find a decent place to eat while starving children, famished teenagers, or peckish grandparents are complaining loudly in your ear and your own stomach is rumbling uncomfortably, you'll appreciate how much knowing *where* you are going, *when* you need to arrive there, and *what* you can expect to eat at those three meals a day can make the difference between unfortunate family feuds and happy tummies that will allow your group to continue on its merry way.

Look around at those families who *didn't* plan ahead like you to appreciate the value of having a workable meal-time itinerary. Those families aren't difficult to find. They're the ones with the tears, howls, and loud harrumphs. Luckily, that won't be you and your family.

Whether it's sitting down to Mickey waffles, bacon, and scrambled eggs with the kids at the Polynesian's 'Ohana character breakfast, complete with a rollicking meet-and-greet session with Lilo, Stitch, Mickey, and Pluto, or toasting your sweetheart with vintage champagne at the Grand Floridian's ultra-luxurious Victoria & Albert's while savoring the 10-course chef's tasting menu, careful planning ahead for your dining pleasure is absolutely key. Without some preparation, memorable meals at the best places in the resort with those you love best simply won't happen.

Don't get me wrong. There will be plenty of time during your visit for spontaneity, for grabbing something delicious on-the-go and savoring it as you head for the next attraction or shop for souvenirs. As long as you think ahead and make a plan, however, you won't miss out on some of the best dining options at Walt Disney World.

As Napoleon Bonaparte observed, "An army marches on its stomach." Well, so does a vacationer, and you have a lot of marching ahead of you. Now, dig in and let's get started!

Digesting the Disney Dining Plan

Originally, the Disney Dining Plan was offered as part of a holiday package at Walt Disney World. It proved to be so popular that it became a regular offering. At first, guests were absolutely delighted with the great value they received for the affordable price. Over the years, that value has eroded. Costs for the dining plans have risen to the point where you should be very sure you will take full advantage of your plan in order for it to make fiscal sense.

Before beginning an in-depth consideration of the merits of the Disney Dining Plan, there is something you ought to keep in mind: Disney is a for-profit corporation and doesn't make business decisions that will cause it to lose money. The Disney Dining Plan has its pluses and minuses, but it is not intended to lose money for the organization. That said, in the first part of this guide we will consider the merits of the various Disney dining plans based on your specific needs and preferences.

Some visitors purchase these dining plans year after and year and are satisfied they are getting good value and convenience for the cost, while others count up hundreds of dollars they've wasted by purchasing dining plans for the family and say "never again." You'll need to carefully evaluate the type of consumer you are in order to determine whether or not the Disney Dining Plan makes good sense for you.

If you can say "yes" to the following, you might be a candidate for one of the Disney Dining Plans:

- I like the convenience of prepaying for things, even if it actually costs me a bit more in the long run.

- My vacations are run on a set schedule. I book FastPasses as soon as possible and don't mind deciding on what to eat, when, and where 180+ days ahead of time.
- I like taking a break from all the action in the parks and sitting down to enjoy a leisurely, full-service meal with the family at least once each day.
- I'm something of a gourmet who enjoys trying lots of unique, exotic dishes and cuisines I wouldn't normally get to taste at home.
- I'll often choose the most expensive item on the menu and rarely skip dessert.
- I'm fine with learning and adhering to a complex set of rules, restrictions, and new vocabulary (table-service credits, ADRs, snack credits, etc.).

Still interested in learning more? Then let's proceed. These dining plans are only available to those guests staying on the grounds of Walt Disney World in one of the many Disney hotels and who book a Magic Your Way vacation package. I highly recommend that you do stay in Disney accommodations. That decision will save you a tremendous amount of time, and there are rooms available at many price levels, from deluxe suites to budget-friendly rooms to campsites. The expansive resort encompasses over 27,000 acres, and staying off-property adds significantly to your travel times to and from the resort every day.

If you decide to stay in two different Disney hotels during your stay at Walt Disney World, and this can be a great way to experience the best of what each hotel has to offer, then you must purchase two separate Disney dining plans. This would be a chance for you to try one of the dining plans for part of your vacation while you stay at one hotel and then eat on your own without a dining plan during the second part of the vacation at a second hotel. See which way you like best.

Just as with booking restaurant reservations, you should book your rooms six months in advance of your arrival. Some luxury villas are part of the Disney Vacation Club and have extremely limited availability. First come, first served means you need to be first!

Staying at a Disney hotel grants you these important free benefits:

- Travel to and from the Orlando Airport by a convenient motor coach called Disney's Magical Express.

- Skip the baggage claim after your flight. Luggage from your airline will be delivered directly to your resort hotel room.

- Get the incredibly helpful MagicBand for every member of your party. More on this handy little gadget later. You'll wonder how you ever got along without it.

- Schedule FastPasses to popular attractions 60 days ahead of time (that's 30 days before people who aren't staying on Disney property can schedule them).

- Transportation by motor coach, monorail, or boat will be available at no charge between parks, to all resort hotels, and to Disney Springs and Disney's BoardWalk, including free parking if you've rented a car.

- In-room free WiFi, which is also available in some restaurants and other public resort areas.

- Extra Magic Hours, hours either before opening or after closing times at the theme parks when only guests staying at Disney accommodations (and a few select others) will be able to come earlier or stay later than other guests in order to enjoy less crowded conditions. Not every park will have Extra Magic Hours every day.

As someone who has vacationed at Walt Disney World many times and stayed both on site and off, I strongly recommend staying in one of the Disney resort hotels. Not only will you receive the benefits listed above, you'll be right in the middle of the action at all times. Lengthy drives through former orange groves and Florida backcountry now bristling with tourist traps, hotels, and apartment complexes at the beginning and end of each day take up far too much of your limited time and energy, and can even kill the Disney vibe you woke up with. Unless you're staying with family or friends in the area, it makes a lot more sense to stay in one of the resort hotels.

Magic Your Way

There are currently some 25 Disney resort hotels, 4 major theme parks, Disney Springs, and the BoardWalk—that adds up to 415+ places to eat including about 90 full service restaurants, 30 of them inside the theme parks! When you book a Magic Your Way vacation package, you can reserve either a room and ticket package or a room, ticket, and dining package. That's when you need to decide if one of the Disney dining plans is right for your needs. You buy it at the same time as you book the Magic Your Way reservations. It might be possible for you to add the Disney Dining Plan at a later time to your pre-existing reservation, and sometimes you may be allowed to do so, but you would need to call and confirm whether that change is possible. Don't count on it. Any addition of the Disney Dining Plan must usually be done a minimum of 48 hours in advance of your arrival. Cases are considered on an individual basis. The time you book your reservation is also the time to make the staff aware of any special dietary restrictions you may have or to make any special food requests known.

Either download the My Disney Experience app free from the App Store online or call (407) 939-5277 to make your hotel reservation. You'll find a large amount of useful information at disneyworld.disney.go.com, too. Disney resort hotels fall into five different price brackets: deluxe villas, deluxe resorts, moderate resorts, value resorts, and campsites. Check out Disney's online descriptions for a complete comparison of what each one has to offer. Prices for lodgings change frequently and without notice and will also vary by season.

Walt Disney World Resort Hotels

All of the hotels on Disney property offer dining options, some of them superlative like Victoria and Albert's, which has earned the rare Five Diamond AAA Award yearly since 2000, and others merely so-so. They are classified as fine/signature dining (the best of the best), unique/themed dining (part of what makes each venue special, including character buffets), casual (table service but relatively inexpensive), food courts (for your grab-and-go needs), lounges (some of them sumptuous, others casual), dining events (check with your hotel when you book your rooms for any special offerings available during your stay), and finally in-room dining (expensive room service, but sometimes it's just exactly what you need).

Deluxe Villas

Expect to pay a premium for this level of luxury. Prices start high and rise swiftly and quite steeply from there, depending on the time of year, size of suite, view, and particular amenities available. You can easily spend more than $2,000 a night or more for a deluxe villa and that doesn't include taxes and fees. Each of the deluxe hotels is special in a different way, and you may already have an idea of where you'd like to stay, but all villas generally offer spacious suites with well-stocked kitchens, laundry facilities in the unit, and multi-bedroom options for larger groups.

Deluxe Resorts

The deluxe hotels are located in the same hotel complexes as the villas, but prices for rooms are somewhat more affordable, depending on the season, although they are definitely priced at the high end of the room cost spectrum. You won't have some of the amenities available at the villas (don't look for complete kitchens or laundry facilities), but the rooms will still be quite nicely appointed with many extras. All of the deluxe hotels offer in-room dining (room service) you can purchase using meal credits from the dining plan.

Moderate Resorts

Rooms in the moderate hotels are an excellent family value. You'll still get the special Disney touches you want, along with plenty of fun, creative themes carried throughout the hotel.

Value Resorts

Families on a tighter budget will appreciate the ability to stay on Disney property without breaking the bank on lodgings. Value rooms are priced at wallet-friendly levels, with discounts depending on the season. Don't look for pricey extras, but you can count on the fact that anything on the resort grounds will be impeccably maintained and clean. Staff will, with very rare exceptions, be helpful and friendly. Best of all, you'll still qualify for the many free benefits listed at the beginning of this chapter. While you can't order in-room delivery service at a value resort, you can still have a pizza meal with beverage and dessert brought right to your room by using two dining plan credits.

Campsites

Prices for a campsite are the lowest in the resort per night, and Disney's 700-acre Fort Wilderness Resort offers one more level of flexibility for families looking to save money while still enjoying a wonderful Walt Disney World vacation. Campsites accommodate up to 10 people, are pet-friendly, and provide water, electrical hook-ups, and cable TV. If you decide to rent a cabin, you can even advance-order an entire pantry full of grocery items that will be waiting for you when you arrive. There are two pools with waterslides, movies under the stars, an exercise trail, horseback and pony rides, bike and watercraft rentals, Chip and Dale's Campfire and Sing-a-long, a white sand beach, and a playground for the children.

What the Disney Dining Plan Does and Doesn't Do for You

You no longer have to worry about budgeting for meals while you're on vacation. It has all been taken care of beforehand. The plan is essentially a voucher system. You pay for what you will eat in advance and receive credits to spend every day at any of the participating places to eat in the parks—and there are many of them!

Credits are the currency you have available to spend on your meals and snacks every day. Your dining plan credits will be encoded onto your MagicBand and scanned when you wish to purchase food. All credits are not created equal. Some credits buy a table-service meal, some a quick-service meal, and some a snack. Some meals are considered two-credit meals (those at very elegant dining venues, at Cinderella's Royal Table with the princesses in the castle, and at the two dinner shows). Sometimes, you might decide to select items from a separate *prix fixe* (fixed price) menu offered at certain locations. That choice requires paying an extra charge in addition to redeeming meal credits. In recent years, many new dining establishments have joined the Disney Dining Plan including the popular Le Cellier Steakhouse in the Canada Pavilion of Epcot. The list of restaurants is fluid. It takes some time to work out contracts at the start of every new year, especially with non-Disney-owned dining establishments. Some may elect to join, while others may decide to drop out.

Sounds difficult keeping up with all those credits you use every day, doesn't it? Don't worry, because at the end of every meal, your remaining credit total will be clearly listed on your check. You can also ask your Disney hotel's concierge to find out where you stand regarding credits spent and credits still available. You are free to spend any unused credits up until 11:59 p.m. on the day you check out of your resort hotel.

There is no charge on the Disney dining plans for children under three. Little ones are free to eat off your plate (literally), or you may want to order something else just for them, but for that you'll need to pay out-of-pocket. At a buffet where you will be serving yourself, you are allowed to get your children under three their own plate plus a beverage at no cost; this isn't true at quick-service or table-service meals. Children are only considered "children" up to age nine, and children on the dining plan are only able to order from the children's menu where one is available, not the adult menu. After they turn ten, they're considered adults and must pay as such and are supposed to order from the adult menu. What happens if your ten or eleven or twelve year old doesn't like anything on the adult menu? Special requests like that are often accommodated by giving the older child a larger portion of something from the children's menu. The over-nine-year-old, in that case, would still be charged a full credit for the meal.

Some things not included with any of the Disney dining plans:

- Multi-serving items intended for more than one person
- Things that come in a souvenir container
- Food and beverages sold at a recreation rental counter
- Things that are considered merchandise (bottle toppers, bottle straps, etc.)

- Certain dining events with special menus available at table-service restaurants

Bear in mind that gratuities are not included (with a very few exceptions—Cinderella's Royal Table, for example), so you are expected to tip the wait staff in addition to what you have already paid for the Dining Plan. With groups of six or more, 18% will be added automatically to your bill, even if one of those six guests is a six-month-old baby who hasn't eaten a thing.

Alcoholic beverages have recently been added to the dining plans, along with non-alcoholic specialty beverages. This certainly adds additional value to choosing one of the plans.

One thing you won't be charged separately for is tax: it's included with the cost of the dining plan, and so you don't have to pay it again as part of your bill.

Tables in Wonderland

About one hundred restaurants at Walt Disney World participate in Tables in Wonderland, a program offering discounted meals for frequent guests. Members save 20% on their dining bills for up to ten people in the party. An 18% gratuity is added to your bill. One big benefit is that the membership comes with free valet parking at resort hotels provided you only come to dine. There are blocked-out dates throughout the year.

Tables in Wonderland is limited to Florida residents, DVC members, and Walt Disney World annual passholders. You must be over 21 to purchase a membership. If you're one of those, and the program seems like a good value because you dine at Disney World often, you can buy an annual membership at the Guest Relations office in any of the four theme parks or at Disney Springs. Once you have your membership card, make sure you don't lose it: there is a $50 replacement charge.

Annual membership costs $175 for Florida residents, and $150 for DVC members and annual passholders. For an additional $50, you can buy a second membership for your spouse or partner.

Some Specialized Dining Plan Vocabulary

Advance Dining Reservations (ADRs) are highly recommended, and in many (if not most cases) they are essential. The best restaurants, character meals, and dinner shows fill up very quickly. If you have a particular favorite or prefer to eat at a certain time, make all of your reservations six months ahead of time. (And before you do that, read "Tremendous Trip #1" in chapter 18 before you book. It will help you maximize your chances to score hard-to-get reservations.) There's really no way around this. Luckily, reservations are fairly straightforward to make online, especially if the restaurant isn't one of the most popular venues or you're going to be there in the off season. Just use the My Disney Experience App, find the restaurant where you want to eat, and click on Find a Table. You'll be asked for the number in your party and can then enter a specific time when you'd like to eat. If that exact time isn't available, times as close as possible to your first choice will be offered. If you find an acceptable time, click to accept that reservation. The My Disney Experience App is intuitive and pretty easy to navigate. Before your trip, you should become familiar with how it works.

It's also possible to call (407) WDW-DINE or (407) 939-3463 and make your meal reservation that way. Speaking directly, politely, and persuasively to a cast member might (in some cases) get you a coveted reservation opening before it's even offered online. Another useful tactic is to check with popular restaurants either online or by phone a day or two before you hope to dine there in an attempt to scoop up a recent cancellation. There are no guarantees that this will work, however.

Once you make an ADR at a particular restaurant for a particular time, you're locked in. This can be a doubled-edged sword. Don't feel like a big, sit-down meal tonight? Sudden change in your plans? If you don't cancel your reservation at least 24 hours in advance, you will be charged $10 per person in your party. That can add up pretty quickly, especially if you're the type who changes plans on the spur of the moment.

Casual Meals are those where you are seated by a host/hostess and receive full service by a member of the wait staff. The food will be decent and sometimes better than that, and it will not be too expensive. In a lot of ways, your experience at a casual place would be similar to what is available back home in many medium-sized communities. Examples include Tony's Town Square on Main Street, U.S.A., Big River Grill and Brewing Works on the BoardWalk, and the ABC Commissary at Hollywood Studios. Quality varies, but there are plenty of good choices.

Unique/themed meals accept reservations. Your dining experience at one of these places is definitely going to be special because of the unusual décor and the types of foods available. This is an experience you would be unlikely to have anywhere else but at a Disney property. Examples are Tusker House at the Animal Kingdom, the Sci-Fi Dine-in Theater Restaurant at Hollywood Studios, 'Ohana at the Polynesian Village Resort, and Raglan Road Irish Pub and Restaurant at Disney Springs. At least one (if not several) of your meals while on vacation at Walt Disney World should be at a unique/themed restaurant.

Character Meals are often the highlight of any Disney vacation, especially (but by no means only) for younger children. Dining with their animated friends come to life is magical. Although that word is often overused in official Disney literature, in this case it's entirely accurate. This is the perfect chance for your family members to interact individually with costumed characters, all of whom will spend time at your table posing for photos and signing autographs. Don't be shy about attending a character meal if you are a solo adult, a couple, or all-adult group, either. They are great for guests of any age. There are many of these delightful meals available, each of which will be explained in detail later. Currently, the most difficult character meal reservation to obtain is Cinderella's Royal Table in Cinderella Castle at the Magic Kingdom. It's also one of the most expensive, costing two meal credits, but gratuity is currently included. In effect, you pay for two meals and eat one. Still, for little ones and their families, the experience is priceless.

Credits, sometimes called *Entitlements,* are the basic currency of your Disney Dining Plan. You spend them throughout your visit until they run out. It doesn't matter if you spend them all in the first few days or spread them out over many days. Your MagicBand keeps track of your totals, so monitor it as you go. More elaborate meals at fine/signature restaurants, the two dinner shows, and any of the many character meals are more costly than quick-service options.

All credits are not created equal. There are table-service credits, quick-service credits, and snack credits. A credit has no set value. You could spend table-service credits at inexpensive counter-service restaurants and order the least expensive items on the menu. Alternatively, you could spend your credits at a Disney fine/signature restaurant and order the most expensive items on the menu. In the first case, you won't get a good return on your financial investment. In the second case, you will.

Dinner Shows can be a delightful and highly enjoyable part of your vacation. The meals are served family-style and feature live entertainment. Any dinner show requires advance reservations. Gratuities are included, so there is no need to tip additionally unless you've ordered alcoholic beverages or other non-included items. The Western-style Hoop-Dee-Doo Musical Revue is located at Disney's Fort Wilderness Resort & Campground. The Spirit of Aloha Dinner Show including hula and fire dancing takes place at Disney's Polynesian Village Resort. The cost for a dinner show is two credits. Disney quick-service dining plan credits cannot be used for a dinner show.

Disney's Healthy Living Initiative is intended to make eating healthier possible, even on a Walt Disney World vacation. On menus, you can identify healthier options for kids' meals by the Disney Check icon. Lower in sodium, sugar, and trans fats, these choices provide a way to help parents encourage healthy eating habits. Instead of the usual fish and chips, pizza, mac and cheese, or fried chicken tenders sided with fries, you'll find options like grilled fish or chicken skewers, steamed veggies, and fruit, for example. Small servings of low-fat milk are also available. Thanks to Disney's Healthy Living Initiative, if adults don't want a dessert at a table-service meal, they are allowed to substitute a side salad, fruit plate, or cup of soup instead. Nice!

If you want even more flexibility, you can visit the front desk of your Walt Disney World Resort Hotel to have your single quick-service meal credit converted to three snack credits that can then be used separately wherever you want.

Disney Signature Restaurants are those special dining experiences that keep you coming back year after year to Walt Disney World. Because their cost is significantly higher than average, you'll need to use two full-service meal credits to eat here. Dress is "resort casual" in most of these lovely establishments. Make every attempt to book reservations six months in advance, as soon as you possible can. Restaurants participating as a part of the Disney Dining Plan vary from year to year. Some are added, while others opt out. Check early in the year of your visit to see a listing of those restaurants that will accept your credits. At press time, participating signature restaurants include:

- BOATHOUSE at Disney Springs
- California Grill at the Contemporary Resort
- Cinderella's Royal Table in Fantasyland at Magic Kingdom
- Cítricos at Grand Floridian Hotel & Spa
- Flying Fish at Disney's BoardWalk
- Hollywood Brown Derby at Hollywood Studios
- Jaleo by José Andrés at Disney Springs, West Side
- Jiko—The Cooking Place at Animal Kingdom Lodge
- Le Cellier Steakhouse at the Canada Pavilion at Epcot
- Monsieur Paul at the France Pavilion at Epcot
- Morimoto Asia at Disney Springs, The Landing
- Narcoossee's at Grand Floridian Hotel & Spa
- Paddlefish at Disney Springs, The Landing
- STK Orlando at Disney Springs, The Landing
- Tiffins on Discovery Island at Animal Kingdom
- Victoria & Albert's Grand Floridian Resort & Spa (not on Dining Plans)

- Wanyama Safari at Animal Kingdom Lodge
- Wolfgang Puck Bar & Grill, Disney Springs, Town Center
- Yachtsman Steakhouse at Disney's Yacht Club

Victoria & Albert's at the Grand Floridian is not on the list of Disney Dining Plan participating restaurants. While it's definitely a fine/signature restaurant, you'll need to pay out-of-pocket to eat there. The dress code is more "dressy," too. Men are expected to wear a sport coat and slacks, and ladies should wear dresses, suits, pants suits, blouse and skirt, or something other than what they've been wearing traipsing around Epcot or the Animal Kingdom all day. If men don't have a sport coat, they can usually be accommodated by the staff since they have a number of these in assorted sizes on hand. Many of those who dine there do so on expense accounts.

Fine/Signature Dining meals are la crème de la crème. They will set you back *two* table service meal credits on the Disney Dining Plan. You are highly advised to book your table six months in advance at the very hottest of the hot tickets such as Flying Fish on the BoardWalk or Le Cellier Steakhouse in the Canada Pavilion at Epcot. At some, like Victoria & Albert's at the Grand Floridian, you'll find out how it feels to be treated like a royal. The service, food, wine, and entire experience is superb, but the V & A is not on any Disney Dining Plan. You'll pay out-of-pocket there, and it's very expensive. A meal at Morimoto Asia, that's Iron Chef Morimoto, at Disney Springs; Cinderella's Royal Table in Fantasyland at the Magic Kingdom; Tiffins at the Animal Kingdom; the Hollywood Brown Derby at Hollywood Studios or at any of the other fine/signature restaurants is a pleasure you won't soon forget. It's the kind of experience that makes a celebration special and can make your vacation at Walt Disney World even more memorable.

Mobile Orders can be a huge time-saver, and lots of locations (currently 23) offer this service. Order your meal on your mobile device app and it will be ready at a special pick-up window when you arrive at the restaurant. Guests with any of the three Disney Dining Plans can redeem meals and snacks in Mobile Order now. Tap "order food" under "my plans" in the app.

Out-of-pocket food or drink expenses are those not covered by your Disney Dining Plan. Gratuities not already covered by the plan, beverages served in souvenir cups, any food purchases made for children under three, food purchases made after all of your meal credits have been spent, or meals at restaurants not participating in the dining plan must all be paid for by you at the time you make the purchase, either by using cash, a credit card, or a Disney gift card.

Pizza Delivery Service is available for guests on the Disney Dining Plan staying at any of Disney's All-Star Resorts, Caribbean Beach, Pop Century, and at both Port Orleans Riverside and French Quarter. Two adult meal credits will provide a pizza entrée, two beverages (alcoholic or not), and two desserts. Gratuity is included, so no tipping is expected.

Private in-room dining is pricey. You'll be charged two credits for just one meal. Gratuity is included. At lunch and dinner, you'll get an entrée, dessert, and your choice of beverage, alcoholic or non-alcoholic.

Quick Service or *Counter Service* meals are those where you pay for the food before you eat. (An exception to this rule is El Mercado de Coronado at the Coronado Springs Hotel where you pay as you leave.) The Quick-Service meal consists of an entrée or a combo meal, and a beverage. It's like a fast-food restaurant in most ways. You order your food at a counter or select it in a cafeteria, pay for it, take it on a tray to a table, and clear the table when you are finished. No reservations are possible at this type of restaurant. Quality varies widely. Some quick-serve places feature a standard burger, fries, and nuggets ho-hum experience, but others offer eye-opening, tastebud-tickling, pleasant surprises, as you'll soon see. Wait until you try Cookes of Dublin at Disney Springs, Sommerfest at the Germany Pavilion at Epcot, or those luscious lobster rolls at Columbia Harbour House at the Magic Kingdom!

Refillable Resort Mugs, also called *Rapid-Fill* mugs, are provided for each member of your party over three years of age if you are on any of the Disney dining plans. The colorful mugs are insulated but not microwaveable and not dishwasher safe. Each holds about 16 fluid ounces. (Guests who are not on the meal plans can purchase the mugs; in that case, the cost is a flat $19.99 for the length of your stay, no matter how long or short your stay is.) Coffee, tea, hot chocolate, and Coke products—even Hi-C and Powerade at certain refill stations but not milk or fruit juice—are the beverages intended for use in these mugs. Water is always free. You can't fill the mugs inside the theme parks, but they are good for use at any Disney resort hotel, regardless of the one where you happen to be staying.

What if you're switching from coffee in the morning to a Coke following an afternoon swim? Look for the mug wash stations located where you refill your mug. Each mug has an RFID bar code that will deactivate it after your stay at a Disney Resort is over. Don't put it through the dishwasher at your deluxe villa if you have one, however—that will render the chip useless!

Snacks are extremely varied and can be identified, for purposes of the Disney Dining Plan, by their small, purple-and-white checkerboard icon. Muffins, individual pieces of fruit, bagels, bottles of water, ice cream treats, an individual box of popcorn, a side-dish in a quick-service restaurant such as a cup of soup, a 20 ounce carbonated beverage, a 12 ounce cup of coffee or tea...the list is practically endless. Lots of emphasis on healthier eating habits means you can now count carrot sticks, apple slices, corn on the cob, a baked potato, or hummus with pita bread as a snack, too.

Table Service or *Full Service* meals means you are seated by a host/hostess and have at least some portion of your meal brought to your table by a server. A buffet meal is still considered a table-service meal since your server brings your drinks and the table is cleared after you leave. In most cases, you'll want to reserve a table well in advance to avoid disappointment. Prime times go very quickly, as do the very popular character meals. Some table-service restaurants are located at the various resort hotels, while others are found in the theme parks and at Disney Springs. Character meals are always table-service meals, as are casual, unique/themed, and fine/signature meals.

A Few Key Restrictions

All guests staying in a room or suite must be on the same dining plan. You can't have the children on the quick-service plan while you and your spouse purchase the regular plan and Grandpa and Grandma choose the deluxe plan. That simply won't fly. Everyone must be on the same plan or everyone must be on no plan at all, if that's what you ultimately decide. Not only must you all be on the same plan, you must all purchase the plan for exactly the same number of nights that you will be staying in the resort hotel. It's an all-or-nothing proposition. You can't decide to forgo the dining plan for the first and last nights of your stay, for example, or extend the dining plan for days on either end of your visit when you aren't staying at a Disney hotel. You can't try it for a few days and then decide to drop it—unless you are splitting your stay between two Disney hotels, that is. In that case, you might decide to try the plan while staying at one hotel and try paying for meals and snacks out-of-pocket at the other to see which way you prefer.

Disney no longer allows guests to "double book" dinner reservations. For example, your party can't book both Cinderella's Royal Table and Be Our Guest for lunch at noon on June 8. What you can do, however, is book your reservations two hours apart. That, the system will allow. In this way, you may book Cinderella at 11:30 and Be Our Guest at 1:30 if you want the ability to make up your mind the day before. Don't forget, however, that you'll be charged a $10 per person fee if you forget to cancel a reservation less than 24 hours ahead of time!

As if this wasn't complicated enough already, there are three possible dining plans from which to choose. Prices change frequently and without notice. You should confirm the latest prices online before your trip.

Three Disney Dining Plans

For the purpose of calculating dining plan costs, Disney decrees that children become "adults" at the age of ten. A child must be between 3–9 years old to qualify for the lower "child" rate.

Quick Service Dining Plan

- Two quick service meals for each day of your stay: an entrée or a combo meal (such as a hamburger and fries, fish and chips, etc.) if available, and a non-alcoholic beverage or an alcoholic beverage where offered for guests over 21 (includes beer, wine, or a mixed drink)
- Two snacks per day
- One refillable resort mug for each guest over 3 years old
- Cost per day: adult $52.50, child $23.78

Regular Dining Plan

- One quick service meal for each day of your stay: an entrée or a combo meal if available, and a non alcoholic beverage or an alcoholic beverage for guests over 21
- One table service meal per day: an entrée, a dessert, and a non-alcoholic beverage or an alcoholic beverage for guests over 21, or one full buffet or family style meal plus beverages
- Two snacks per day
- One refillable resort mug for each guest over 3 years old
- Cost per day: adult $75.49, child $27.98

Deluxe Dining Plan

- Three complete meals for each day of your stay in any combination your choose. Meals include one appetizer, one entrée, one dessert, and and one non-alcoholic beverage or one alcoholic beverage for guests over 21. You may opt for three full service, sit-down meals every single day if you'd like, or you may choose any combination of full service and quick service meals, including full buffet meals.
- Two snacks per day
- One refillable resort mug
- Cost per day: adult $116.25, child $43.49

If you need information and can't wait, call 407 WDW DINE (407 939-3463). You may also ask your question by email sent to guest.mail@wdw.disneyonline.com.

The Free Disney Dining Plan

Yes, you heard right! On selected dates, Walt Disney World will offer the regular dining plan for "free" to its guests who stay at the Disney resort hotels and purchase Park Hopper admission tickets. (You could pay to upgrade the plan to deluxe if you're so inclined.) There's one caveat, though, and it's a big one. If you sign up for the free dining plan, you are not eligible to qualify for any discounted promotions for your room or on the price for admission tickets to the park. If you aren't already getting any discount on your room or tickets, then it's a great deal, of course. Most people, however, find that the discounts they can qualify for on accommodations and park admission tickets will offset any savings the free Disney Dining Plan would provide. If your party is relatively small and you like to stay at the deluxe hotels, it's doubtful you'd save money with this offer. It might make sense for a large group staying at a value hotel, though.

So, there you have it—the basics of the Disney Dining Plans. Let me assure you that it not only sounds complicated, it *is* complicated. My best advice? Those of you who are intrigued by the plan and think that the ease of pre-paying for meals is attractive ought to give it a try. You might want to start with the regular plan. You'll get to sample the snacks, grab one quick service meal, and have one nice, sit-down, table service meal every day. By the end of your visit, you should have a good idea of whether or not the dining plan made sense for your family.

If you're anything like most guests, you'll be spending plenty of cash eating at Walt Disney World no matter how you do it. Comestibles are costly, in most cases considerably more costly than the very same things would be off-site. Many guests are shocked by this fact, so prepare yourself for it ahead of time. Expect to pay a hefty premium, as much as a third more, for the considerable convenience of dining while you're on Disney property. Some meals are well worth it, others not nearly so much. We'll get to all of that in the chapters to come.

For now, take a little time to review the pluses and minuses of participating in a Disney Dining Plan; talk it over with the other members in your group. You have just two ways to go. Either take a leap of faith and try out one of the dining plans that best suits your needs and your budget or see how much you spend eating on your vacation without the dining plan and calculate whether it could have actually saved you any money or not—and that requires a lot of keeping track of every food purchase.

As noted at the beginning of this chapter, there are those who swear by the merits of the Disney Dining Plan and couldn't imagine a Walt Disney World vacation without it, just as there are others who've tried it once and say every bit as adamantly *never* again. The choice is all yours. No matter which way you select, it's hard to go too far wrong while dining at Walt Disney World.

About the Dining Reviews

In the following chapters, I indicate the cost of eating at each Disney quick-service or table-service restaurant with a range of prices:

* *   \$14.99 and lower
* **   \$15-\$34.99
* ***   \$35-\$59.99
* ****   \$60 and higher

Depending on how finicky you are, you can enjoy a good meal at the low end of the range or splurge on the high. Of course, Disney frequently changes its prices—usually upwards—so if cost is a crucial factor in your decision to eat at a specific restaurant, check the menu beforehand. For up-to-the-minute, guaranteed accurate information, you should check only the menus on the official Walt Disney World website. Use the menus cribbed on Disney fan sites with caution.

Unless otherwise indicated, the cost range is per adult. If the restaurant offers a Tables in Wonderland discount, you'll see the designation "TiW" after the cost range.

The credit "cost" for each meal is designated with "S" (Snack), "Q" (Quick Service), or "T" (Table Service), depending upon what kind of Disney Dining Plan (DDP) credit it requires.

Reservations are *always* recommended at table-service restaurants. At the more popular ones, like Cinderella's Royal Table, 'Ohana, and Chef Mickey's, reservations might as well be *required*, as they're snapped up quickly. (At some venues, like Disney's dinner shows, reservations really *are* required.)

During less busy seasons, you might get lucky as a walk-up and score a table. It never hurts to try. But if you know your dining plans in advance, avoid possible disappointment and book a reservation.

The dining reviews are ordered by DDP credit type—snack, quick service, table service—and then alphabetically within each of those categories. Usually, there are snack items available at locations designated as accepting quick-service credits, so when you see a venue designated as "quick service", assume that you can use snack credits there, too, for some items. In contrast, table-service locations rarely if ever have snack items available. Food kiosks and stores that sell food items, whether eligible for the dining plan or not, are organized at the start of each section. A few venues are not on the dining plan; their reviews are placed wherever it makes sense to put them.

It's like reading a manufacturer's warranty, isn't it? I don't know about you, but I've built up an appetite...

The Magic Kingdom, Part One

Main Street, USA, Adventureland, Frontierland

If you're anything like most guests, this is the one theme park you'll definitely want to visit during your Walt Disney World vacation. Whether you are the youngest child or the most senior member of the group, you will find the Magic Kingdom is the place where dreams really do come true.

This Disney theme park, the first one to open on October 1, 1971, is well-organized and loaded with places where you can grab something tasty on the go, sit down for a quick bite for lunch, or enjoy a leisurely dinner after a big day of fun. First, we will consider where to find what you'd like to eat on Main Street, U.S.A., followed by Adventureland, Frontier-land, Liberty Square, Fantasyland, and Tomorrowland. That way, you can easily turn to the section in this guide where you happen to be at any given time and check out the food and beverage offerings you'll find there. You can also take a "let your fingers do the walking" tour through the pages of this book and consider each theme park well before you arrive to determine when and where you'd like to make those key dining reservations. We'll tour clockwise through the park.

Walt Disney World now makes every effort to accommodate special dietary needs and food allergies. Kosher, low fat, low sodium, sugar free, gluten free, peanut/tree nut safe, lactose intolerant, vegan, vegetarian, and other special diet menus are currently available, but be sure to ask (preferably in advance of your arrival) and then confirm again with your server. Several of these choices are noted on the menus. Times have changed since the park opened in 1971, and healthy alternatives now play a major role in dining options.

Main Street, U.S.A.

Walt Disney intended Main Street to represent a typical, small American town at the turn of the last century from 1900 to about 1910. It's based on a combination of three towns: Marceline, Missouri, where Walt spent a happy part of his growing-up years; the Henry Ford Museum and Greenfield Village, also called the Edison Institute, in Dearborn, Michigan; and Ft. Collins, Colorado, where Harper Goff, principal designer of the original Main Street in Disneyland, grew up. It will also look familiar if you've seen *Lady and the Tramp,* since Main Street is an echo of Lady's hometown, too. At Walt Disney World, however, the area was changed to represent not just Midwestern America but other areas of the country as well, including New England. In fact, if you look closely, you'll see that each of the buildings in the middle of Main Street, the area known as the Four Corners, is done in a different architectural style. You might not notice it, but Main Street is paved with resilient asphalt to make walking less fatiguing for tired feet.

Walt Disney said: "For those of us who remember the carefree time it re-creates, Main Street will bring back happy memories. For younger visitors, it is an adventure in turning back the calendar to the days of their grandfather's youth."

Main Street, U.S.A. Kiosks, Wagons, and Carts

- Stop by the Main Street **Ice Cold Refreshment Stand** near the central hub on your way to the castle for fresh fruit, cold drinks, and various snacks.

- There are also **Popcorn Carts** located on Main Street and throughout the park. The smell is practically irresistible—you can always share a warm box of popcorn as you stroll down the street. More than five million boxes are sold every year. You will also find refillable souvenir buckets if you just can't get enough. Try not to spill! Popcorn is the bane of those busy sweepers.

- There is an **Ice Cream Cart** and an **Ice Cream Stand** on Main Street, the cart in front of the Town Square Theatre and the stand to the left of the central hub as you face the castle. Both are well-supplied with Mickey ice cream bars, Mickey ice cream sandwiches, frozen bananas, and frozen fruit bars. The stand on your way to Adventureland also has Mickey pretzels, churros, cotton candy, and both have Coke products.

- To the right of the central hub, you'll find a **Popcorn and Ice Cream** cart on your way to Tomorrowland. Check out the big souvenir buckets for popcorn.

Note: Exact locations may vary. You can count on finding bottles of Dasani water being sold at just about any kiosk, wagon, cart, or counter. A bottle of Dasani water costs one snack credit if you're on the Disney Dining Plan.

Taste of Magic Kingdom Park VIP Tour

DDP: No / Cost: $$$$
Type: Varies; Snack

This is a new experience, one guaranteed to interest park veterans and newcomers alike. If you want to see what's behind the counter and taste some of the most renowned foods the Magic Kingdom has to offer, this $99 plus tax VIP tasting tour might be the perfect way to start off your resort vacation. A knowledgeable Disney Tour Guide conducts a small group of guests through three hours of food-related fun. You'll meet the creative minds behind the Disney meals and snacks and get the chance to try lots of different flavors, both sweet and savory. You'll even get to taste an item in development that isn't available on any menu yet. As of now, tours are scheduled on Monday, Tuesday, Friday, Saturday, and Sunday. You must be at least 16 to participate. Check-in is at Tony's Town Square Restaurant on Main Street. Theme park admission is required to participate and is not included in the price. Special dietary restrictions can't be accommodated on tour. You can book online or call (407) WDW-DINE.

Casey's Corner

DDP: One credit (Q) / Cost: $
Type: American; Quick Service; Mobile Orders; Lunch, Dinner

Inspired by the all-American pastime, the famous 1888 poem by Ernest Thayer, and the Disney cartoon from 1946, this spot has a "Casey at the Bat" ballpark theme. Craving a foot-long chili-cheese dog? How about some of those addictive corn dog nuggets? Bacon macaroni and cheese on your dog? Plant-based loaded-slaw dog? The hot dogs are all beef, and there are usually a few limited-time, seasonal offerings, currently corned beef hash. You'll find hot dogs and more at Casey's Corner, a red, white, and blue quick-service restaurant on the left side of Main Street facing the castle and adjacent to the hub. Listen to the pianist tickle the ivories playing old-time tunes and relax with a selection of hot dogs, fries, brownies, cotton candy, Cracker Jack, and everything else kids (or adults!) might desire. No Disney check meals here. No carrot sticks or yogurt substitutions, but you can get apple slices instead of fries. Casey's is all things indulgent when you feel like swinging for the bleachers with a calorie splurge that might hit a home run.

The Crystal Palace

DDP: One credit (T) / Cost: $$$ (TiW)
Type: American; Character Buffet/Family Style; Breakfast, Lunch, Dinner

Past Casey's heading toward Adventureland is one of the prettiest dining spots in the Magic Kingdom. One of the most delightful aspects of dining here is being joined table-side by friends from the Hundred Acre Wood: Winnie the Pooh, Tigger, Piglet, and Eeyore.

Having a meal at the Crystal Palace is like dining in a Victorian glass conservatory. Ceilings soar, white walls are covered with decorative architectural embellishments, and lush greenery adds to the period authenticity. Meals are served buffet style. Breakfast offers made-to-order omelettes, bacon and eggs, potatoes, Mickey waffles, cereals, fresh fruit, breads and pastries, and just about any breakfast item you can imagine. Lunch and dinner include salads, soups and breads, carved meats, fish, chicken, pasta, peel-and-eat shrimp, and house-made sweets and ice cream. You won't leave this "palace" hungry.

Main Street Bakery

DDP: One credit (Q) / Cost: $
Type: American; Quick Service; Snacks

If you're missing your Starbucks favorites, be it frappuccino, espresso, latte, smoothie, iced coffee, or hot chocolate, don't worry—you'll find them all here. The bakery is on the right side of the street just past the Four Corners. Add delicious Disney baked goods or pastries from La Boulangerie for a snack or quick breakfast. What you *won't* find here nowadays are the ever-popular giant, gooey cinnamon rolls. Look for them instead at Gaston's Tavern in Fantasyland.

Main Street Confectionery

On the right corner as you're facing the castle and just across Town Square, you'll find this sweet shop filled with character-themed treats. Employees are able to make creative suggestions, and the results are delightful. Try Mickey-shaped Rice Krispie treats with ears dipped in chocolate or a caramel chocolate-covered apple that looks like Mickey's famous red shorts. Everything to satisfy your sweet cravings is on colorful display here. Watch the action in the back of the store as cast members make cotton candy, English toffee, peanut brittle, fudge, and gigantic caramel apples—they can slice to make them easier to share.

Plaza Ice Cream Parlor

DDP: No / Cost: $
Type: American; Quick Service; Snacks

At the end of Main Street on the right, you'll find this turn-of-the-twentieth-century gem. Hand-scooped ice cream treats abound at this quaint, old-fashioned shop. You can get scoops, sugar-free sorbet, or a decadent waffle-bowl ice cream sundae. Fat-free treats are available, too. Try a Main Street Split, a Minnie Sundae, or an Apple Blossom Sundae—warm apple pie with caramel sauce, whipped cream, and two scoops of ice cream. Bring your appetite! Flavors are currently vanilla, strawberry, cookies 'n cream, tofutti and rice dream, chocolate, mint chocolate chip, fat-free vanilla chocolate swirl, and no-sugar raspberry sorbet.

The Plaza Restaurant

DDP: One credit (T) / Cost: $$ (TiW)
Type: American; Casual; Breakfast, Lunch, Dinner

Just past the ice cream parlor on your right at the end of Main Street and facing Cinderella Castle, you'll find this quintessentially American restaurant that offers something sure to please most members of your party. Walls of mirrors, wrought-iron chairs, and a 1900s ambience make the Plaza a welcome respite where you can regroup while enjoying a hearty breakfast (not always offered). Fill up on the classic all-American platter, Mickey waffles, omelettes, steak and eggs, ham and eggs Benedict, and more. Appetizers like wedge salad, loaded fries, or seasonal soups get your meal started at lunch or dinner. Entrées remind you of home cooking: meatloaf, chicken, cheese steak, tuna, or fried green tomato sandwiches; brisket, vegetable, or Angus burgers, a lobster Cobb salad, and chicken with strawberries salad. Any room left for dessert? Try one of the many fountain specialties including milk shakes, ice cream sundaes, seasonal specialty cakes, sometimes a slice of caramel apple pie à la mode, and seasonal butterscotch bread pudding with vanilla ice cream. Prices are the same at lunch and dinner.

Tony's Town Square Restaurant

DDP: One credit (T) / Cost: $$ (TiW)
Type: American/Italian; Casual; Lunch, Dinner

This pretty little Italian-American restaurant is filled with light from its many windows and has lacy, wrought-iron chairs and pots of hanging ferns. Dine on the outdoor terrace and you'll look right onto Main Street, so there's always plenty to watch as you wait for your meal. If it looks familiar, that's because it's based on Tony's trattoria from *Lady and the Tramp,* the one where the canine sweethearts shared a plate of spaghetti—and a kiss.

You'll find traditional Italian appetizers like meats and cheeses, pasta fagioli soup, fried mozzarella with creamy tomato sauce, and calamari. Entrées such as chicken

Parmigiana, rigatoni, spaghetti, shrimp scampi, gnocchi, pizza, and American favorites like fish or steak. Tony's features Italian specialty desserts such as tiramisù, gelato, cannoli, and occasionally (if you're lucky) a chocolate-hazelnut budino that's pretty spectacular. There's a nice Italian wine selection from Umbria, Veneto, and Tuscany as well as Birra Moretti Lager. Prices at lunch and dinner are the same.

Tony's has a **Disney Festival of Fantasy** dining option. For $54 for adults and $19 for kids ages 3-9, you can eat here and receive a voucher for admittance to a VIP reserved viewing area to watch the parade later.

Adventureland

Leaving Main Street behind, you'll cross a short bridge and see in front of you the impressive entrance to Adventureland. You'll find yourself surrounded by luxuriant jungle foliage and a wild, exciting, tropical atmosphere. The area is further divided into an Arabian Village section and a Caribbean Plaza. You'll note plenty of Polynesian influences in the carved Tikis, masks, and decorative wooden poles. When he opened Disneyland in 1955, Walt Disney's concept of Adventureland was influenced by the 1951 Bogart/Hepburn film, *The African Queen*.

Walt said: "To create a land that would make this dream reality, we pictured ourselves far from civilization, in the remote jungles of Asia and Africa."

Adventureland Kiosks, Wagons and Carts

- Miles from the usual park fare, there's a **Spring Rolls** (usually veggie or pork and currently a house-made Philly cheesesteak spring roll) wagon. Sometimes there are cheeseburger spring rolls, corn dog nuggets, and chocolate chip cookies.

- Another treat during busy seasons is the Adventureland **Nut Cart** near the Jungle Cruise where you'll find glazed almonds, ice-cream, and frozen treats.

- The Adventureland **Popcorn and Ice Cream Cart** offers a welcome snack for busy guests on the go. Check for the purple-and-white checkerboard snack icon if you're on the Disney Dining Plan. It also offers frozen bananas and cotton candy.

Aloha Isle

DDP: One credit (S) / Cost: $
Type: American; Quick Service, Mobile Orders; Snacks

If you've never tried the immensely popular pineapple Dole whip cup or float, here's your chance. Look for it behind the Enchanted Tiki Room. This unique, addictive snack is relatively low in fat and calories, gluten-free, vegan, and non-dairy. This is true even if you get the pineapple/vanilla swirl version. Indulge in this refreshing and delicious snack without guilt! Fresh pineapple spears and pineapple juice are also served here. A recent addition is one of Walt Disney's all-time favorite desserts, pineapple upside down cake, only now it comes topped with Dole whip, vanilla Dole whip, or Swirl. Walt's old-fashioned favorite has been updated!

Jungle Navigation Co. Ltd. Skipper Canteen

DDP: One credit (T) / Cost: $$ (TiW)
Type: African/Asian/Latin; Casual; Lunch, Dinner

The Skipper Canteen is one of the first buildings you'll see on your right as you enter Adventureland. It boasts three differently themed dining rooms: the Falls Family Parlor, the S.E.A. Room, and the largest of the three, the Mess Hall. The Skipper Canteen attempts to capture all the rollicking, wild fun of the Jungle Cruise attraction. It succeeds!

You'll see that influence in the menu titles: Falls Family Falafel, Lost and Found seasonal soup, and Orinoco Ida's Cachapas (corn pancakes). It provides adventurous new African, Asian, and Latin flavors as well as several unique entrées, even for those "well-seasoned" guests who've visited the Magic Kingdom many times. If some of those in your group prefer a slightly tamer dining experience, don't worry. There are plenty of American-style choices on the menu, too. Pork, steak, curried vegetable stew, whole fried fish, lamb chops, and "a lot at steak" salad (very tasty with chimichurri vinaigrette).

Desserts like Quick Sand! (jasmine rice pudding, mango sauce, hibiscus meringue, lemon curd, and pineapple) or

Kangaloosh! (African-inspired chocolate cake with caramelized bananas, caramel-cashew ice cream, topped with coffee dust) are just two of the sure-to-please sweets at this walk-on-the-wild-side Magic Kingdom culinary experience. Kids have plenty to pick from on their create-your-own entrée menu. Kids desserts have fun, creative presentations sure to impress young explorers like red candy lava swirls erupting from an ice cream sundae. Dining here is a welcome change from the usual park fare, and the restaurant itself is a delightful experience in every way. It's a wonderful addition to Adventureland.

Sunshine Tree Terrace

DDP: No / Cost: $
Type: American; Quick Service; Snacks

Just over the bridge on your way into Adventureland, you'll find the towering Swiss Family Robinson Treehouse, and with it, the Sunshine Tree Terrace. Citrus swirl, a delicious orange cream float (yes, please), soft serve vanilla ice cream, a refreshing raspberry-lemonade slushy, and lots of kinds of cool drinks will be a welcome break on a warm, steamy, Florida day.

Tortuga Tavern

DDP: One credit (Q) / Cost: $
Type: American; Quick service; Lunch, Dinner

Count yourself lucky if Tortuga Tavern is open when you happen to visit Adventureland because it's often closed. The tavern is usually only open during times when the Magic Kingdom is exceptionally busy. It's a great spot for delicious jerk-smoked brisket sandwich served with pineapple-coconut slaw and house-made chili-lime chips. Try a unique dish called ropa vieja, Caribbean-style slow-cooked shredded beef served over white rice. Grab a plain turkey leg or order an all-beef hot dog you can top with either jerk-smoked brisket or ropa vieja. For a different kind of snack, how about black bean salsa with plantain chips? The rum cake will have you saying "yo-ho-ho," and you'll soon be ready to take a voyage on the Pirates of the Caribbean attraction, which is located just across the walkway from Tortuga Tavern.

Frontierland

Continue through Adventureland and you'll find yourself in the rootin,' tootin' old West back when living on the frontier meant wide-open spaces and facing down danger on all sides. When Frontierland opened in Disneyland in 1955, Walt Disney explained it this way: "It is here that we experience the story of our country's past. The color, romance, and drama of frontier America as it developed from wilderness trails to roads, riverboats, railroads and civilization. A tribute to the faith, courage and ingenuity of our hearty pioneers who blazed the trails and made this progress possible."

Tom Sawyer and Huck Finn grew up in Hannibal, Missouri, while Walt and his brother Roy explored the rural environs of Marceline, Missouri, but kids from everywhere will appreciate the good times to be had in Frontierland. Modern sensibilities are perhaps somewhat less likely to be fascinated with this historical period as people were sixty-plus years ago, but you'll find a few satisfying dining opportunities when your party is ready to take a break from the attractions, both wild and tame.

Frontierland Kiosks, Wagons, and Carts

- Winding your way through Frontierland, you'll find snack carts chock-full of appealing items. **Churros** are long, thin donuts, Mexican style and dusted with cinnamon and sugar. The churro cart also sells **Mickey Pretzels**.

- **Turkey Legs** are offered by a cart seasonally but only during very busy times.

- **Popcorn and Ice Cream** can be found at yet another. They also sometimes carry cotton candy and cinnamon-glazed almonds. The carts make it easy for your group to catch up with some calories as you mosey through Frontierland.

The Diamond Horseshoe

DDP: One credit (T) / Cost: $$-$$$
Type: American; Casual; Lunch, Dinner

You'll find the Horseshoe next door to the Liberty Tree Tavern. It's the first restaurant on the border between Frontierland

and Liberty Square. Like several other dining venues in this area, Diamond Horseshoe will only be open during very busy times of the year, like the Thanksgiving and Christmas holidays, and some weekends. There's a player piano on the stage that doesn't—play, that is. Nothing currently is being featured on the picturesque stage, but perhaps there may be entertainment by the time you arrive. Guests are certainly clamoring for some. Most recently, the menu has been an all-you-care-to-enjoy meal with salad and cornbread, pulled pork, ham, beef, turkey, sausage, "cowboy" beans, baked mac and cheese, smoked stuffed peppers, and corn on the cob. There have recently been sandwiches and veggie entrées added to the menu. Grilled chicken sandwich, roasted beet salad, cowboy macaroni, a mixed green salad, and a smoked beef brisket sandwich gives you more to choose from than previously, but nothing on the menu is very exciting. Gone are those yummy "campfire" brownies for dessert, brownies with toasted marshmallow cream on top, but you'll still find layered cherry cheesecake, banana pudding, and a rich, buttermilk chocolate cake. Lunch and dinner are priced the same.

Golden Oak Outpost

DDP: One credit (Q) / Cost: $
Type: American; Quick Service; Lunch, Dinner

Near Splash Mountain, this cozy Western counter is open only during busy seasons and some weekends. Fare is very basic: chicken nuggets, chili queso (cheese) fries, waffle fries, jalapeño poppers, fried spicy cauliflower with creamy ranch, warm chocolate chip cookies, a dulce de leche milkshake, a rocky road milkshake, fountain beverages, and frozen lemonade.

Pecos Bill Tall Tale Inn and Café

DDP: One credit (Q) / Cost: $
Type: Southwestern/Mexican; Quick Service, Mobile Orders; Lunch, Dinner

Feel free to rustle up some rib-stickin' grub with a decidedly Southwestern influence in this casual dining establishment, famous for its huge help yourself toppings bar. Burgers, fajitas, taco salads, burritos, and loaded nachos are the main courses.

There are Disney check meals for kids with Smucker's Uncrustables or a veggie rice bowl, as well as standard kids meals with mini-corn dogs, pork carnitas, a chicken rice bowl, and mac and cheese. Lots of beverage choices are on hand. Desserts include mini-churros and Greek yogurt. Find seating indoors or out.

Prairie Outpost & Supply

This sweet shop is worth a visit, but it might take some hunting to find (it's next to Pecos Bill). It's well stocked with chocolate-dipped pretzels, lollipops of many kinds, a colorful spectrum of jelly bellies, hand-made chocolate candies, and attractive Disney-style sweets available in pretty souvenir containers to take to teachers, family, or friends back home.

Westward Ho Refreshments

DDP: No / Cost: $
Type: American; Quick Service; Snacks

Across from Pecos Bill on your way to Big Thunder Mountain Railroad, you will find this simple kiosk that resembles a rustic cabin. When it's open, only during busy seasons, corn dogs are often on the menu. Currently the little stand is offering bacon and egg breakfast sandwiches on a multigrain croissant. Hot and cold beverages, fountain drinks, chips, muffins, and chocolate chip cookies are usually available.

You're certainly going to do more than eat and drink while you're visiting Walt Disney World, and getting through even half of the Magic Kingdom in a day will leave your schedule jam-packed. If you're planning to see it all in a single day, a definite possibility if you budget your time carefully, turn the page and you'll find dining and snacking choices to enjoy while your party heads for the second half of the park. If you're splitting your Magic Kingdom visit over two days (or more), get a good rest tonight and you'll be ready for a hearty breakfast in the morning. Hope you made that reservation six months ago for the charming Be Our Guest restaurant in Fantasyland!

The Magic Kingdom, Part Two

Liberty Square, Fantasyland, Tomorrowland

Liberty Square

Way back in the early 1950s when Disneyland was still just a dream, Walt hoped to include a nod to early American history positioned off Main Street, U.S.A. That didn't happen in Anaheim, but as the country's Bicentennial birthday approached and Walt Disney World was in the planning stages, Walt's original idea became Liberty Square. Flags of the thirteen original colonies are proudly flown here. You'll see many authentic colonial-period antiques on display in the area, which is the smallest of the themed "lands" in the Magic Kingdom. A bell made from the same mold as the original Liberty Bell was cast in 1989 and brought to Liberty Square, a gift from Philadelphia. The Liberty Tree, originally an elm, that played such a prominent role in Boston's early history and in Walt Disney's film *Johnny Tremaine* was honored when a hundred-year-old oak found on the property was transplanted to the area. A younger oak then was grafted to the original tree. Look for the two lanterns signaling "two if by sea," just as Paul Revere once did, except that in Liberty Square, they're visible in the upper window of a replica of Philadelphia's House of Burgesses instead of Boston's Old North Church.

Liberty Square Kiosks, Wagons and Carts

- On busy days, a kiosk selling **Cheese Pizza** will be open.

- Some different, healthy choices are found at the **Liberty Square Market**. Try corn on the cob loaded with spices or a baked potato. Fresh is the order of the day. Find grape tomatoes and lots of fresh fruit on tempting display. Seating is available at tables, some of it shaded. You may not even need lunch afterward!

Columbia Harbour House

DDP: One credit (Q) / Cost: $
Type: American; Quick Service, Mobile Orders; Lunch, Dinner

Lobster rolls are the big draw here, and you'll hear guests raving about them. If you're a lobster fan, stop by. It's just down the walkway that leads to the Haunted Mansion. Two other hearty sandwiches are an all-white tuna and a hummus with tomato and broccoli slaw. They all come with chips. The grilled salmon and rice is a tasty option. Disney check meals for kids feature all-white tuna sandwiches, Smucker's Uncrustables, or a salad with chicken. Three other kids options are chicken nuggets, chicken and fish nuggets combo, or mac and cheese. You can order soups, salads, and sides that vary but include items like corn cobbette, hush puppies, green beans and carrots, veggie chili, broccoli, or rice. An adult entrée called "Trio Platter" features shrimp, fish, and chicken with hush puppies and choice of green beans and carrots, apple slices, or fries. Cake sometimes, seasonal cobblers, and yogurt round out the bill of fare.

Liberty Tree Tavern

DDP: One credit (T) / Cost: $$-$$$ (TiW)
Type: American; Casual; Buffet/Family Style; Lunch, Dinner

Tucked in right beside the Diamond Horseshoe, you can choose the all-you-care-to-enjoy Patriot's Platter, which comes with family-style servings of turkey, prime rib, pork roast, herbed stuffing, mashed potatoes, vegetables, and mac and cheese. It also comes with a salad and Johnny Appleseed's warm bread pudding topped with vanilla crème anglaise. That's an excellent pick here if you're famished; it's delicious and filling. You can order from an a la carte menu instead if you prefer. Try crab and lobster dip, corn fritters, or clam chowder to start. Entrées are pasta, seared salmon salad, or an Angus cheeseburger. End with a cupcake, fruit cup, seasonal cheesecake, or—but only sometimes—a real wow of a Boston cream pie. Disney check meals for kids are pasta or a chicken and apple salad, with cheeseburger or chicken nuggets on the regular kids menu. It's like dining in a colonial inn two hundred and fifty years ago. The detailed décor adds quite a bit to the enjoyment of your bountiful repast.

Sleepy Hollow

DDP: No / Cost: $
Type: American; Counter Service; Quick Service; Snacks

Not quite ready for a big meal but still craving a hearty and delicious snack? Stop here! Notice the quaint little brick building? It is a scale model of Washington Irving's house on the Hudson River. You won't regret a visit. This little stop is *de rigueur* for serious Magic Kingdom foodies in the know. Lots of things on this inventive menu aren't available elsewhere in the park. You'll find Sleepy Hollow as you leave Liberty Square on the way to Cinderella Castle. Satisfy your hunger with a big sweet-and-spicy chicken waffle and house-made chips, funnel cake topped with powdered sugar or seasonal ice cream flavors, made-to-order ice cream cookie sandwiches, or Belgian waffles topped with strawberries and whipped cream. The waffle stuffed with Nutella and fresh berries is fantastic, and if you're a serious corn dog fan, this is definitely the place for you! There are lots of beverage choices on hand, too. Sit with your snack at outdoor tables that have a perfect view of the castle and smile as everyone who walks by stops to ask in awe, "Where'd you get *that*?"

Fantasyland

For many guests, this is the land that brings back fond memories of childhood favorite stories and characters. The Disneyland version was very dear to Walt Disney's own heart. He said: "Here is a land of imagination, hopes and dreams. In this timeless land of enchantment the age of chivalry, magic and make-believe are reborn and fairy tales come true. Fantasyland is dedicated to the young and the young at heart, to those who believe that when you wish upon a star your dreams do come true."

When you think of the best-known Disney animated films, Fantasyland is where you'll find them brought to life in family-friendly fashion. Keep in mind, as you plan your visit, that this area gets progressively busier as the day goes on, so come early to avoid long waits.

Fantasyland Kiosks, Wagons, Carts

- The new part of Fantasyland known as the Enchanted Forest features a popcorn cart like no other—it's **Maurice's Amazing Popping Machine**. It was designed by Belle's father and also serves frozen treats. Hot dogs are only offered from a kiosk in this part of Fantasyland when the park is extremely busy.

- The Storybook Circus area has a **Pretzel Stand** with melted cheese for pretzel dipping and **Churros** to dip in chocolate sauce. A well-stocked **Popcorn Cart** is parked here, too, serving it up fresh and hot.

- If you want a different kind of popcorn snack, try the house-made caramel corn at **Big Top Treats**. It's made fresh every day. Candy apples, cookies, and (adorable!) fanciful cupcakes shaped like Dumbo and other characters are featured at Big Top as well.

- **Prince Eric's Market** near the Seven Dwarfs Mine Train has frozen lemonade and those jumbo smoked turkey legs that weigh in at about a pound and a half each.

Even if you didn't manage to get a reservation at the super-popular Be Our Guest Restaurant, you won't go hungry in Fantasyland!

Be Our Guest

DDP: One credit (T) / Cost: $-$$ (TiW for dinner only)
Type: French; Unique/Themed, Fast Casual; Breakfast, Lunch, Dinner

If you've spoken to friends who've recently visited Walt Disney World, you've probably heard about how difficult it is to nab a reservation at this extremely popular, surprisingly elegant, deliciously inventive French restaurant. Start six months in advance if you want a hard-to-get reservation here. Find it at the base of the Beast's castle in the Enchanted Forest area of Fantasyland. There is an order ahead feature for breakfast and lunch only where you are able to pre-order your meal online up to 30 days in advance, but make your reservations up to 180 days before you hope to dine here.

Breakfast and lunch are "casual." Dinner is "special and unique." There are three dining rooms: the dark and brooding medieval West Wing with the famous rose under glass; the light, airy, and sumptuous Ballroom complete with chandeliers and views of softly falling snow through the windows; and the sweet Rose Gallery (only used for lunch) with twirling figures of Belle and the Beast. American appetites can easily find something wonderful, but the French touch is just as enticing.

Breakfast is hearty enough to please even Gaston. In fact, choose the Feast á la Gaston if you're famished—scrambled eggs, bacon sausage, roasted potatoes and fresh fruit will quell any hunger pangs you may have. Eggs, bacon, veggie quiche, croque madame, meats and cheese with a toasted baguette all come sided with fresh fruit. Look for heavenly croissant donuts on the menu. If you've never tried one, they are amazing, but this presentation rather gilds the lily by adding banana-caramel sauce, pastry crème, and chocolate ganache, plus a selection of pastries. If you're a purist, get a plain one over at the Refreshment Port in Epcot. Hard to beat!

Lunch features the yummy croque monsieur sandwich, along with carved turkey and roast beef sandwiches, braised pork, tuna salad niçoise, quinoa salad, and veggie quiche. Desserts are a hard-to-choose-from variety of specialty cupcakes and French pastries.

Dinner is lavish—a bit more extensive and adventurous. Escargot, charred octopus, and the delightful Maine lobster bisque join the starters that include charcuterie, French onion soup, spiced tuna, or mixed field greens. Select from among beef (a nice center-cut filet), pork, chicken, lamb, and fish entrées. Just now there's a seafood bouillabaisse. Desserts rotate. Now, there's a almond macaron, a dark chocolate truffle, or a white chocolate "Chip" cup served with "the gray stuff—it's delicious." It's a white chocolate shell cup filled with cookie créme.

Kids have an extremely nice listing of choices tailored to younger preferences. They can create their own entrées, add the sides they like, and also create their own desserts. Yay!

Drinks here are just as special as the menu. Non-alcoholic beverages in souvenir light-up cups are appealing for kids. An impressive list of fine wines from California and France pairs well with the menu. European breweries are well represented. You'll find it hard to go wrong at Be Our Guest—providing you can get a table. *Everyone* wants to eat here!

Cheshire Café

DDP: No / Cost: $
Type: American; Counter Service; Quick Service; Snacks

Continue walking past Storybook Circus until you see the Mad Tea Party with its spinning teacups. Beside it is this sweet café named for the enigmatic, grinning feline in *Alice in Wonderland*. If you've come early in the day and are looking for a quick, convenient breakfast, look no further. In busy seasons, find an assortment of cereals, muffins, whole fruit, juice, coffee (hot or iced), and hot cocoa that will hit the spot. If you want to try something unique, order the Cheshire Cat Tail. Don't be put off by the name. It's a darling pastry with pink and purple stripes. There's also a Wonderland Slushy. Seating is available on a covered patio or at tables under shady umbrellas.

Cinderella's Royal Table

DDP: Two credits / Cost: $$$-$$$$ (TiW)
Type: American; Character; Fine/Signature; Breakfast, Lunch, Dinner

Cinderella Castle has always been the iconic symbol for Walt Disney World, and not only is it one of the best scenic backdrops in the park, you'll have the chance to see it from the inside if you book a character meal here during your stay—but it'll cost you two credits on the Disney Dining Plan (though you won't have to leave a tip, as an 18% gratuity is included).

It's hard not to feel like royalty in this restaurant. As you enter, you'll have the opportunity to be photographed with Cinderella herself against a lavish background. The dining room resembles a medieval banquet hall complete with soaring ceilings, bright heraldic banners, and stained glass windows. The Fairy Godmother often plays hostess, while some combination of Cinderella, Snow White, Ariel, Jasmine, Sleeping Beauty, and/or Belle drop by your table for a chat. If your little Princess happens to be wearing the same costume as one of the girls, expect she'll receive a compliment on her good taste! Let's face it, you're not here for the food as much as you are for the experience of dining in the castle and meeting the princesses.

Don't expect to linger. Courses come back-to-back. Still, you can find just about whatever your royal heart desires on the menu...including Cuvée Dom Pérignon champagne for $350! Breakfast is traditional with inventive options such as shrimp and grits, beef tenderloin and egg, a traditional breakfast platter, or caramel apple stuffed French toast. You'll find healthy choices and vegetarian entrées at each meal. Healthy kids meals are available, naturally, but so are kid-friendly indulgences. The welcome trend of allowing kids to create their own entrees and desserts applies here. Ask for allergy-free choices if you need them.

Lunch and dinner menus are the same: pork, beef, chicken, fish, vegetable couscous, each prepared in a way sure to please the most demanding Prince or Princess, no matter their ages. Chocolate mousse ("The Clock Strikes Twelve") or sometimes flourless chocolate cake, sugar-free lemon sorbet, occasionally carrot-pineapple cake (billed as Bruno-the-Horse's favorite), a citrus chiffon cake, or the Jaq and Gus cheesecake and peaches are adult desserts, and the build-your-own cupcake, seasonal sorbet, or a yogurt parfait for the younger guests are sure to finish your regal dining experience to perfection. Don't miss this one! It's a reservation you must make early if you hope to reserve a table.

Disney Early Morning Magic—Fantasyland

DDP: No / Cost:$$$$
Type: American; Quick Service; Continental Breakfast

Only on select Sundays and Tuesdays from 7:45 a.m. until 10:00 a.m., you can breakfast at Cosmic Ray's Starlight Café in Tomorrowland and the enter Fantasyland to enjoy the Many

Adventures of Winnie the Pooh, Seven Dwarf's Mine Train, Peter Pan's Flight (some days have been blocked out), Princess Fairytale Hall, It's a Small World, Mad Tea Party, and Under the Sea before the area is open to others. You must have a valid park admission. The charge of $79 for adults and $69 for kids 3-9 is in addition to regular admission. You'll need to purchase this package in advance either online or by phone and pre-pay. After 9:00 a.m., other guests will be admitted to Fantasyland, but breakfast will be served until 10:00 a.m., so you might wait to eat until after you've ridden the attractions. Popular American breakfast favorites are on the menu, and it's all-you-care-to-enjoy.

The Friar's Nook

DDP: One credit (Q) / Cost: $
Type: American; Counter Service; Quick Service; Lunch, Dinner

Walk through the castle and immediately turn right to find this quick-serve counter. Need a fast snack for the kids or something heartier? Loaded buffalo chicken tots, creamy bacon mac and cheese, creamy bacon tots, a brat and tots, an all-beef hot dog and tots, or the fried Twinkie with vanilla, strawberry, caramel or chocolate sauce should do the trick. Kids can choose an uncrustable or tots and cheese sauce. Lots of fountain beverages, a lemonade slushy, chocolate and low-fat milk, and iced coffees are available from the drinks menu.

Gaston's Tavern

DDP: No / Cost: $
Type: American; Quick Service; Snack

Just past Be Our Guest is the he-man-style Gaston's Tavern. Indoor tables can be hard to secure when the park is busy, so have one member of the party save a spot while the rest place the order at the counter. Those famous cinnamon rolls are the big draw here. You can ask for an additional cup of frosting at no extra charge if you need it. Gaston also appreciates a good chocolate croissant. Le Fou's Brew is cool in the summer (100% sugar-free frozen apple juice with a touch of toasted marshmallow and passion fruit-mango foam on top) and warm in the winter (hot cocoa with a hint of toasted marshmallow topped with whipped cream and sprinkled with crushed candy cane). It's a cult favorite with a big following. Get it in a souvenir stein or goblet to remember the experience. You'll also find apples with caramel dip, hummus and chips, veggies and dip, mini Babybel snack cheese, a trio of macarons, and cups of fruit to round out the snack selection. Be sure to try out Gaston's oversized chair beside the fireplace. You'll feel right at home.

Pinocchio's Village Haus

DDP: One credit (Q) / Cost: $
Type: Italian; Quick Service, Mobile Orders; Lunch, Dinner

Walk through the castle, pass by the carousel on your right, and on your left adjacent to It's a Small World, you'll find this casual, Italian counter with tables and umbrellas out front. If you're a fan of flatbreads like pepperoni, meat lovers, margherita, and gourmet cheese, this is your kind of place. You will also find chicken Parmesan, chicken Alfredo, or Caesar salad with chicken, chicken nuggets, antipasto salad, penne pasta, and a chicken Parm sandwich. Disney check meals are available (turkey sandwich or uncrustable), the usual kid favorites like flatbreads, pasta and chicken nuggets, and gelato, yogurt, or a chocolate chip cookie for desert. The tomato basil soup and breadsticks make a nice, quick lunch. There are all the usual beverages to go with your meal, and allergy-friendly items are available on request.

Storybook Treats

DDP: No / Cost: $
Type: American; Quick Service; Snacks

When you're craving something cool and sweet, soft serve ice cream at Storybook Treats may be just what you want. Indulge with a chocolate chip cookie sundae with hot fudge, hot fudge sundae, strawberry sundae, float, or soft-serve ice cream—vanilla, chocolate, or swirl. The Peter Pan float is lime soft serve, Sprite, and a chocolate feather! Lots of cool beverages are available to quench your thirst.

Tomorrowland

When Disneyland opened in 1955, Walt Disney said about Tomorrowland: "A vista into a world of wondrous ideas, signifying man's achievements...a step into the future, with predictions of constructive things to come. Tomorrow offers new frontiers in science, adventure and ideals: the Atomic Age...the challenge of outer space...and the hope for a peaceful, unified world."

By the time Tomorrowland opened at Walt Disney World in 1971 with only two attractions up and running, the company rethought the concept a bit. The future has a habit of catching up with the present, so here, the future took a pause in the 1950s. Robots and U.F.O.s, streamlined rocket ships and the atomic energy—you'll find that spirit here. Walt also observed, "Tomorrow can be a wonderful age. Our scientists today are opening the door of the Space Age to achievements that will benefit our children and generations to come. The Tomorrowland attractions have been designed to give you an opportunity to participate in adventures that are a living blueprint of our future." You'll find large, counter-service dining choices here. Snack options abound, but don't expect to teleport into any fancy restaurants or character meals. It's all casual and quick in this land of the future.

Tomorrowland Kiosks, Wagons, and Carts

- **Cool Ship Cooling Station** has a constantly rotating menu, but cool drinks are always available, usually with Mickey pretzels and occasionally corn dogs, too.
- Only on busy days, **Space Dogs** near the PeopleMover sells hot dogs, and a **Turkey Legs Cart** may be found only during busy times near the Astro Orbiter.
- Smell popcorn? Yes, a **Popcorn Cart** is located in Tomorrowland, too, and it's right beside an **Ice Cream Cart**.

Auntie Gravity's Galactic Goodies

DDP: No / Cost: $
Type: American; Quick Service; Snacks, Breakfast (busy seasons)

Journey past Cosmic Ray's and you'll come to Auntie Gravity's on the same side of the walkway. It forms a triangle with Cool

Ship and the popcorn and ice cream carts near the entrance to Space Mountain. This is the perfect place for a quick, grab-and-go breakfast (but only during busy seasons) or a mid-day snack. Muffins, whole pieces of fruit, assorted cereals and milk, and fruit smoothies will pair well with coffee, hot or iced, and cocoa. Vanilla, chocolate, or swirl ice cream can be put into a float, cup, cone, or sundae.

Cosmic Ray's Starlight Café

DDP: One credit (Q) / Cost: $
Type: American; Counter Service; Quick Service; Mobile Orders; Lunch, Dinner

Walking past the Mad Tea Party teacups through the "back door" into Tomorrowland, the first quick-service dining place you'll see is this modern, counter service restaurant. It will be on your right. It's great for a casual meal. You can fill up the gang with hearty pulled pork sandwiches, grilled chicken sandwiches, half a rotisserie chicken with mashed potatoes and green beans, cheeseburgers with bacon, a Greek salad, chicken nuggets, and a plant-based sloppy Joe. Sides are fries, a Cutie Mandarin orange, and cheese dip. You'll find a Disney check uncrustables meal and many kid-appealing entrées like nuggets, a salad with turkey and mac and cheese. The toppings bar is a pleasant surprise with add-ons like sautéed mushrooms and onions, grilled onions, sriracha, aioli, and jalapeños. Ray's has desserts, too, sometimes there are more choices, but right now it's just S'mores.

The Lunching Pad

DDP: One credit (Q) / Cost: $
Type: American; Quick Service, Mobile Orders; Lunch, Dinner

Walk 180 degrees around the Astro Orbiter and PeopleMover. On the opposite side facing toward the central hub, you'll find this name-tells-all counter—although it could just as well be called the Dining Pad, but that wouldn't be a pun. Hot dogs come with apple slices or chips, barbecue pulled pork sand-wiches come topped with slaw and sided with chips, and there are churros, assorted chips, cheese stuffed pretzels or cream cheese pretzels on the menu. Frozen carbonated beverages come with souvenir straws. How about a Space Ranger slushy with a candy straw? Orange juice, milk and soy milk, regular or chocolate milk, coffee and tea, and many other beverages (like Fanta!) are sold here.

Tomorrowland Terrace Restaurant

DDP: One credit (Q) / Cost: $
Type: American; Quick Service, Mobile Orders; Lunch, Dinner

Sit on the pretty outdoor terrace overlooking Cinderella Castle for a gorgeous backdrop at your lunch or dinner. Tomorrow Terrace is open seasonally during busy times. A 1/3 pound Angus bacon cheeseburger with apple slices or fries should quell any rumbly tummies. There is also a plant-based BBQ cheese-burger. Slightly lighter fare like Asian chicken lettuce wraps are served, along with selections like chicken strips, and a roasted turkey BLT or a buffalo chicken salad. Coconut tres leches cake is sometimes seasonally available, and a rocky road brownie, and Greek yogurt can be enjoyed alone or with a meal. Disney check meals (Smucker's Uncrustables) are on the menu as well as other entrées kids will enjoy (mac and cheese, chicken strips). There's a great view of Happily Ever After fireworks at night.

The restaurant is currently offering a **Fireworks Dessert Party at Tomorrowland Terrace** where you'll enjoy a gorgeous selection of some of the best of park treats, both sweet and savory, and have a reserved viewing seat to watch Happily Every After fireworks.

- The cost is $84 for adults and $50 for children 3-9, tax included and no tip expected. You can book reservations up to 180 days before the event. Always keep in mind that the fireworks may be cancelled without notice, due to unforeseen circumstances or weather.

- If you don't need to sit to enjoy the show, you can purchase the package for a standing-room area for $69 for adults and $41 for kids 3-9, tax included and no tip expected. If you chose this option, you'll enjoy dessert at Tomorrowland Terrace and be escorted to a reserved standing-room viewing area at the nearby Plaza Gardens to watch the fireworks.

- The final dessert option happens following the fire-works when your day at the park is coming to a sweet conclusion. The cost is $69 for adults and $41 for kids 3-9, the same as the second option. You'll come for a private, reserved viewing spot at Plaza Gardens before the show. Your dessert over at the Terrace comes afterwards.

You've just taken a culinary tour through the Magic Kingdom, starting on Main Street, U.S.A. and heading clockwise around the entire park focusing on the many places to satisfy just about any appetite, from the heartiest to the lightest, the most adventurous to the most selective. You'll also find options here to accommodate every budget. Some of your choices are sit-down, fancy affairs like Cinderella's Royal Table, some are delightful character meals/buffets like the Crystal Palace, and some are inventive new dining adventures like Skipper's Canteen. Whether you feel like a quick bite of something satis-fying on the run, such as Casey's corn dog nuggets, or you're eating healthy and looking for fresh fruit, Greek yogurt, or perhaps that famous pineapple Dole Whip treat, you're sure to find it at the Magic Kingdom.

Next, let's take a stroll through Epcot, the theme park many guests consider to be the Holy Grail of Walt Disney World dining experiences. As Julia Child exuberantly has encour-aged, "Bon appétit," and you're going to need a good appetite while visiting Epcot!

Epcot, Part 1

Future World, Canada, United Kingdom, France, Morocco, Japan

Epcot is, without a doubt, the theme park with the most appealing, international selection of good things to eat. It's also the location of the world-famous Epcot International Food & Wine Festival every year. The park opened in 1982, eleven years after the Magic Kingdom. With eleven pavilions from as many nations, it's like a mini-around-the-world vacation extravaganza. One thing you'll notice is that this park is divided into two distinct halves, a Future World and a sort of permanent World's Fair called the World Showcase. In this chapter, we'll cover all of Future World as well as the pavilions of Canada, the United Kingdom, France, Morocco, and Japan.

Originally, Walt Disney envisioned his grand plan in the Florida countryside as a social experiment he called the Experimental Prototype Community of Tomorrow, EPCOT for short. That's right, the word was spelled in all capital letters back when it was an acronym. It was to have been a place where people would live, work, and play together in security and harmony. Public transportation would be plentiful and would feature PeopleMovers and monorails. The self-contained community would show the rest of the world how life should be lived. Believe it or not, there wasn't even a theme park in the original plans for Walt Disney World at all, let alone four of them! Investors refused to sign on, however, without a built-in "draw," something like the hugely popular Disneyland in Anaheim. Thus, the Magic Kingdom was created. Walt passed away in 1966, five years before the grand opening of

Walt Disney World, and never saw his Florida plan realized. Still, his dream is the one responsible for its creation.

Look for some new plans in development at Epcot. IllumiNations, the extravagant fireworks production since October of 1999, will be replaced by a new show. A Guardians of the Galaxy roller coaster ride, a Ratatouille attraction, and a new table service restaurant next to Mission: SPACE are on the drawing board, all of which will be welcome additions to the park.

At this point, the "living, working, and playing" concept has largely been set aside in favor of a recreation destination where families can come for vacations without ever needing to leave the extensive grounds, all 27,000+ acres of them. Epcot is large, too. The Magic Kingdom is about 100 acres inside the park perimeter, while Epcot is more like 300 acres—and we'll cover them all in this guide. Don't be surprised if you need lots of refueling stops!

Future World

The giant, silver sphere known as Spaceship Earth anchors the first "land" of Epcot and is the representative symbol of the park itself. All things fast-paced and streamlined will be found here, from amusement park rides you can design and try out for yourself, to a working test track for cars of the future. Everything looks ahead, and the emphasis is on technology. The Seas and The Land are two large areas contained within Future World, both of them providing guests with appealing choices for meals.

Future World Kiosks, Carts, and Wagons

- The **Test Track Cool Wash** station is a small kiosk near the busy Test Track. When it's open during very busy times, you'll find slushies, drinks, and sometimes snacks.

- **Popcorn Carts** move around, but if you find one, it might offer some unusual, savory, gourmet flavors.

- A **Turkey Leg Cart** is sometimes open when the park is very busy.

- The **Land Cart** near The Land Pavilion offers fresh fruit and cheeses, **Mickey Pretzels** with dipping cheese, a veggie plate, hummus and pretzels, and lots of beverages including beers.

- **Espresso Coffee and Pastries** may be found in front of the Universe of Energy.
- Look for a **Popcorn and Pretzel Stand** in front of Mission Space.
- You'll see a **Popcorn and Ice Cream Stand** between Electric Umbrella and the fountain.

Coral Reef Restaurant

DDP: One credit (T) / Cost: $$ (TiW))
Type: Seafood/American; Unique/Themed; Lunch, Dinner

As you walk through the main entrance to Epcot, you will come to The Seas on your right. The Coral Reef is next to the Nemo & Friends attraction. It sometimes offers dining events; check in advance of your trip to see what might be available during your visit.

Lunch and dinner here are termed unique/themed dining experiences, and they certainly are. One request well worth making is to ask for a seat near the enormous circular saltwater aquarium, the biggest one in the world. At more than 200 feet across, it's home to some 4,000 sea creatures. The 165 feet in diameter Spaceship Earth could be fully immersed in the aquarium without touching the sides!

The specialty food here, naturally, is seafood, but you'll find many other items on the menu as well. The entire experience feels like you're dining underwater; from the ceiling to the lamps to the carpeting, everything is in shades of watery blues and greens. There is no difference in price between the lunch and dinner menus. This is the newest trend throughout Walt Disney World—hoping to save money at lunch isn't a valid strategy these days.

There is a large selection of appetizers including an old-fashioned "colossal" shrimp cocktail, lovely lobster bisque with cream and brandy, spinach and ricotta ravioli, and more. Entrées include pork, chicken, steak, mahi mahi, lobster, shrimp and grits, and salmon, along with tempura-fried cauliflower and vegetables. Enhancements feature a shrimp skewer, lobster mac and cheese, crab Oscar, and Jonah crab claws. Desserts are inventive. Try a chocolate wave with raspberry gelato, an angel food cake with no sugar, the popular Key Lime Tart, and a warm vanilla custard-filled Strudel with Prosecco ice cream and hazelnut praline that's pretty spectacular. Kids meals lean toward the "create-your-own" variety where they can pick from a nice variety of appetizers, entrees, sides, and desserts. This is a wonderful, welcome trend that makes pleasing both children and their parents a lot easier. The illusion of dining "under the sea" will ensure that this restaurant is an entertaining choice.

Electric Umbrella

DDP: One credit (Q) / Cost: $
Type: American; Quick Service, Mobile Orders; Lunch, Dinner

On the left side of the fountain, as you're walking into the park past Spaceship Earth, you'll find a fast, counter service restaurant for lunch or dinner. There is seating inside, so rest your feet and dig into some cheeseburgers, chicken nuggets, a chicken breast salad, veggie quinoa salad, mojo pulled pork burger, or vegetarian three-cheese flatbread. A turkey sandwich or uncrustable are the Disney Check meals, but kids can order many of the above choices on their own menu plus the ever-popular mac and cheese. If you have room, finish up with a chocolate cupcake, a mixed fruit cup, a sugarless brownie, or a piece of red velvet cake.

Fountain View

DDP: One credit (Q) / Cost: $
Type: American/Bakery Cuisine; Quick Service; Snacks

For a pick me up shot of espresso or a tall, cool frappuccino, look for the big fountain just past the silver dome of Spaceship Earth. Fountain View will be to the right as you walk toward the World Showcase. Customizable coffee, smoothies, teas, refreshers, hot cocoa, and all your favorite Starbucks signature beverages like white chocolate mocha or caramel macchiato are found right here. Seasonal beverages are offered, along with a selection of portable baked goods to go with your beverage.

Garden Grill

DDP: One credit (T) / Cost: $$-$$$ (TiW)
Type: American; Family Style; Character Buffet; Breakfast, Lunch, Dinner

In The Land Pavilion, one level above Soarin' and Sunshine Seasons, is the charming Garden Grill, a family-style restaurant where tables are visited by costumed characters, usually Chip 'n' Dale and sometimes Mickey and/or Pluto or other pals. There are occasionally dining events, so ask about them in advance of your vacation. The restaurant rotates slowly to give everyone a view of four different themes (desert, prairie, rainforest, and farmhouse) throughout the course of the meal.

Cuisine is American with some of the offerings grown on-site in the Living with the Land greenhouses. It's an all-you-care-to-enjoy, hearty harvest meal. For breakfast, expect the usual filling fare of bacon, ham, or sausage and eggs, Mickey waffles, Chip's sticky bun bake, fruit, and sometimes biscuits with gravy. Lunch and dinner usually include warm bread, beef, turkey, carved pork with apple chutney, mashed potatoes, mac and cheese, garden veggies, herbed stuffing, and the meal is topped off with a fresh berry shortcake. There are many specialty drinks, beers, wines, and non-alcoholic beverages. This is a fun place to dine for all ages!

Sunshine Seasons

DDP: One credit (Q) / Cost: $
Type: Global/American; Quick Service; Fast Casual; Breakfast, Lunch, Dinner

This restaurant is virtually all things to all guests, boasting a tremendous variety of fresh and tasty items on its menu. Find it in The Land Pavilion, which will be on your right as you move toward the World Showcase. Once you're there, the first thing it do it get a table. Sometimes they're in short supply. It can be a tad overwhelming—walk through the length of the restaurant so as not to miss any of the counters. Each counter has its own specialties: Asian Noodles (usually Mongolian beef and vegan korma, and other rotating items such as sweet and sour chicken with jasmine rice), Soups and Salads (things like chicken corn chowder, black bean soup, pumpkin soup, chili, seared tuna with Asian noodle salad, Caesar salad), Sandwiches (sometimes fish tacos, too), the Grill (salmon, pork, chicken), and a Kid's Zone for Disney check meals that seems to have something for just about every child (Smucker's Uncrustables, chicken wrap, salmon, chicken drumstick). All kinds of beverages and desserts, both sinful (try the spectacular Minnie rose gold cupcake if it's in stock!) and healthful (vegan fruit desserts), can be found in the grab-and-go stations. This is a great place to take a break and relax while satisfying food preferences for every member of your party. Items rotate seasonally and frequently, but you will always find plenty of good things. This should be a no-stress chance to take a minute, pause and refresh, and sample something delicious during your busy day.

Taste Track

DDP: One credit (S) / Cost: $
Type: American; Quick Service; Snacks

Taste Track has lots of ice cream treats, from sundaes to floats to ice cream cookie sandwiches and waffle cones, at this little snack venue located near the entrance to Test Track. It's only open seasonally.

World Showcase Promenade

Eleven pavilions representing Canada, the United Kingdom, France, Morocco, Japan, the United States, Germany, Italy, China, Norway, and Mexico ring a scenic, 46-acre lagoon. There are step-saving tips like taking one of the two ferry boats across the lake, but if you are like most of us, you'll want to see something of every country. That means walking—and plenty of it. This theme park is so large that it makes sense to visit Epcot over two days if you possibly can.

Promenade Refreshments

DDP: One credit (Q) / Cost: $
Type: American; Quick Service; Lunch, Dinner

For a casual snack or quick meal, stop here before getting started on your trip around the Showcase—but remember, there are many international delights waiting to be sampled just a few steps ahead. There are all-beef hot dogs or chili dogs with ranch kettle chips, alcoholic beverages including several beers, and fountain drinks here. There is also soft-serve orange, vanilla, and swirl in a waffle cone. Find nearby benches under shady trees that overlook the lake. Exotic birds often dart around looking for any crumbs that might fall.

Refreshment Port

DDP: One credit (Q) / Cost: $
Type: American; Counter Service; Quick Service; Lunch, Dinner

Not to interject myself into your party's private discussion, but if you're talking snack options at this point, please allow me to highly recommend the warm croissant donuts (known elsewhere as cronuts) at the Refreshment Port. Sugar and spice and everything nice—including soft serve on top, if you so desire—makes this stop a definite *yes!* Are you feeling exceptionally throw-calorie-counting-to-the-wind today? Then try the hot cocoa with Godiva liqueur. Beef brisket poutine and traditional poutine are the current specialties. Sometimes, chicken nuggets and fries are on the menu, too. But don't pass up the cronuts; you won't find them just anywhere.

Canada

Canada Kiosks, Wagons, and Carts

- Keep an eye out for a cart called **Popcorn** in Canada. Where else would you find maple-flavored popcorn? The cart carries Moosehead and Blanche de Chambly draft beers, available with souvenir steins, as well as seasonal chilled maple café and Crown Royal maple whiskey. Maple is the order of the day in Canada, as you'll soon see.

Le Cellier Steakhouse

DDP: Two credits (T) / Cost: $$$ (TiW)
Type: Canadian; Fine/Signature; Lunch, Dinner

Le Cellier recently joined the Disney Dining Plan, and because of the expensive menu selections, it will cost you two dining plan credits. It is immensely popular. Reservations are hard to come by, so start your quest for a table as soon as possible. Six months before your vacation is not too soon to begin. Le Cellier is intended to be just what it sounds like, the romantic wine cellar of a lovely Canadian château.

For starters, guests rave about the cheddar soup featuring Nueske's applewood smoked bacon (the best!). Seasonally, there are heirloom tomatoes, charcuterie (currently from the larder: "pig, pig, and more pig" with five kinds of pork and artisanal cheeses/accompaniments), and a variety of salads, P.E.I. mussels, as well. Entrées are both satisfying and beautifully prepared. Filet mignon, maple-brined chicken breast, châteaubriand for two, Angus rib-eye, and steamed Asian-style dumplings make for choices to delight the most reticent palate. Not on the dining plan but tempting nonetheless (these are out-of-pocket expenses) are enhancements like Gorgonzola-creamed spinach, Brussels sprouts, lobster mac and cheese, asparagus with sauce Béarnaise and more. Unfortunately, the wowza seafood sampler for two is no more. If you have any room left for dessert, you won't be disappointed. A chocolate maple Yukon bar, warm pecan and brown butter tart, maple crème brûlée, strawberry cheesecake, and some sugar-free delights remain to be savored at your leisure. A chocolate addition to dessert would be welcomed, however.

For children already cultivating a sophisticated palate, the create-your-own-entrée meals are grilled chicken and seared salmon, each with two side selections. Steak, mac and cheese, grilled cheese, pasta, and a decadent "chocolate moose" (mousse) will hit just the right notes for children. Maybe adults can get that last one, too?

Le Cellier is justifiably celebrated for its superlative wine list, and you'll receive expert advice on pairings from the sommelier. The regions of Côtes du Rhône and Saint-Estephe, France, plus Napa, California, provide the wine. You may be tempted by the icewine flight: Château Des Charles Vidal, Inniskillen Vidal, and Neige Apple. It's easy to understand Le Cellier's stellar reputation. Some items come and go, but a few of the tried and true hits would be warmly welcomed back.

United Kingdom

United Kingdom Kiosks Wagons, and Carts

- The **UK Beer Cart** during busy seasons serves British draft beers and ales in souvenir cups. Pear cider is on the menu. Pair a drink with house-made, seasoned, potato crisps—we call those "chips" on this side of the pond.

Rose & Crown Dining Room

DDP: One credit (T) / Cost: $$ (TiW)
Type: British; Unique/Themed; Lunch, Dinner

For a relaxed dining experience, take a break either inside or on the outdoor patio. Patio tables are great for watching IllumiNations (just through the end of summer, 2019, at which point it will be replaced with an all-new night-time extravaganza) at night. Fare is traditional British. For starters, try the Coronation Salad, St. James smoked salmon (sometimes), potato-leek soup, house-made meat pie (sometimes), Scotch egg, or UK cheese platter. Main courses are crowd-pleasers. Go British, of course, but everyone should be able to find something appealing. Fish and chips, bangers and mash, Welsh pub burger, shepherd's pie, vegetable crumble, corned beef and cabbage, Scottish salmon, and chicken masala curry are among the many UK favorites. Kids can create their own appetizers, entrées, and desserts. They are American-kid friendly.

Ever long to try Yorkshire pudding, mushy peas (crushed and surprisingly tasty), or bubble and squeak (a pan fried vegetable mixture)? Here's your chance. Rotating tarts, cakes, scones, sticky toffee pudding, and English trifle are the sweet treats.

Flights of Scotch are available, single malt, Macallan, and Johnnie Walker, along with 2 oz. pours of half a dozen varieties of Scotch. There are many other beverages for both kids and adults. Be sure to check out the twenty kinds of "pub blends," which are half one thing and half another, like bass ale and Guinness, cider and Guinness, and plenty more, so 'ave a seat, guv'ner, and tuck in!

IllumiNations Dining Package (soon to be called Epcot Forever) takes place at the Rose & Crown for a dinner at 8:00

p.m. Seating is outside on the patio overlooking the lagoon. The menu is *prix fixe a*nd includes alcoholic beverages. The price is currently $85 for adults and $35 for children 3-9 with tax and tip included. You must purchase a separate admission to Epcot. In case of inclement weather, the dinner takes place under a covered area of the patio. Call 48 hours before if you need to cancel or you'll be billed in full.

Rose & Crown Pub

DDP: No / Cost: $
Type: British; Unique/Themed; Lunch, Dinner

Casual, Cockney, and cozy, this pub welcomes you to sit a spell and enjoy a snack or meal and a drink. Table service is available. Traditional British pub grub is exactly what you'll find here: battered banger and chips (sausage and chips, or fries as we call them), fish and chips, and Scotch egg (hard boiled egg wrapped in sausage and deep-fried). The drink menu is filled with lagers, stouts, ales, wines and sangria, pub blends, Scotch whiskey and whiskey flights, port, cognac, and house specialties like the Welsh Dragon, the Leaping Leprechaun, and the English Rose. Lift a glass, and lift your spirits! The same beverages available at the main restaurant may be ordered here.

A **Rose & Crown Dining Room & Pub Tea Experience** is being offered. If you want to try a genuine British tea, the pub has that covered with Twinnings teas and typical tea-time treats at 9:30 am on Friday, Saturday, and Sunday in season. Reservations are highly advised, and the Disney Dining Plan is not accepted. Cost is $35 and includes tips on brewing the perfect "cuppa" tea.

Yorkshire County Fish Shop

DDP: One credit (Q) / Cost: $
Type: British; Quick Service; Lunch, Dinner

This pretty, picturesque counter restaurant serves up—you guessed it—that old British (and American!) favorite: fish and chips. Piping hot and crispy fresh, it's a real winner. They've recently added chicken and mushroom pie. Also try genuine Victorian sponge cake with jam and buttercream or a piece of whole seasonal fruit. Fountain beverages are available, and so is Bass Ale or Harp Lager Draft.

France

France Kiosks, Wagons, and Carts

- **Crepes des Chefs de France** is a charming kiosk featuring oh-so-sweet crepes with Nutella (Europe's favorite taste sensation), lemon, strawberry, or sugar. Don't forget, you can put ice cream on top! Add an espresso, a cappuccino, or even a Kronenbourg 1664, a beer brewed in Alsace, France.
- **Le Vins des Chefs de France** is a chance to sample Chardonnay, Vouvray, Cabernet, Merlot, Beaujolais, and other regional French wines. Non-alcoholic beverages are also available and a refreshing orange slushy, with or without a shot of Grand Mariner or Grey Goose citron.

Chefs de France

DDP: One credit (T) / Cost: $$ (TiW for lunch only)
Type: French; Unique/Themed Dining; Lunch, Dinner

For some reason, when other restaurants are packed, you can sometimes find a table open here in France. It's not due to any lack of excellence with the cuisine nor the service. This establishment makes you feel like you've happened upon a French bistro in one of the Parisian arrondissements. The menu was first created by three famous French chefs: Paul Bocuse, Gaston Lenotre, and Roger Vergé. Jerome Bocuse, Paul's son, still manages the Epcot French restaurants today. Look for photos on the wall of the original chefs.

Nouvelle cuisine changes seasonally, and you may order from either an a la carte or the *prix fixe menu*. If you're not feeling quite adventurous enough to try the cassolette d'escargots (snails in casserole), perhaps you'll find the satiny bisque de homard (lobster bisque) more to your liking. Charcuterie, a marvelous soupe à l'oignon gratinée (French onion soup), a selection of French cheeses, crisp salads, and salmon fumé (smoked) are some other prelude options. You can't go far wrong with just about anything here. Beef, seafood, pork, trout, duck, flatbreads, and many spectacular vegetarian plates are currently available. Naturally, the desserts are sheer perfection. Crème brûlée, gateau au chocolat (chocolate cake), a strawberries and cream cake with raspberry sauce (seasonal), an apple tart with vanilla ice cream (seasonal) or other assorted sorbets will finish your meal très bon in the French style. The cream puff swan filled with chocolate mousse and served with chocolate ice cream and chocolate sauce should please any chocolate fan in addition to being so absolutely gorgeous that it is difficult, but certainly not impossible, to dig in!

If you prefer, the three-course *prix fixe* meal allows no substitutions, but there are plenty of appealing choices; it provides the opportunity to try the best of the choices on the menu at this lovely bistro.

L'Artisan des Glaces

DDP: No / Cost: $
Type: French; Quick Service; Snacks

Head to the back of the France Pavilion and look for a picturesque tower. Therein, find all manner of ice cream and sorbet to tempt and delight the palate. Try an ice cream martini for something unique and strictly for adults, or make the kids happy with a chocolate macaron ice cream sandwich. Recent interesting additions include the café glacé iced cappuccino with ice cream, the croque glacé with ice cream pressed in a warm, homemade brioche, and a coupe de dimanche with two scoops of ice cream in a waffle bowl that includes whipped cream and sauce. Flavors change seasonally, but there are always plenty of them from which to choose.

Les Halles Boulangerie-Patisserie

DDP: One credit (Q) / Cost: $
Type: French Cuisine/Bakery; Quick Service; Lunch, Dinner

Want a taste of France but aren't ready for a full, table-service meal at this point in your day? Currently, the menu includes sandwiches like ham and cheese, Brie and apples, chicken and cheese, turkey B.L.T., a three-cheese tartine, and a salad Niçois. Not everything here remains the same, but you can count on the high quality of what's on the menu. Find tasty foods here that are very different from the usual park fare. French hot and cold sandwiches, salads, croque monsieur, vichyssoise, quiche

(Lorraine and Florentine), or perhaps a lovely lobster bisque with half a fresh-baked baguette are sure to satisfy your craving for something fresh and delicious—but wait! Save room for a sweet from the tremendously extensive selection that includes chocolate croissants, palmiers (cinnamon or chocolate elephant ears), beignets, cookies, puff pastries, chocolate mousse, and many, many more. You'll find plenty of alcoholic and non-alcoholic beverages to accompany your selections, no matter what they might be. This is a stop well worth making!

Monsieur Paul

DDP: Two credits (T) / Cost: $$$
Type: French;. Fine/Signature; Dinner

Just upstairs from Les Chefs de France, you'll find the très elegante Monsieur Paul. Again, if you want a full-service dinner and don't have an advance dining reservation, try here, especially if you're willing to dine earlier or later than usual. You can sometimes find a table on relatively short notice, especially during the off season, but reservations are recommended.

It bills itself as "gourmet dining" with "inventive twists on traditional French cuisine." The setting is romantic with a wonderful view overlooking the lake, especially from the window seats. It is worth noting that there is a "strict dress code," and here it is:

"Appropriate attire for men includes khakis, slacks, jeans, dress shorts and collared shirts; appropriate attire for women includes capris, skirts, dresses, jeans and dress shorts. Attire that will not be permitted includes tank tops or hats for gentleman, swimwear, cut offs or torn clothing. In addition, while T-shirts are allowed, T-shirts featuring offensive language and/or graphics are not."

There's an indulgent *prix fixe* menu which will set you back two dining plan credits *plus* $30.50. The menu features appetizing preparations of chicken, fish, duck, beef, lamb, pork, and a large selection of appetizers (oxtail soup with truffles, chilled Maine lobster, upside down caramelized onion tart, and more) and desserts like the stunning chocolate sphere (yes, please), warm chocolate almond cake, caramelized apples, and meringue. An exceptional children's menu is also available. It is indeed a splurge, but the first-rate food at Monsieur Paul makes it an eminently satisfying one!

Morocco

Morocco Kiosks, Wagons, and Carts

- A **Spice Road Table Juice Bar** counter is attached to the restaurant of the same name that serves alcoholic slushy drinks and beers. Ice cream (house made) and baklava is sold here as well. If you're looking for juice, however, look elsewhere. Despite the name, they don't have it.

Restaurant Marrakesh

DDP: One credit (T) / Cost: $$ (TiW)
Type: Moroccan, Mediterranean; Unique/Themed Dining; Lunch, Dinner

The smallest of the eleven pavilions, Morocco nevertheless offers you some exciting dining opportunities, especially if you want to try something off the beaten gustatory path. A family-friendly belly dancer (yes, it's possible) entertains on the hour, accompanied by live musicians. Northern Mediterranean foods served in a sultan's palace setting is an escape from the ordinary. And, unlike most other Disney World restaurants nowadays, lunch entrées at Marrakesh are less expensive than those at dinner.

Adventurous appetizers feature thin layers of pastry with fillings such as beef and eggs, seafood, or chicken. There are also soups, salads, and some samplers for two if you'd prefer to try a variety. Entrées with couscous abound. Try it with chicken, lamb, beef, or veggies. Roast lamb, lemon chicken, shish kebobs, and salmon offer choices to please most. Want to try several different kinds of specialties? You can order the 3-course *prix fixe* meal called "Taste of Morocco." Children will find many American-style choices like chicken or fish nuggets and fries, a hamburger, or they might like to try the beef kebab and a Moroccan-style pasta dish.

Desserts with pastry and vanilla ice cream or a fruit salad with mint ice cream complete the experience. Recently, warm beignets with sweet cream have joined the dessert menu. Don't overlook the long list of specialty drinks, like Casablanca Sunset,

Marrakesh Express, and Sahara Splash. Dining here is a lovely experience and definitely one you won't find around every corner.

Spice Road Table

DDP: One credit (T) / Cost: $$ (TiW)
Type: Moroccan; Unique/Themed; Lunch, Dinner

On the lagoon side of the Morocco Pavilion, look for this full-service restaurant with lots of atmosphere. There's a romantic, candlelight dinner available, and you can sit right on the water to watch the fireworks show.

There are so many Mediterranean small plates that it would be hard not to find something you'd like to try! Among them are hummus and olives, fried calamari, garlic shrimp, rice-stuffed grape leaves, chicken roll, hummus fries, and fresh fish cakes. Three lamb sliders, yellow fin tuna, rack of lamb, vegetable platter, roast chicken, and a mixed grill skewer are among the entrées, with beef sliders, NY strip steak, fish croquettes, bow tie pasta, and chicken nuggets featured on the children's menu. How about a chocolate pyramid for dessert, saffron and pistachio custard, or a selection of baklava? Live a little by trying something from the extensive list of inventive specialty drinks showcasing this region of the world. Moroccan beers and non-alcoholic beverages are also available. Remember to request a table by the water—you'll be glad you did.

Tangierine Café

DDP: One credit (Q) / Cost: $
Type: Moroccan, Mediterranean; Quick Service; Lunch, Dinner

Shawarma is a long skewer of roasting lamb, chicken, or other meat from which slices are cut, and you'll find lots of it at this counter. Get it on a platter sided with hummus, tabouleh, and couscous salad served with fresh Moroccan bread. Chicken, lamb, or falafel wraps come with couscous and lentil salad. There's a kefta (meatball) platter, saffron rotisserie chicken, and a vegetable platter. For kids, hamburgers and chicken tenders are on the menu. A variety of sides are served. Try a glass of Moroccan wine, sangria, or imported or domestic beer with your meal. Non-alcoholic beverages including a delicious frozen fruit drink are available, too.

Japan

Japan Kiosks, Wagons, and Carts

- **Kabuki Café** is a handy place to sample quick Japanese snacks like miso soup, edamame, sushi, and kakigōri (refreshing shaved ice, flavored and sweetened). Offerings vary with the seasons.

- Hot or cold sake is available at the **Garden House Beverage Stand**, and there's also a sake bar found inside the Mitsukoshi Department Store. While you're there, have a look at the truly spectacular selection of Mikimoto pearls.

Katsura Grill

DDP: One credit (Q) / Cost: $
Type: Japanese; Quick Service; Lunch, Dinner

Maybe you're not quite ready to jump into the deep-end of Japanese dining. In that case, this little counter may be precisely right for you. Everything is very reasonably priced and the choices are many. Take the stairway up to the counter and find tables, covered or out in the fresh air. Sushi, noodles (both ramen and udon), shrimp and chicken teriyaki, chicken and beef teriyaki, chicken cutlet curry, and other selections will give you a taste of the Orient without being more than you bargained for. Rice, edamame, and miso soup are side orders. Desserts may include green tea cheesecake, green tea ice cream, and azuki (red bean) strawberry ice cream. Kids' versions of most of the entrées are on the menu. Hot or cold sake, plum wine, and a variety of Japanese beers, specialty drinks, and non-alcoholic beverages are available to accompany your meal. The setting is quiet and leafy-green; this is a great place to take a break and recoup your energy.

Teppan Edo

DDP: One credit (T) / Cost: $$ (TiW)
Type: Japanese/Asian/Sushi; Unique/Themed; Lunch, Dinner

Climb the wide flight of stairs outside and ascend to the Far East. Teppan-style dining means your chefs will prepare your meal from a center grill while you watch, and diners have the opportunity to speak directly with those preparing the food. It's an interactive experience, so be prepared for that.

Appetizers are authentically prepared Japanese-style ribs, tempura, edamame, miso soup, and tofu. Sushi many ways comes next: order volcano roll, spicy salmon tartare roll, shrimp tempura roll, or perhaps you'll opt for a sushi sampler to try several. Entrées will please both Western and Eastern tastes. They are served with salad, rice, udon noodles (thick, wheat flour noodles), and vegetables. Filet mignon, strip steak, julienne beef, salmon, chicken, shrimp, scallops or a seasonal vegetable medley provide guests with not only a great meal but an exciting show watching it all prepared with flair right in front of them. There are several options to combine two entrées, if you simply can't make up your mind. Pair your meal with hot or cold sake, beer, or perhaps a sake cocktail. There are plenty of options for children here with many non-alcoholic beverages, too.

In addition, the list of enhancements is extensive and will make it possible for you to create a customized meal exactly to your specifications. These attractive add-on extras are not included with the dining plan. If you want to try grilled lobster, Wagyu steak (fork tender and sublimely succulent), or tuna tataki, be prepared to pay out-of-pocket. Dining at Teppan is both entertaining and tasty—now *that's* a great combination.

Tokyo Dining

DDP: One credit (T) / Cost: $$ (TiW)
Type: Japanese; Unique/Themed Dining; Lunch, Dinner

You'll feel like you've stepped into a serene and upscale downtown Tokyo dining establishment. Attention to detail is impeccable. Even the napkins are folded to look like origami art! Ask for a window view to watch the fireworks at night. You'll find prices are a bit more reasonable here than at many of the Epcot dining establishments, and the service is superlative.

Starters like edamame, spicy calamari tempura, cassva flour and panko-crusted shrimp set the tone for a traditional Japanese meal. Lunch and dinner menus and prices are almost identical, with lunch having slightly fewer items on the menu, but both meals have many choices to fit most people's preferences. There are soups (vegetable miso, seafood, asari clam miso) and salads that will please most diners from a simple garden salad to the tuna-salmon-poke salad. Steak or chicken, tempura or sushi rolls, nigiri sushi, or sashimi (which is raw seafood for the adventurous), and many ways of enjoying them transport you to downtown Tokyo. With colorful names like Firecracker Rolls, Dragon Monster Rolls, Spicy Crunchy Rolls with Volcano and Dynamite Drizzle, you'll want to expand your sushi dining horizons. Conversely, lots of rice and noodle dishes or teriyaki and tempura meals are available for the more conservative diners among your party. There is also a nice filet mignon with a plum wine reduction and seasonal veggies. The chef's creation bento box is a fun way to sample many of the house specialties. Kids also have somewhat tamer choices such as tempura nuggets or California roll. Green tea and ginger or mango mousse cakes are the dessert offerings, along with soft-serve ice cream. Count on a good experience when you visit Tokyo Dining.

Takumi-Tei

DDP: No / Cost: $$$$
Type: Asian/Japanese/Seafood/Sushi Cuisine; Fine/Signature Dining; Dinner

Opening in the summer of 2019, the newest dining addition to the Japan Pavilion promises a blending of fine Japanese craftsmanship and the world of nature. It will be housed in the Japan Pavilion Pagoda. Guests are told to "immerse yourself in a truly creative dining experience in a sublime setting at Takumi-Tei—Japanese for house of the artisan."

Those artisans better be prepared to put on some khakis and a collared shirt because this restaurant will enforce a dress code like the one at Monsieur Paul's. It reads: "In order to preserve the atmosphere of this dining experience, Guests are asked to adhere to the dress code. The minimum dress code is required—and dressier attire is also welcome. Please review the minimum dress code requirements: Men must wear khakis, slacks or dress shorts and collared shirts. Jeans may be worn if in good condition. Sport coats are optional. Women must wear Capri pants, skirts, dresses or dress shorts. Jeans may be worn if in good condition. Not permitted are tank tops, flip-flops, swimsuits, swimsuit cover-ups, hats for gentlemen, cut-offs, torn clothing and t-shirts with offensive language and/or graphics." Takumi-Tei is definitely intended to be a bit more formal than most park places to dine.

Official Disney literature says, "Delight your senses in this stunning setting when you dine on brilliantly prepared dishes. At Takumi-Tei, you'll dine in one of 5 rooms, each inspired by a natural element—water, wood, earth, stone or washi paper. Every area will feature beautiful, handcrafted works of art honoring the element that brought it to life. The beauty of Japan is featured both in its art and in its cuisine. Dine on creatively prepared, Japanese-inspired dishes from a multi-course tasting menu, featuring a traditional Japanese tea service. Guests may also enjoy signature cocktails, premium sake, wine and craft beer.

For the ultimate experience, dine on an exclusive menu at the Chef's Table in the Water Room. This space is beautifully designed to immerse diners in a tranquil setting that reflects the balance between nature and Japanese art." Expect great food priced accordingly—and make reservations!

Congratulations, weary world travelers! You have successfully navigated all of Future World and are now at the half-way point in Epcot's World Showcase. Your dining and snack choices have been abundant and, at least among most of the pavilions, truly international. If you are dividing your time at Epcot between two (or more) days, enjoy a pleasant night's rest before returning. You've certainly earned it. If not, turn the page because we're forging ahead to some of the best eating places in all of Walt Disney World.

Epcot, Part Two

American Adventure, Italy, Germany, China, Norway, Mexico

Rounding the halfway point of the World Showcase Lagoon, you'll encounter some of the most appealing and tasty snacks available anywhere on Disney property, as well as some of the best restaurants Walt Disney World has to offer. The central body of water, besides being 47 acres in surface area, requires a full 1.2 mile perimeter walk to completely circle it on foot—and that doesn't count your side trips through the eleven pavilions. That's why you definitely need to take into account the substantial distances you'll cover when planning rest and refreshment stops, particularly if there are small children or seniors in your party. This second half of the World Showcase contains the pavilions of the United States, Italy, Germany, China, Norway, and Mexico. Ready? Get set. Go!

American Adventure

American Adventure Kiosks, Wagons, and Carts

- Feeling parched and longing to wet your whistle? "Purveyors of Fine American Ale" at **Block & Hans** will do the job. They serve a variety of American craft brews. Pair it with a Mickey pretzel and cheese sauce, take a seat, and watch the world go by.

- The **Fife & Drum Tavern** has enough on hand for a filling refreshment stop: turkey legs, waffle ice cream cones, the American Dream (a red, white, and blue slushy drink), and popcorn. You'll also find root beer floats, hard orange soda, and a long list of beers, wines, and non-alcoholic beverages. There is plenty of shady seating nearby.

- The name says it all at the **Funnel Cake Stand**. Get one plain or make it fancy with soft-serve ice cream, cookies and cream, chocolate sauce, or powdered sugar. Take home a kit if you want to duplicate this treat once the vacation comes to an end.

- An **Espresso Coffee and Pastries** stand has opened lately on the edge of American near Italy. Check it out for all your coffee and tea needs, hot chocolate in season, the frozen flame (passionfruit and strawberry seasonally), and you have the option to "make it spirited" by adding a shot of Gray Goose vodka, Kahlua, or fireball cinnamon whisky to your beverage choice.

Liberty Inn

DDP: One credit (Q) / Cost: $
Type: American; Quick Service; Mobile Orders; Lunch, Dinner

With so many other attractive, international choices, you might want to skip this familiar menu, but if it's exactly what you and the kids are craving, it will definitely hit the spot. Burgers, surf and turf, a fried chicken sandwich, barbecue pork, Cobb salad with chicken, a patriotic chicken salad (red craisins, white chicken, and bleu cheese), nuggets, fries, a grilled veggie burger, foot-long all-beef hot dogs, and fries or apple slices are familiar and comfortable for a quick meal or snack. Kids have Disney meal choices, pasta and marinara or a chicken and apple salad. The regular kids menu has a cheeseburger or chicken nuggets. A marshmallow cookie crunch cupcake, mixed fruit cup, or apple pie cheesecake will be a sweet end to your meal at the Liberty Inn.

Refreshment Outpost

DDP: One credit (Q) / Cost: $
Type: American; Quick Service; Lunch, Dinner

For a fast refueling stop, grab an all-beef hot dog with chips or something sweet like soft-serve in a waffle cone, an ice cream float, or a frozen slushy made with lemonade or Coke. There are fountain drinks and some alcoholic drinks like draft beers and some creative concoctions: frozen brown elephant (frozen Coke and Amarula cream liqueur), outpost lemonade with vodka, and mango Starr with Starr African rum.

Italy

Italy Kiosks, Wagons, and Carts

- If it's time to refresh the troops, find something cool and sweet from the **Gelato Stand** in a cup, cone, or waffle bowl. Flavors change frequently.
- **Via Napoli** has a pizza window if you don't have time to sit down and savor a meal right now. Otherwise, try Via Napoli itself. Most folks agree that it's the best pizza at Walt Disney World.

Tutto Gusto Wine Cellar

DDP: No / Cost: $S
Type: Italian; Lounge; Snacks

There's more than wine in this cellar. Think of it as an Italian wine cellar with meats and cheeses. Order "plates for two or more" with cuisines representing the many distinct regions of Italy. Try something familiar like meatball sliders, ravioli, or panini, or branch out from the usual Italian-American fare with insulata di mare (salad of the sea) with lemon shrimp, squid, and octopus. You can also fill up on a great array of panini, beef, salmon, and chicken dishes, and pasta like lasagna, ravioli, spaghetti, and lots more goodies. Cannoli, strawberries and marscapone (in season), tiramisù, chocolate Nutella cake, and other dessert "shooters" complete the bill of fare. It feels like a real Italian wine bar.

Tutto Italia Ristorante

DDP: One credit (T) / Cost: $$ (TiW)
Type: Italian; Unique/Themed Dining; Lunch and Dinner

Dine in Old World charm under the glow of chandeliers surrounded by realistic murals of ancient Rome. You will find the lunch menu less extensive and less expensive than dinner, but you'll enjoy wonderful Italian food no matter when you arrive.

The grande antipasto misto is a great way to share samples of many of the appetizers with your dining partner. There are about ten other tempting choices for appetizers, with arancini being a stand-out (shrimp and lobster fried risotto balls). For lunch, choose from Italian salads with chicken added if you're making it a meal, pasta, paninis, and beef and fish main courses. Dinner has much of the same with some interesting additions and higher prices. Risotto with shrimp, tagliatelle with campagnoli (hot and spicy Italian sausage), cheese tortellini with prosciutto and peas, lasagna alla Bolognese, and good old baked ziti or spaghetti, as well as inventive beef, fish, and chicken entrées are plentiful. Desserts include tiramisù, sorbetti e gelati, panna cotta, a lemon ricotta cheesecake with marinated strawberries, cannoli, and a warm hazelnut chocolate cake with vanilla gelato and chocolate sauce that's hard to forget. Kids should have no problem with the choice of mozzarella sticks, spaghetti, chicken tenders, and cheese or pepperoni pizza on their menu. What a delightful way to say ciao to Italy!

Via Napoli Ristoranti e Pizzeria

DDP: One credit (T) / Cost: $$ (TiW)
Type: Italian; Unique/Themed Dining; Lunch, Dinner

The consensus is that this is where you'll find the best pizza in all of Walt Disney World. It's true, but you'll find plenty of other Italian favorites here, as well. Head to the back of the Italy Pavilion to find Via Napoli. Nick Valenti is in charge of sending to your table the best of what southern Italy has to offer.

Mozzarella Caprese (tomato and fresh mozzarella salad) or prosciutto and melon are sure-fire hits to start your culinary tour. Food is baked in three ovens—with names! Your dinner will be cooked in Stromboli, Etna, or Vesuvius, all famous volcanos of the region. They even have faces, and you can see the fire flickering in their open mouths. Colorful travel posters of Italy line the walls. Many kinds of fresh pasta, Parmigiana to please just about everyone in your party, chicken and Caesar salads, and more than 24 choices of pizza made fresh to order will leave your group happy with appetites well-satisfied. The mezzo-metro pizza is half a meter (more than 19.6 inches) across!

The range of toppings is incredible—just about anything you want on a pizza, you can have on it at Via Napoli. You will find signature specialty pizzas like a white pizza with smoked salmon, a four cheese, a broccolini full of veggies, a spicy picante, and other inventive pies.

Kids can choose from pizza Marg, bocconcini (breaded, with fried bites of mozzarella), and spaghetti with meat-balls on their own menu plus a chocolate or vanilla sundae or a vanilla gelato cookie sandwich should suit them for dessert. Four kinds of Italian beer, wine and sangria by the glass, and specialty drinks like Sicilian Sunset, Via Vesuvius, or a Via Napoli Sangria are on hand to accompany your meal. There are plenty of non-alcoholic beverages, too. Via Napoli is perenni-ally popular for good reason!

Germany

Germany Kiosks, Wagons, and Carts

- Check out the little bar in the back of **Weinkeller**, adja-cent to the Biergarten, for a variety of German wines. You can get cheeses to pair with them.
- The Germany **Hövels** stand and **Germany Bier** stand both offer a variety of beers from the different regions of Germany, and they sell pretzels as well.

Biergarten

DDP: One credit (T) / Cost: $$$ (TiW)
Type: German; Unique/Themed Dining; Lunch, Dinner

It's always October here at the Biergarten! Next to Sommer-fest and billing itself as a "boisterous buffet," you'll serve your-self up heaping helpings of hearty German food. Octoberfest seating means you will find large, banquet tables where several families are seated together. As you eat, you'll hear lots of rous-ing, lively German folk music. Feel free to clap along or sing if you know the words. The vibe here is rollicking and relaxed.

Cold salads include potato, tomato, cucumber, cabbage, and pasta. Lots of the offerings are seasonal, so expect them to change frequently. They come with pretzel rolls and house-made pickles. Entrées feature items such as pork schnitzel, spätzle (noodles), German meat loaf, sauerbraten, roast pork, beef, platters of sausages, and mac and cheese, along with chicken and fish dishes. Apple strudel, cheesecake, chocolate cookies, Black Forest cake, and others bring your lavish buffet to a sweet conclusion. You'll find the menu well-stocked with German beers, white wines, red wines, schnapps, and shots. There are, of course, non-alcoholic beverages aplenty. Let the oom-pah-pah music begin!

Karamell-Küche

DDP: One credit (S) / Cost: $
Type: German/American; Quick Service; Snacks

This quaint little establishment will remind you of the pictur-esque caramel shops you've seen in the Werther's Originals advertisements, and sure enough, Werther's is the sponsor. Caramel presented in a virtually endless array of preparations is the order of the day. You'll find tempting caramel apples, caramel popcorn, caramel dipped chocolates and strawberries (and pineapple and grapes, too), caramel marshmallows, cara-mel pretzels, and more hand-crafted caramel treats than you've ever imagined, made right here in this sweet-smelling caramel kitchen. As many ways and combinations as you can imagine caramel creations being concocted, this shop has more! It will be difficult for children (or adults, for that matter) to choose among them, so you might want to pick up a few items while you're here to take home or enjoy later back at your hotel room.

Sommerfest

DDP: One credit (Q) / Cost: $
Type: German; Quick Service; Lunch, Dinner

A quick stop at Sommerfest's counter will have you feeling like you've just dropped in on a casual, Bavarian café for the afternoon or evening. Brightly painted Alpine motifs deco-rate the buildings that surround you. Tables outside let you enjoy German music coming from the nearby Biergarten while munching on reasonably priced brats, frankfurters, nudel gratin (baked mac and cheese with a custard-like texture), and cold potato salad with eggs. The restaurant also specializes in authentic, hand-twisted pretzels. Finish in German style with the deliciously rich Black Forest cake (chocolate and cherries) or Bavarian apple strudel. A selection of German beers, bourbon shots, and Riesling wine are available, as well as plenty of non-alcoholic drinks.

China

China Kiosks, Wagons, and Carts

- The pretty pagoda called the **Joy of Tea** offers much more than just tea. Have a chicken curry pocket or a pork and vegetable egg roll or—if you can't decide—sample both by ordering the Lucky Combo! Hot and cold assorted teas, lucky red bean ice cream, ginger ice cream, alcoholic beverages featuring plum wine, schnapps, gin, and vodka, draft beer, and smoothies or soft drinks will accompany that snack nicely. Joy no longer offers the wonderful barbecue pork bun—please bring it back!

Lotus Blossom Café

DDP: One credit (Q) / Cost: $
Type: Chinese; Quick Service; Lunch, Dinner

If your party wants something fast and delicious, either for a meal or just a snack, walk through the red pillars of the Lotus Blossom. Dine either inside or outside under the eaves. You'll be delighted with the reasonably priced menu. Maybe the pot stickers and pork and vegetable egg rolls are exactly what you need to keep you going today. You'll recognize your favorite Chinese take-out items like orange chicken, Mongolian beef noodles, shrimp fried rice, Sichuan spicy chicken, and vegetable stir-fry. Draft beers, plum wine, smoothies, teas, and fountain beverages are served, along with caramel ginger or lychee ice cream.

Nine Dragons Restaurant

DDP: One credit (T) / Cost: $$ (TiW)
Type: Asian/Chinese; Unique/Themed; Lunch, Dinner

Dine in an elegant setting under the soft glow of Chinese lanterns at Nine Dragons where contemporary Chinese cuisine meets traditional. The price is reasonable and the service is some of the most attentive in the entire park.

You'll recognize familiar appetizers like pot stickers, spring rolls, and dumplings. The Chinese steamed buns are exceptionally savory and choices include braised pork and chili aioli, fragrant chicken, and General Tsao's chicken. Whether you'd like to try salt and pepper shrimp, honey-sesame chicken, roast duck salad, Kowloon spare ribs, Kung Pao chicken or shrimp, shrimp typhoon, fragrant five-spiced fish, or vegetable and tofu stir-fry, there is a wealth of mouth-watering items from which to choose. An excellent value is the Nine Dragons Family Dinner Set. It includes your choice of soup, entrée, and dessert. Banana cheesecake egg rolls, Chinese ginger cake, and ice cream are the featured desserts. You'll usually be able to find a table here, and it's always a good choice for food, service, and value.

Norway

Norway Kiosks, Wagons, and Carts

- Stop by the **Norway Drink Cart** if you feel like having something cool to drink. A glass of wine or beer, fountain beverages and bottled water are sold, as well as Mickey ice cream treats and a croissant doughnut that's out of this world.

Akershus Royal Banquet Hall

DDP: One credit (T) / Cost: $$$-$$$$ (TiW)
Type: Norwegian/American; Character Buffet; Breakfast, Lunch, Dinner

This medieval castle is the perfect place in Epcot to meet Disney princesses. If Cinderella's Royal Table was sold out when you called to reserve a table, Akershus might still have openings. There are no guarantees on exactly which princesses will appear on any given day, but some of the princesses who usually attend are Princess Aurora (Sleeping Beauty), Belle, Ariel, Snow White, and Cinderella.

Breakfast here is traditional American fare served family style, but there is also a grand Norwegian smorgasbord buffet: smoked pork, dilled salmon gravlax, roasted turkey, cheeses, garnishes, and more. It's filled with so many great treats that everyone should find plenty to like. Lunch and dinner feature Norwegian specialties, so be aware of the menu when planning a visit. The choices are wide enough to please just about everyone. First comes a "Taste of Norway," which includes seafoods, cheeses, fruits, salads, salads, fruits, and cured, sliced meats. Next, pan-seared salmon, wonderful Norwegian meatballs, seared pork tenderloin, chicken, beef (sometimes), and a cheese and spinach stuffed pasta dish are some of the main courses. Kids have the create-their-own selections option with chicken, beef, Norwegian meatballs, salmon, mac and cheese, or pizza, plus choice of two sides. For dessert, you'll have a tempting assortment of Norwegian-inspired sweet treats that make it difficult to pick just one. Guests in your party might find themselves wanting to share bites of the many, lovely baked goods.

Kringla Bakeri og Kafe

DDP: One credit (Q) / Cost: $
Type: Norwegian; Quick Service; Snacks, Lunch, Dinner

This unassuming little café is one of the nicest surprises in all of Epcot. Those in the know never fail to stop here for the justifiably famous bakery treats, accompanied by a good cup of coffee. If you're looking for more than a quick snack but aren't quite ready for a full Norwegian meal at Akershus, try the succulent Norwegian meatballs (seasonally), the ham and fresh apple sandwich (sweet apple chutney, Jarlsberg and Muenster cheeses—wow), Norwegian club sandwich, or a smoked salmon and egg bagel. Try a Norwegian chef salad, and the uncrustable is another popular pick for children.

Something this place excels at is pastry—*lots* of pastry. Once you try the Norwegian school bread, you'll be signing up for extra classes! It's a not-overly-sweet cardamom bun filled with vanilla cream custard and coated with toasted coconut. The Viking chocolate mousse is scrumptious and comes with small cookie horns stuck into the sides of a frozen chocolate Viking hat. It's delightful! Chocolate pretzels, the troll horn, snow globe, and a cinnamon loaf of epic proportions will make everyone in your group want to linger just a little bit longer in Norway. Do not miss this café!

Frozen Ever After Dessert Party is your chance to try some of the most lovely treats (sweet and savory) and beverages while enjoying the Epcot fireworks. During the seasonal dessert party, you'll watch the show that happens over the water from the comfort of your table with unobstructed views and toast the end of a special day with sparkling specialty beverages, alcoholic and non-alcoholic. Afterwards, you'll take a ride on the popular Frozen Ever After (saves having to use a FastPass) attraction in the Norway Pavilion. Prices are $79 for adults and $47 for kids 3-9, which includes tax and gratuity (separate park admission ticket is required). Don't expect to meet the Frozen characters, however. It is not a character Meet-and-Greet. As with all outdoor events, weather may cancel the show, but the dessert party will be moved to a nearby indoor location. Reservations are required.

Mexico

Mexico Kiosks, Wagons, and Carts

- **Choza de Margarita** serves drinks like signature **Margaritas** served on the rocks, frozen Margaritas, and Mexican beers. This newer kiosk, a thatched hut, also has quick snacks (tacos, empanadas, guacamole, chicken tostada, etc.) to grab-and-go.

La Cantina de San Angel

DDP: One credit (Q) / Cost: $
Type: Mexican; Quick Service; Breakfast (seasonally), Lunch, Dinner

This cantina is right on the lagoon overlooking the water next to La Hacienda. Don't expect to find an American-style breakfast here. The menu is definitely spicy. Eggs with cheese, chilies, tortillas, and chorizo (Mexican sausage) will certainly wake you up! A milder children's option is available. Lunch and dinner menus are the same, and also feature traditional Mexican food. You can order chicken and rice, tacos (including beef, chicken, or fish tacos), empanadas (here, that means fried flour tortillas filled with cheese), Mexican salad, and nachos. Beans and rice are served with most of the entrées. For kids, mac and cheese, cheese empanadas or chicken tenders are available. Desserts are churros (Mexican donuts) and paletas (fruit popsicles) or Mickey ice cream. Mexican sodas (called jarritos), Coke products, hot cocoa, and coffee accompany the meals. There are plenty of alcoholic beverages, too, like Margaritas, draft beer, tequila, and sangria. All that, and you can watch the fireworks while having dinner—but remember to ask for a table overlooking the water.

La Cava del Tequila

DDP: No / Cost: $
Type: Mexican; Lounges; Beverages

Over 200 kinds of tequila are available in this cave of wonders, not to mention some of the best Margaritas this side of the border, along with Mexican beers and wines. Chips and salsa or guacamole can accompany your drink selections.

La Hacienda de San Angel

DDP: One credit (T) / Cost: $$
Type: Mexican; Unique/Themed; Dinner

Look for this quaint, Mexican restaurant right on the water. The dinner menu at La Hacienda is both extensive and inventive. You will find many traditional Mexican favorites, but there are also more exotic offerings to tempt you. Entremeses (appetizers) include a light spring salad, cream of corn soup with crisp tortilla strips, barbecued beef with black beans and chorizo (spicy sausage), shrimp and chorizo, and several kinds of fresh cheese sauces, guacamole, and various chili sauces with chips and tortillas. There are interesting plates "for two," one with several varieties of seafood and one with beef and chicken. These come with beans and vegetables. Entrées have enough diversity to please most palates. Steak, chicken, a taco sampler platter, chile relleno with shrimp, or short ribs with potato purée all come with housemade corn tortillas and rice. Finish the meal with volcán de chocolate (lava cake with raspberry sauce), fruit sorbets, empanada de manzana (puff pastry filled with caramel apples, dulce de leche ice cream, and caramel sauce), or the well-known Mexican flan (custard). Service is friendly and attentive, and the flavors are definitely zesty! With grand windows overlooking the lagoon, the view of the fireworks show at night is simply spectacular.

San Angel Inn Restaurante

DDP: One credit (T) / Cost: $$ (TiW)
Type: Mexican; Unique/Themed Dining; Lunch and Dinner

One of the nicest perks of dining at San Angel Inn Restaurante is sitting beside the water indoors in perpetual blue twilight watching the little boats go drifting by, filled with guests on their way to the Gran Fiesta Tour Starring the Three Caballeros: Donald Duck, Panchito Pistoles, and José Carioca. The architecture is modeled in the style of a seventeenth-century hacienda. In the background, a Mayan pyramid is colorfully illuminated. Look for carved stone heads in the Olmec style.

The menu here is like taking a trip to Mexico. In fact, Epcot's version is based on the famous San Angel restaurant in Mexico City. For starters, try the Aztec soup, Acapulco-style shrimp cocktail, chicken tostadas, guacamole, queso fundito (Monterrey jack cheese melted with spicy sausage, poblano peppers and onions and served with flour tortillas), or Caesar salad. The main courses aren't your typical Mexican-Amrican takeout fare. Far from it! You'll find beef, pork, chicken, and fish well-prepared and spiced carefully, sided with authentic sauces, and some combination of rice, beans, or vegetables. Mole poblano is grilled chicken with a classic mole sauce—pine nuts, spices and just a hint of unsweetened chocolate. There are two chef's recommendations that should please hearty appetites. Try the braised short rib, tamale, poblano pepper stuffed with shrimp, queso fresco (fresh cheese), and black beans, or the Veracruz-style catch of the day served over roasted potatoes and a Mexican vegetable medley. Kids can order tamer entrées such as grilled chicken, chicken tenders, cheese quesadilla, or mac and cheese. Lots of signature beverages and Margaritas are available to accompany your meal. Bavarian cream with fresh berries (seasonal), caramel ice cream, cheesecake with caramel sauce, a traditional vanilla flan (custard with caramel sauce), Mexican fruit sorbets, or chocolate mousse should allow you to savor the ambience here at San Angel before leaving Mexico behind.

It's hard to find a prettier, more romantic dining spot anywhere at Walt Disney World, and the food is outstanding. Dining at San Angel is always a treat.

Your head may be spinning and your feet may be protesting by this point in the evening, but your stomach should be very happy. After all, visiting eleven countries is a tall order in just a day or two. Add Future World Epcot to that agenda and you will definitely need a good night's sleep to get rested and ready for more adventures tomorrow. If you thought Epcot was big at 300 acres, just wait. The Animal Kingdom is the second largest theme park in the world, boasting 500 lush acres! Your party can count on finding plenty of good things to eat and drink in order to maintain the stamina to cover such large distances, and those dining options are exactly what you'll find in the next chapter.

Disney's Animal Kingdom, Part One

Discovery Island, Africa, Rafiki's Planet Watch

Dining choices in the Animal Kingdom are extensive and range from the tame and familiar to the wild and exotic—a lot like the animals you'll encounter here. Those comfortable walking shoes you packed can expect a serious workout today!

The 500-acre Animal Kingdom opened on Earth Day, April 22, 1998, the fourth of the four big Disney theme parks to open in Orlando. It has been expanded and updated several times since then, and more big changes are on the horizon. Coming here is a wonderful way to introduce children to the idea of animal and habitat conservation; education is a big part of the park's mission.

Now that Pandora—the World of Avatar has opened, the entire area has experienced a big uptick in attendance. The new land added an additional twelve acres to the already huge Animal Kingdom. You'll see floating islands and bioluminescent plants, and you can dine at the Satu'li Canteen, a spacious restaurant displaying objet d'art from the Na'Vi culture and décor reflecting this gorgeous new world.

Whether you arrive by car or Disney bus, you'll pass a Rainforest Café on the left as you face the entrance gates. It's not inside the park, but because of the restaurant's animal theme, it's a perfect fit for this location. Keep it in mind. You might want to eat here at some point before, after, or even during your visit.

On our "dining safari," we will proceed clockwise and pass through the Oasis, Discovery Island, Africa, Rafiki's Planet Watch, Asia, Pandora, and finally DinoLand, U.S.A. If you notice a kaleidoscope of different ideas and kinds of exhibits, you're right. That's because the original concept for Disney's Animal Kingdom, as explained by Michael Eisner at the opening ceremonies back on April 22, 1998, was pretty wide-ranging and ambitious: "Welcome to a kingdom of animals...real, ancient and imagined: a kingdom ruled by lions, dinosaurs and dragons; a kingdom of balance, harmony and survival; a kingdom we enter to share in the wonder, gaze at the beauty, thrill at the drama, and learn."

To that list, let's add "and eat," because you'll undoubtedly be doing a lot of that while you're here.

Rainforest Café at Disney's Animal Kingdom

DDP: One credit (T) / Cost: $$
Type: American; Unique/Themed; Breakfast, Lunch, Dinner

This wild café is located just outside the park gates. The menu here is typically American. What you get, in addition to good food and excellent service, is the ambience of eating in a tropical rainforest filled with animated animals, stars overhead, and even the occasional rainstorm accompanied by lightening and thunder. The bar stools all are painted and designed to resemble the back half of various beasts—zebras, giraffes, tigers, and others. Little ones might find the realism a bit overwhelming, especially the loud sounds of the simulated storm. If you can rouse everyone out of bed early enough (it opens at 8:30 a.m.), you might want to plan a stop at this interesting restaurant before you even pass through the entrance turnstiles to the Animal Kingdom.

Breakfast items are "Jungle Classics" or "Rainforest Favorites," and the kids menu is very appealing. Breakfast includes omelettes (including egg white omelettes), eggs Benedict, Tonga toast (this is amazing!), waffles, steak and eggs, oatmeal and fruit, breakfast slider sandwiches, and a hot and spicy Mexican breakfast pizza called Pie of the Viper. "Fun-sized" kids menu options are great—this place loves children. Mimosas, Jungle Fever Bloody Marks, many kinds of specialty coffee drinks, and juices are on the breakfast menu.

At lunch and dinner, the menus and prices are the same. Rainforest is known for its large menu with items guaranteed to please just about anyone. Start off with beef lava nachos, crustacean crab dip, or maybe an ahi poke tower. Burgers, sandwiches, and fries? Check. Pasta and flatbreads? Check. Soups, salads, seafoods? Check. Beef, chicken, pork? Check and double check! You can even try some reasonably priced add-ons (often referred to nowadays as enhancements) like coconut shrimp, onion rings, shrimp scampi, and St. Louis spareribs. Kids have plenty of entrees like grilled chicken, hot dog, popcorn shrimp, mini-burgers, mac and cheese, pizza, pasta, and some great pork spareribs with sides like apple-sauce, fresh fruit, corn, steamed veggies, and more.

A favorite dessert here is the sparkling volcano. It used to come lit with an actual sparkler, but now the sparkle is a decoration inserted into the top. It's plenty big enough for three or four to share. Brownies, vanilla ice cream, whipped cream, and hot fudge and caramel running down the sides of the mountain make it easy to understand this dessert's enduring popularity. If that's too much, then cheesecake, sorbet, a root beer float, or Key lime pie ought to keep the gang happy.

The place is formulaic, but that formula continues to work exceptionally well. The décor and the food are both lots of fun. There's a spectacular aquarium and gift shop for added interest.

Safari Bar

DDP: No / Cost: $
Type: American; Lounges; Snacks and Beverages

Just outside the gates leading to the Animal Kingdom is the Rainforest Café's Safari Bar. The lounge stocks plenty of draft and bottled beers, some of them unusual like Funky Buddha Pineapple Beach, and at present has wines from California, Italy, and New Zealand. The place is known for some wild specialty cocktails and signature cocktails that are bright, bold, and lots of fun. You can try a Cheetah Rita, Mongoose Mai Tai, Panama Punch, Fireball Smash, or a couple of signature martinis. If you're feeling like a little something, or even a big something, you can order from the full restaurant menu. That's a great option, especially when it's impossible to get a table in the popular Rainforest Café!

Discovery Island

Discovery Island Kiosks, Wagons, and Carts

- **The Feeding Ground** is the clever name for a popcorn wagon on Discovery Island. You can find frozen lemonade for the kids and adult beverages here, too.

- **The Smiling Crocodile** is located on the way to the bridge leading to Asia. It's just before you get to the Eight Spoon Café on the opposite side of the walkway. It currently features a turkey BLT on ciabatta bread and a pimento-cheese BLT, but offerings do change. Both come with bread-and-butter pickles, and you can wash it all back with a cold beer or fountain beverages.

- **Eight Spoon Café** is a small walk-up kiosk as you leave Discovery Island and head over the bridge to Asia. Baked mac and cheese either plain or with pulled pork or shrimp and sweet chili sauce, Mickey pretzels with cheese dipping sauce, and assorted chips are available, along with fountain beverages and water.

- **Isle of Java** is near the bridge that leads to DinoLand, U.S.A. If you want coffee or a morning beverage, Isle has you covered. There's an Island Cappuccino with white chocolate and Captain Morgan spiced rum, too. Pair your drink with muffins, elephant ears, bagels, or a Danish. Isle also has apple cider donut holes with an apple cider glaze.

Creature Comforts

DDP: One credit (S) / Cost: $
Type: American; Quick Service; Snacks

Past Pizzafari on the same side of the walkway, you'll come to Creature Comforts. Everything's coming up Starbucks at this delicious-smelling counter-service establishment. The long list of hot, cold, and specialty coffee drinks is sure to please anyone looking for a pick-me-up, caffeinated or not. Tea, hot cocoa, milk, or fruit beverages should provide just what you're looking for if coffee isn't your thing. In addition, there are some interesting seasonal choices, currently some iced caramel or iced cinnamon drinks. If you'd like to make this a quick breakfast stop or just want a satisfying snack, pick up a Starbucks specialty coffee drink for yourself and pair it with a scone, muffin, danish, croissant, yogurt, pumpkin or banana bread, or a slice of iced lemon pound cake.

Flame Tree Barbecue

DDP: One credit (Q) / Cost: $ (TiW)
Type: American; Quick Service; Mobile Orders; Lunch, Dinner

Almost directly across from Pizzafari on the opposite side of Discovery Island is Flame Tree Barbecue. Barbecue ribs (if you're ravenous, get the full rack of St. Louis-style ribs) chicken, pulled pork, fruit salad, and smoked turkey are menu favorites here. Can't choose? There's a ribs, chicken and pulled pork sampler with baked beans and coleslaw. Sides are fries and onion rings, and they also have Mandarin oranges. Disney check meals for kids are Smucker's Uncrustables. Additional kids choices are a baked chicken drumstick, a turkey sandwich, or an all-beef hot dog. For dessert, items rotate, but right now the salted caramel apple crisp cupcake is a sweet finish to a meal here. There are beers and wines to pair with your food, in addition to lots of non-alcoholic beverages. For the adventuresome imbiber, check out the Mandarin orange vodka lemonade; it's guaranteed to beat the heat.

Nomad Lounge

DDP: No / Cost: $$
Type: African/American; Lounge; Snacks, Drinks

Nomad is next to Tiffins, Discovery Island signature dining restaurant. If you weren't able to get a table at Tiffins, you can still sample some of the flavors right here, accompanied by a tremendous selection of alcoholic and non-alcoholic beverages. The small plates change with the season and are now the irresistible chicken satay with spicy peanut sauce and cucumber salad, Wagyu beef sliders, a nice charcuterie, "impossible" burger sliders (they are veggie, but it's hard to tell that), a tuna poke bowl, smoked pork ribs, a selections of artisanal cheeses, and a truffle poutine. Be sure to try the Tiffin's signature bread service with extras like fig tapenade and maybe a Taste of Tiffins dessert (if available) or churros with vanilla cream and chili-strawberry. With names like the Tempting Tigress, the Snow Leopard Salvation, or Jenn's Tatoo, choosing a specialty cocktail might pose quite the challenge!

Pizzafari

DDP: One credit (Q) / Cost: $ (TiW)
Type: Italian; Quick Service; Mobile Orders; Lunch, Dinner

As soon as you cross the bridge leading to Discovery Island, Pizzafari will be on your left. Colorful paintings of wild birds and animals in motion enliven the walls of its several dining rooms. A casual atmosphere makes for relaxing dining. Flatbreads like shrimp, pepperoni, cheese, and veggie are offered, along with salads including chicken Caesar. Garlic knots and tomato basil soup could make a meal by themselves. Disney check meals for kids include Mickey pasta with turkey marinara sauce or Smucker's Uncrustables, but kids could opt for cheese pizza or mac and cheese on their menu instead. Desserts are sometimes chocolate mousse and tiramisù, either one always welcome, but as of now only cannelloni cake is available.

Pizzafari Family-Style Dining

DDP: One credit (T) / Cost: $$
Type: Italian; Table Service; Dinner

Have a Caesar or Caprese salad to start, followed by pepperoni pizza, baked ziti, fettucini Alfredo with chicken, and mini-cannolis for dessert. It's served up family style and the mood is casual. Tables in Wonderland discount doesn't apply to this meal. The cost is $19.99 for adults and $11.99 for children ages 3-9, tax not included but no tip is expected. Beverages including alcoholic beverages are included in the dinner price.

Terra Treats

DDP: One credit (S) / Cost: $
Type: Gluten free/allergy free; Quick Service; Snacks

A little kiosk on the far side of Discovery Island just before the bridge that leads to Africa, Terra Treats is worth noting. Selections include hummus and veggies, buffalo chicken wings, a fresh fruit cup, and rice chips.

Tiffins

DDP: Two credits (T) / Cost: $$$
Type: African/Asian/Latin; Fine/Signature; Lunch, Dinner

Adjacent to Pizzafari, the popular Tiffins is creating a lot of gastronomic buzz. (Wondering what a "tiffin" is? It means a light lunch, but a lot of the entrées here are hardly in the light category.) Tiffin's is considered to be one of the best places to eat among all the restaurants in the four Disney theme parks. The cuisine is a mixture of African, Asian, and Latin influences, but it is intended to appeal to average American tastes so remain undaunted and give it a try. You won't be disappointed.

The appetizers include charred octopus, a selection of artisan cheeses, avocado and tomato salad, spiced chickpea falafel, charcuterie, mushroom soup and others depending upon the season. There's always a selection of Tiffin's delicious signature breads. A rotating list of favorites like chicken, lamb, pork, halibut, duck, Wagyu beef, shrimp and grits, and braised lamb shank are joined on the list of entrées by whole fried fish and a terrific pan-seared Alaskan halibut with fingerling potatoes and haricot verts (green beans). Vegetarian crispy sadza (corn cake) with seasonal veggies appears, too. Add an enhancement like lobster mac and cheese or Brussels sprouts. Lunch offers you a chance to "taste two" from a long list of gourmet offerings. Create-your-own entrées for kids are pan-seared fish, shredded beef tacos, grilled chicken breast, grilled shrimp, and "impossible foods bunny chow" with beverage.

The desserts are equally exotic: passion fruit tapioca crème with chocolate crumble, guava mousse with lemon curd, whipped cheesecake and espresso sponge, and a yummy South American chocolate ganache with caramelized banana and cocoa nib tuile (a baked wafer), among several others. The beverage menu is extensive, with lots of non-alcoholic beverages plus beers and wines from around the world. There are many creative cocktails on the menu, too. The three dining rooms each have a different theme carried out with careful attention to detail. Some have framed drawings used in the early conceptions of the Animal Kingdom. Tiffin's is your opportunity to try something unusual—and fabulous!

Tiffins is currently offering a **Festival of the Lion King Dining Package** that includes a meal at the restaurant (either before or after the show and safari), VIP seating for the show (you'll be close to the action), and you will be escorted to your guided safari through the savanna. This package is a significant time-saver. You don't need to use FastPasses to see the show or take the safari, plus you are booked for the nicest restaurant in the Animal Kingdom. Tier I costs are $99 for adults and $49 for children 3-9. Price doesn't include tax and tip. Cancel within 48 hours of you'll be charged in full. You'll need to make reservations and space is limited. The time it takes to enjoy this event is about 3.5 hours, and you must have a valid park admission ticket. Everything is subject to change or cancellation without notice. For Tier II, costs are $74 for adults and $29 for children 3-9; price doesn't include tax and tip. With this choice, the safari is not included.

Africa

Africa Kiosks, Wagons, and Carts

- **Caravan Road** is a kiosk on the pathway between Africa and Asia. When it's open, which is only during busy times of the year, it serves semi-exotic items like teriyaki beef sliders, Asian noodle salad, and edamame. It also offers Coke products and water.

- **Dawa Bar** is located outside Tusker's. Lots of alcoholic drink options are served, including draft and bottled beer, red and white wine, and cleverly concocted cocktails. Dawa sells breakfast beverages, too, like an African Bloody Mary.

- **Harambe Fruit Market** right across from Kilimanjaro Safaris is your stop for fresh seasonal fruits such as pineapple spears, strawberries, clementines, dried fruits and nuts, fruits with cheese or cheese crackers, and non-alcoholic drinks. Mickey pretzels with cheese dip and mini Babybel cheese and chips are also served at Harambe.

- Check out **Mahindi** near the bridge to Discovery Island for frozen "Jungle Juice" and popcorn, cinnamon glazed almonds or pecans, chips, fountain beverages, and beer.

- Leaving Africa and heading along the path into Asia, contemplate a visit to **Mr. Kamal's**, an oasis featuring chicken dumplings with ponzu (a Japanese citrus sauce), seasoned fries, hummus and veggies with a mini pita, with fountain beverages.

- **Zuri's Sweets Shop** is tucked just behind Mombassa Marketplace. Sweet treats are all the rage at Zuri's, many of them with an animal theme. Savory candies and lots of health-conscious treats like almonds, granola, and yogurt pretzels are also stocked. Cookies, candies, bins of bulk goodies, various nuts, and snacks for everyone, both healthful or indulgent, are on display.

Harambe Market

DDP: One credit (Q) / Cost: $
Type: African; Quick Service, Mobile Orders; Lunch, Dinner

Inspired by African street vendors, walk right up and place your order at the counter. Chicken, pork sausage, ribs, or a vegetable bowl, sided with varied salads. Kids may want a Disney check grilled barbecued chicken skewer, or from the kids menu either corn dogs or barbecue ribs. Harambe occasionally serves warm malva cake (of Cape Dutch-African origin, it contains apricot jam and has a spongy caramelized texture) for dessert. Currently, you'll find safari cake (coconut cake with pineapple-coconut mousse) and pineapple-coconut, watermelon, or passion fruit shave ice. Alcoholic and non-alcoholic beverages are available.

Circle of Flavors: Harambe at Night is a seasonal event centered around five African animals, the leopard, Cape buffalo, African elephant, lion, and rhinoceros. It starts at the train station with a musical reception, light snacks, and specialty beverages. Board the Wildlife Express Train to a meeting with favorite characters from The Lion King at Rafiki's Planet Watch. The train takes you back to the Harambe Market for a "street fest" with music, family-friendly savory foods, themed desserts, kids activities, and more. Cost is $125 for adults, $99 for children 3-9. Check online or call to see if it's being offered while you're visiting.

Kusafiri Coffee Shop and Bakery

DDP: No / **Cost:** $
Type: American; Quick Service; Snacks, Breakfast

This little counter is right next to Tusker House. Grab a cup of steaming coffee or cocoa and pair it with a Mickey Mouse-shaped cinnamon roll large enough for two to share. Breakfast wraps, Danish pastries, croissants, muffins, elephant ears (naturally), fresh fruit, yogurt, and milk and cereals should prepare you for your trek through the Animal Kingdom. Later in the day, come back for sandwiches (smoked turkey, hot roast beef, and tomato and mozzarella) sided with curry-spiced chips. Those breakfast pastries will still be around and cookies, too. Lots of juices, fountain beverages, and coffee drinks are always available at Kusufari. It's fresh and tasty when you need something quick and good.

Mahindi

DDP: No / **Cost:** $
Type: American; Quick Service; Snacks

This little hut serves popcorn and souvenir popcorn buckets, nuts (cinnamon-glazed almonds or pecans), chips, Coke products, and beer.

Tamu Tamu

DDP: One credit (S) / **Cost:** $
Type: American; Quick Service; Snacks

Stop here if your party is looking for something cool, quick, and delicious. If you wanted the malva cake at Harambe but didn't find it on the menu, order the warm malva cake sundae covered in vanilla ice cream and caramel sauce. The Mickey ice cream sundae, a double chocolate chip ice cream/cookie sandwich, the always ever-popular Dole Whip (with or without coconut rum or dark rum), chocolate-covered espresso beans, and many fountain beverages ought to cool everyone off on a warm day.

Tusker House Restaurant

DDP: One credit (T) / **Cost:** $$$ (TiW)
Type: African/American; Character Unique/Themed; Breakfast, Lunch, Dinner

A "tusker" refers to a large bull elephant, and Tusker House is a great place for you to interact with Donald Duck, Daisy, Mickey, and Goofy in their safari garb. There are parades through the restaurant and children are invited to march along. Characters will pose for pictures at your table and sign autographs. You'll find one of the nicest, most extensive selections of menu items anywhere in the resort at Tusker's bountiful buffet. Those in your group should be able to find plenty to keep them satisfied, regardless of personal preferences.

Breakfast fare is fresh fruits, pastries (warm cinnamon rolls, lemon poppyseed bread, croissants,), eggs, meats, Mickey waffles, quiche, fresh fruits, Simba and Nala waffles, potatoes, oatmeal with toppings, cereals, African mealie pap (a breakfast porridge), beef bobotie (spiced meat with an egg-based topping), banana bread pudding, and the kitchen sink—well, almost! Lunch and dinner feature American and "African-inspired" selections like salmon, pork, beef sirloin, chicken, potatoes, mac and cheese, corn dog nuggets, deli meats and cheeses, vegetarian offerings, couscous salad, tofu, fruits and salads, cakes, cookies, brownies, tarts...and the list goes on and on. You will not leave Tusker House craving anything more. Both children and adults will find much to celebrate here! It's one of the best and most entertaining dining experiences in the Animal Kingdom, and when you add in beloved characters wearing safari garb, it's a real "can't miss" Disney dining experience. Many guests find that a trip to the Animal Kingdom just isn't complete without a meal at Tusker House.

Rafiki's Planet Watch

You've taken the narrow gauge Wildlife Express Train all the way out to see Rafiki, the wise bird from The Lion King. Chip and Dale may be there, too, dressed for a safari. You'll see animal conservation up close and personal, and guests can even touch some of the inhabitants here in the Affection Section. Your party will learn about behind-the-scenes care of the animals and have a chance to interact with staff veterinarians while viewing a real examination room. You'll see plenty of nutritious snacks on hand, ready to feed to the well-cared-for animals.

For the longest time, Rafiki's Planet Watch had no food or beverage stations for human beings, a puzzling omission since you've literally been tripping over kiosks, wagons, carts, quick-serve counters, and table-service restaurants from the moment you entered the park.

But that's changed. Rafiki's Planet Watch now has an **Ice Cream Cart**. Cue the animal noises.

Your expedition through Disney's Animal Kingdom heads to Asia next, and then the newest land in the park, Pandora—the World of Avatar, before wrapping up at DinoLand, U.S.A. The first part of this theme park was filled with fantastic places to dine. The second part doesn't contain nearly the variety of options; if you find yourselves at a loss as to where to eat, you might consider revisiting one of the relatively close restaurants in Africa, Discovery Island, or maybe the Rainforest Café on your way out through the Oasis. At this point in your trek, you will no doubt begin to appreciate the sheer size of Disney's Animal Kingdom.

Disney's Animal Kingdom, Part Two

Asia, Pandora, DinoLand, U.S.A.

Asia

Asia Kiosks, Wagons, and Carts

- **Warung Outpost** is one of the first things you'll pass in Asia traveling clockwise through the park. It's right outside the entrance to Flights of Wonder. Think chips, Mickey pretzels, and lots of drinks, both alcoholic and not. Margaritas and strawberry freezes are available, too.

- **Drinkwallah** is situated on the water across from the Yak and Yeti Restaurant. Frozen Coke, whole fruits, and chips enjoyed in the shade ought to perk everyone up.

- **Royal Anandapur Tea Company** is beside Drinkwallah. Seasonal beverages will vary, and many come hot, iced, or frozen, but you can always count on plenty to drink. Chips and cinnamon glazed almonds and pecans are offered as of now.

- A **Pretzel and Nuts Cart** is located next to the Mahrajah Jungle Trek. It also sells ice cream and frozen lemonade plus a strawberry fruit cup.

- About four **Ice Cream Carts** are dotted throughout Asia. All the usual goodies are there from frozen bananas, fruit bars, frozen lemonade, and of course Mickey's ice cream bar and ice cream sandwich.

- You can't miss the bright blue **Anandapur Ice Cream Truck**—and you shouldn't! (It's the last thing you'll pass before coming to the Thirsty River Bar on the way out of Asia heading for DinoLand.) Soft-serve vanilla, chocolate, or twist ice cream in a waffle cone, floats, and fountain beverages will cool you off on the warmest afternoon.

Caravan Road

DDP: No / Cost: $
Type: Asian; Fast Casual; Snacks

If you need a little something, Caravan has a good teriyaki beef slider with pickled cucumber, edamame, and assorted fountain beverages. Various specials appear seasonally, more of them during busy times of the year, and vegetarian offerings are generally available. It's right across from the big Tree of Life.

Rivers of Light Dessert Party

DDP: No / $$$$
Type: American; Desserts

If you're around in the evening, come to the Rivers of Light Asia View area terrace just across from Expedition Everest. You will definitely want to watch the 15 minute Rivers of Light spectacular show, and if you want to make the experience even sweeter, come to the dessert party where you'll choose from a varied and beautiful array of themed sweets and savory treats. Drinks are included, both alcoholic and non-alcoholic specialty beverages. Prices are currently $79 for adults and $47 for children 3-9. Price includes tax, and tip is not expected. It doesn't include a ticket to the park, however, so you'll need a valid park admission. Make reservations at (407) WDW-DINE. If you wish to cancel, do so at least 120 hours before the event or you'll be billed in full. In case of inclement weather, the dessert buffet will be held inside at Flame Tree.

Rivers of Light Dining Package

DDP: One credit at Tusker House (T); Two credits at Tiffins (T) / $$-$$$$
Type: Varies; Breakfast, Lunch Dinner

Two restaurants participate: Tiffins and Tusker House. At Tusker House, breakfast with the package starts at $39 for adults and $24 for kids 3-9. Lunch or dinner starts at $52 for adults and $32 for kids 3-9. At Tiffins, Lunch or dinner starts at $68 for adults and at $26 for kids 3-9. The prices don't include taxes or gratuities. At your meal, you'll get a voucher that admits you to reserved seating for one of the night-time shows. Booking this is a bit complicated—you can't book the dining package until about 3 months prior to your dinner, unlike your other dining reservations. If the show itself is cancelled for any reason, you'll still be on the hook for your dinner reservation, and the fee won't be refunded in this case. Seats are not assigned at the show. It's first come, first served. There are several showings per night, but your reservation time determines which show you can attend. You will enter the Rivers of Light theatre view area at the DinoLand entrance. Get there 15-35 minutes before showtime. If you're planning to eat at Tusker House or Tiffins already and planning to stay until evening, this is something to consider. The food will be great and the show is definitely well worth seeing.

Thirsty River Bar and Trek Snacks

DDP: No / Cost: $
Type: Asian; Quick Service; Lounge; Snacks

Past the bright blue Anandapur Ice Cream Truck, you'll find this convenient place to pick up a snack on your way to Expedition Everest. This little kiosk tries hard to be all things to all people. An oldie but goodie, the frozen banana (covered in chocolate and nuts), is delicious—and you can pick one up right here. Popcorn, ice cream treats, frozen juices, and all-day beverages are served anytime. For a quick snack, hummus with veggies and pita or Smucker's Uncrustables are available. Mickey pretzels, chips, and popcorn are on the menu. So are frozen lemonade, a strawberry fruit bar, and a chocolate chip cookie. The drink selection is wide, and includes the Khumbu Icefall, the Flying Yak (non-alcoholic), and the Himalayan Ghost, to name just a few. Lots of beers, ales, and a few wines are sold at Thirsty River Bar, too.

Warung Outpost

DDP: No / Cost: $
Type: American/Mexican; Quick Service; Lounge

Close to Mr. Karaml's and Carvan Road, you'll come upon a Margarita motherlode with three different kinds served separately or layered in case you want the trio of flavors in your glass. Mickey pretzels and cheese dip or chips are available here, as well as non-alcoholic Shangi-La Berry Freeze. Kali River Mango, Bali Hai Strawberry, and Maharaja Lime are the Margarita flavors and Triple Yeti Blast combines all of them. A couple of beers and a frozen cocktail complete the beverage options.

Yak & Yeti Quality Beverages

DDP: No / Cost: $
Type: Chinese; American; Quick Service; Lounge

Feel like you only have time for a grab-and-go snack or quick meal? Then this is your answer in Asia, though it might be a little hard to find. Look behind the Yak & Yeti Local Foods Cafés. It's not something you'd notice if you weren't specifically looking for it. Seating is outdoors. The cuisine is Chinese, the options are limited, but it will be fast and tasty, and sometimes that's just right. Choices vary seasonally, but right now there's an Asian chicken wrap, a ginger chicken salad, and the good old turkey leg served with chips. Sides are pork egg rolls, a mini mango pie, assorted chips, and a mini chocolate silk cake. Specialty drinks like the Yak Attack or Frozen Emperor Margarita are popular choices. Lots of cold draft beers are on tap as well as Beso del Sol (Kiss of the Sun) Sangria and the usual wide variety of fountain drinks and non alcoholic beverages. Any of the foods like turkey leg with chips, egg rolls, and a ginger chicken wrap or salad are easily portable and will get you on the way to your next destination.

Yak & Yeti Local Foods Cafés

DDP: One credit (Q) / Cost: $
Type: Pan-Asian; American; Quick Service; Breakfast, Lunch, Dinner

Maybe you don't feel like devoting the time to a lengthy, sit-down meal. Instead, try this open-air café for similar types of food without the wait, especially if you don't have a reservation already booked at the Yak & Yeti Restaurant and you can't get a table as a walk-up. Continue past the restaurant and you'll see the exotic cafés that resemble those you'd find in remote parts of Asia. The cuisine is Pan-Asian, and most of it will be quite familiar to Americans. For breakfast, there are scrambled eggs with bacon or sausage, fruit salad, hash browns, or a yogurt parfait. Kids have a cereal combo, French toast, and a pancake and sausage stick. For lunch or dinner, this café has Kobe beef hot dogs or cheeseburgers, teriyaki beef bowl with white rice, honey sesame chicken, an Asian chicken wrap, a ginger chicken salad, roasted vegetable masala, and Korean rib tips with fries. Many kinds of egg rolls, fries, and chicken fried rice are available as sides. Kids can pick from cheeseburgers, Smucker's Uncrustables, and chicken strips. Try the mini mango pie, mini chocolate silk cake, or frozen lemonade if you want a little something for dessert.

Yak & Yeti Restaurant

DDP: One credit (T) / Cost: $$
Type: Asian/Chinese/Seafood/American Cuisine; Unique/Themed; Lunch, Dinner

Dine amid décor featuring genuine art and artifacts from the Nepalese region of Asia inside the lovely, cool Yak & Yeti. Despite the "Asian-Fusion" cuisine, many of the menu items will be familiar, but among them you will also find some surprising, exciting combinations.

Appetizers are pot stickers, firecracker shrimp, wok-fried green beans, and pork egg rolls. From there, move on to the "shareables," plates meant for two: tasty and crisp lettuce cups, dim sum basket, ahi tuna nachos, and big island tuna poke bowl. There are half a dozen soups and salads from house specialties to seared tuna to pork wonton soup with chicken broth and veggies. Specialties of the house are salmon, chicken, shrimp, duck, and fish. Several kinds of wok-cooked dinners include sweet-and-sour chicken, Korean barbecue ribs, and crispy honey chicken. In addition, there are many kinds of bowls of various lo mein noodles. Under the grilled meats section of the menu, Kobe burgers are fantastic, there are

Korean BBQ ribs (different from the wok variety but equally yummy), glazed Angus rib-eye steak, a catch of the day, and teriaki chicken. Kids choose from among chicken tenders, mac and cheese, teriyaki chicken, cheeseburgers, mini corn dogs, tempura chicken, chicken fried rice, noodles, and pork egg rolls. There are eight kid-friendly side orders and chocolate pudding or a chocolate chip ice cream sandwich for dessert.

Even the adult dessert list is extensive, ranging from good old New York cheesecake to warm pineapple upside-down cake with vanilla ice cream and caramel sauce, to mango pie or sorbet, and fried cream cheese wontons with vanilla ice cream and skewers of fresh pineapple.

Dining at this interesting place is a feast for all the senses.

Pandora

The newest addition to the Animal Kingdom opened on May 27, 2017. The land is inspired by James Cameron's Avatar, released in 2009 and still the highest-grossing film worldwide to date. It consists of two main attractions, the Avatar Flight of Passage and the Na'vi River Journey. On the first, you'll catch a ride on a banshee for a 3D viewing experience. The second is a gentle glide down a mysterious river where plants glow with their own eerie bioluminescence amid a lush, alien jungle. You can also hike through the unearthly Mo'ara Valley to glimpse floating mountains and the glowing plants and animals that inhabit this strange, new world. You'll find some novel and fun places to eat here, both of them casual. There's a lounge with drinks and snacks as well as a quick service restaurant with fare different from anywhere else in Walt Disney World. If you've never had passion fruit boba balls sitting on top of your food and drinks, get ready!

Pandora—The World of Avatar
Kiosks, Wagons, and Carts

- Pandora is just getting started, but you'll already find some unusual, one-of-a-kind snacks sold at various locations here. On the **ACE Mobile Treats** cart, you'll find the "fruits of Mo'ra" fruit bar and some refreshing drinks like Zico watermelon raspberry coconut water or mountain berry blast. Even the Power-C vitamin water is dragonfruit flavored.

- **Telyu Gummi Candy** is supposed to be a source of protein for the inhabitants of Pandora, but this candy is all sugar—dragon fruit, lemon, and fruit punch—and looks like garden-variety grubs on a stick. Celia fruit gummi candy tastes suspiciously like earthly strawberries. Kids will have fun with them. Pandoran tree spores are actually just brownie bites covered with purple or blue coconut. The Expedition Trail Mix looks just like ordinary trail mix. The same goes for Pandoran sugar crystals on a stick. The blueberry almond popcorn is mostly notable because it's blue. One item to buy more for its looks than its flavor is the pretty Vein Pod—krispy treats have made their way across the galaxy. The pods are large enough to share and covered in white chocolate tinted green with lacy veins of regular chocolate. Don't expect to find churros and popcorn in Pandora.

Pongu Pongu

DDP: One Credit (S) / Cost: $
Type: American/Na'vi; Quick Service; Breakfast, Lunch, Dinner

Translated from Na'vi as "Party Party," Pongu Pongu is a tucked-away quick-service restaurant just across the walkway from the Satu'li Canteen. It's run by "a friendly expat" who visited Avatar and never returned. Find "out-of-this-world" drinks topped with pretty passion fruit boba balls. There are several non-alcoholic fruity drinks and many cocktails sold here, some of them glowing with bioluminescence. Pricy souvenir mugs boost the price, but you do get a glowing unadelta seed on top of your drink. A new treat to try here is the pongo lumpia, based on street food in the Philippines and Indonesia, that combines a sweet cream cheese and pineapple filling that's encased in a crispy, egg-roll-type outside. Try some! Pair them with Hawkes' Grog Ale, namely bright green beer, if you're feeling particularly adventurous.

This place has already gone from being originally billed as just snacks and drinks to serving three meals a day. At breakfast, you can now find a sausage and egg biscuit, French toast sticks, and the surprisingly tasty pongo lumpia. At lunch and dinner, there's a "colossal" pretzel with beer cheese sauce and, again, pongu lumpia—but that's about it. The menu is very limited but may expand if it proves popular. Mostly, however, it's better known for the wild drinks that glow and often include boba balls.

Satu'li Canteen

DDP: One Credit (Q) / Cost: $
Type: American/Na'vi; Quick Service; Mobile Orders; Lunch, Dinner

The restaurant resembles an old Quonset hut, an outpost in the galaxy where you can refresh and refuel the members of your expedition. As soon as you arrive here, try the latest My Disney Experience app on your iPhone or other mobile device to order your food, thus saving time waiting in line to place your order. Pay online, too. You'll receive a notification once it's ready, and you'll pick it up at the "Mobile Order Pick Up" sign. Because Satu'li Canteen is "owned and operated by Alpha Centauri Expeditions," the emphasis is on the fresh, natural bounty of Pandora.

Breakfast has recently been discontinued, but check over at Pongu Pongu if you're looking for a quick morning meal. Lunch and dinner mostly feature bowls with a protein (chicken, beef, fish, chili-garlic shrimp, or crispy, fried tofu), a grain, and a vegetable component. It's worth noting that the vegetarian options are more creative than usual; most things are served with crispy veggie chips and veggie slaw with creamy dressing. Sadly, those handy and savory cheeseburger bao buns are no longer intended for adults, but you can still get them on the children's menu. The "Teylu" all-beef hot dog wrapped in Parker House roll dough went over well with a picky eater in our party recently. Kids can always try the mild cheese quesadilla. Several Disney check meals for kids are smaller versions of the adult bowls. Those fancy, colorful, other-worldly drinks from Pongu Pongu are on the menu here as well, in case you missed them.

Don't expect everything to look familiar on Pandora. The blueberry cream cheese mousse with passion fruit curd resembles a work of Na'vian art. The same goes for a gorgeous, rounded chocolate cake (it's flecked with gold!) with banana cream, goji berries, and a cookie. Both are odd-looking but taste great. You might even say they are out of this world!

DinoLand, U.S.A.

DinoLand Kiosks, Wagons, and Carts

- On the path from Discovery Island to DinoLand, look for the **Trilo-Bites** kiosk. "Buffalo chicken chips," sometimes turkey legs, ice cream floats, fountain beverages, soft serve ice cream, and Sea Dog Sunfish draft beer should hold you until the next meal. Let's hope the darling Boneyard Bounty (ice cream, gummy worms, cookie crumbles) might make a return appearance.

- You'll find a cute stand called **Dino Diner** near the Fossil Fun Games. Grab something on the run from this counter that looks just like a 1950s streamlined trailer. Nachos supreme (loaded!) called corn chip pie, churros, a chili cheese dog, and all-beef hot dog, chips, frozen Coke or lemonade, and other beverages, both alcoholic and not, are sold here, too.

- A **Popcorn wagon** is nearby, as well, and throughout Dino-Land you'll come across several mobile **Ice Cream Carts**.

Dino-Bite

DDP: No / Cost: $
Type: American; Quick Service; Snacks

At Dino-Bite, you'll find assorted flavors of Häagen-Dazs hand-scooped ice cream in a waffle cone, hot fudge sundaes, cookies, chips, Mickey pretzels, ice cream sandwiches, chocolate chip cookies, and fountain beverages. There are several beers here, too. This snack stop ought to keep the kids in your party, both big and the small, satisfied while visiting our prehistoric past. Unfortunately, the Bugs Sundae is not available, but it just might return at some point.

Restaurantosaurus

DDP: One credit (S) / Cost: $ (TiW)
Type: American; Quick Service; Mobile Orders; Lunch, Dinner

Adjacent to the Boneyard, an archaeological dig, you can dine dino-style amid fossil replicas and "dig décor." There are lots of tables with umbrellas to provide welcome shade. The kids menu is designed to please most kids with Disney meals—a Smucker's Uncrustable and a turkey wrap. There are other kid-friendly options, too, like chicken nuggets and cheese-burgers. Adults will find the typical array of Angus burgers, chicken dishes, chili-cheese hot dogs, and a vegetarian black bean burger sided with fries, apple slices, or salad. Clam chowder or potato soup is another option in winter months or a grilled chicken salad with Mandarin oranges and cran-berries in warmer months. Sides like guacamole, chili-cheese fries, and jalapeño poppers round out the choices. For dessert, there's a warm chocolate caramel brownie and a lotus cupcake. Safari Amber, Bud Lite, or a Margarita with José Cuervo tequila are served along with the standard fountain bever-ages, lemonade, chocolate milk, and juices.

Whether your safari here lasts one day, two days, or longer, you'll certainly cover a lot of territory in Disney's Animal King-dom. The next and final one of the four Disney theme parks to explore is Disney's Hollywood Studios. The dining options there range from the sublime where you can relive the glory days of Hollywood at the Brown Derby to the ridiculous (but extremely cool) Sci-Fi Dine-In Theater, where you'll sit in modi-fied convertible cars and eat your meal while watching trailers for old science fiction and horror movies and you'll encoun ter just about everything in between. Be sure to check out the new Toy Story Land if you haven't already, and, if you visit after August 29, 2019, the even newer Star Wars: Galaxy's Edge.

Disney's Hollywood Studios, Part One

*Hollywood Boulevard, Echo Lake,
Muppet Courtyard, Toy Story Land*

Tucked among several well-known, outstanding attractions and shows at Disney's Hollywood Studios, you'll find some equally outstanding places to dine. Sure, there are plenty of run-of-the-mill, quick-service counters selling the usual nuggets, burgers, and fries, but there are also a few restaurants that will pleasantly surprise you. You just have to know where to look for them.

Hollywood Studios, the third of Walt Disney World's four theme parks, opened on May 1, 1989. It's somewhat larger than the Magic Kingdom and considerably smaller than either Epcot or the Animal Kingdom. It comes in at about 135 acres and has the least regular footprint of them all, which makes getting around with any kind of organized plan a bit more challenging.

Echo Lake is intended to be the central "hub," but it's not quite that simple. Hollywood Studios is actually shaped something like the head of Oswald the Rabbit, one of Walt's earliest animated creations. Muppet Courtyard is his open mouth. His round face is comprised of Pixar Place, Commissary Lane, Animation Courtyard, and Echo Lake. Heading up one of Oswald's two long ears, Hollywood Boulevard, you'll encounter the Tower of Terror and Rock 'n' Roller Coaster. The other ear, really just a path, ends at the outdoor arena where the Fantasmic! show happens. There's no way to follow a regular clockwise route through this park, so we'll simply take it one area at a time.

Although two new areas have been added to the park, the basic 135 acre footprint hasn't changed. How does that work? Toy Story Land, 11 acres, occupies the spot where the old Studios Backlot Tour and a few "backstage" areas used to be. Star Wars: Galaxy's Edge comes in at 14 acres but displaces the former Streets of America location. Star Wars at both Disneyland in Anaheim and Walt Disney World in Orlando are clones with virtually identical blueprints.

Hollywood Studios has undergone several revisions (and a name change) since it opened and has been branded and re-branded over the years. The original affiliation with MGM has been dropped like a hot (acrimonious) potato. At one point, part of this park was an actual, working film studio. It's still in the process of finding a distinct identity, but with the new Star Wars: Galaxy's Edge and Toy Story Land additions taking their bows, it's become a whole lot more exciting.

On opening day, then-CEO Michael Eisner said: "The World you have entered was created by The Walt Disney Company and is dedicated to Hollywood—not a place on a map, but a state of mind that exists wherever people dream and wonder and imagine, a place where illusion and reality are fused by technological magic. We welcome you to a Hollywood that never was—and always will be."

Nostalgia still plays an important role here, and California's idealized version of Hollywood during the 1930s-1940s is the period being celebrated.

Hollywood Boulevard

The first area to explore is Hollywood Boulevard, named for the original street in California. It's the main thoroughfare funneling guests into the rest of the park, a lot like Main Street, U.S.A., does in the Magic Kingdom. There's a replica of the Crossroads of the World statue as you enter the street, a nod to the first outdoor shopping mall on Sunset Boulevard. The original statue, however, doesn't have Mickey Mouse striding cheerfully atop the globe, but there's a lot of shopping here, just like the shopping center in California. This area is also a venue for parades and street performers. At the opposite end of the boulevard is an exact re-creation of Grauman's Chinese Theatre with hand and footprints of the movie stars in cement like the ones you've seen in all those old newsreel clips. On the boulevard, you'll also find a re-creation of the first Brown Derby restaurant, and it's one of the nicest places for lunch or dinner in the entire resort. Just don't expect to see Lucy and Desi sipping cocktails at the next table.

Hollywood Boulevard Kiosks, Wagons, and Carts

- Past the main entrance, look for the red-and-white striped awning of the **ICE COLD Coca Cola** kiosk. Juices, a cherry slushy, Coke products, iced coffees, a variety of chips, chocolate chip cookies, Mickey ice cream bars, and Mickey ice cream sandwiches are available here.

- At the fork where Sunset Boulevard meets Hollywood Boulevard, you'll find a well-stocked **Ice Cream** kiosk loaded with Mickey bars, ice cream sandwiches, frozen bananas with nuts and chocolate, Nestle's orange cream bars, frozen orangeade, frozen lemonade, cotton candy, bananas, fountain beverages, and several kinds of beer.

- Glazed peanuts and almonds, ice cream bars, frozen fruit bars, Coke products, frozen lemonade, and beer are available at a little **Nuts and Ice Cream** cart on Hollywood Blvd.

- Three **Popcorn Carts** dot this area of the park. In addition to popcorn, two also sell Mickey pretzels with cheese sauce, all kinds of Coke beverages, and some souvenir Star Wars steins.

- A mobile **Pretzel and Churro** cart is usually found at the end of the boulevard. In addition to Mickey pretzels with cheese sauce and churros, it usually carries whole fruit, Mickey ice cream bars, ice cream sandwiches, Coke beverages, Yeungling and Sam Adams beers, and Angry Orchard Crisp Apple Hard Cider. Carts can move around.

The Hollywood Brown Derby

DDP: Two credits (T) / Cost: $$$ (TiW)
Type: American; Fine/Signature; Lunch, Dinner

For the best, most elegant, as-close-as-it-gets taste of what glamorous old Hollywood was actually like, you've simply got to book a table at the Brown Derby. Service is impeccable but never intrusive. Menu selections are not only inventive but beautifully prepared and plated. The quality of the food is excellent. It's a splurge in every way, but this is one of the reasons why you came to Walt Disney World, for superlative dining experiences different from those available anywhere else. It's quintessential Hollywood at its finest.

Start with the beef carpaccio with capers, lemon-mustard aioli, black salt and shaved Parm, roasted Roma tomato soup (good!), blue lump crab crispy wonton, or ahi tuna crusted with togarashi (Japanese chili) and crispy nori (edible seaweed). Tempting entrées like char-grilled filet of beef, duck breast, rack of lamb, a charred Cheshire pork chop, Faroe Island salmon, Bell & Evans chicken, the classic Cobb salad, and several others will satisfy your appetite indulgently. Not currently on the menu, regretfully, is that melt-in-your-mouth Wagyu burger, but you can still get it in slider form at the lounge next door.

To add yet another level of indulgence, consider an "enhancement" to your entrée, such as a cold-water lobster tail, shrimp skewer, or Georges Bank seared sea scallops. Warm blueberry cobbler, a dark chocolate crèmeux with apricot marmalade and white chocolate amber ring (yes, please), cappuccino crème brûlée, banana toffee cake, or the elegant signature grapefruit cake (it never disappoints) will bring your meal at the Brown Derby to a memorable close. Many premium teas are available as well as a very nice selection of exceptionally good wines.

Children will dine every bit as decadently as the adults with their own fabulous menu. The create-your-own kids meal here raises the bar with pan-seared black grouper, grilled beef or chicken, or vegetarian pho. Of course kids could instead opt for chicken noodle soup, grilled cheese sandwich, or a hot dog on their regular menu.

Two other special experiences happen here. You can get the Fantasmic! Dinner Package (first feast at lunch or dinner and then head to your reserved seats for Fantasmic!) or Dine with a Disney Imagineer (lunch is four courses in the Bamboo Room), both of which are guaranteed to "wow" even the most blasé of guests.

If you're going in Hollywood style, this is the place to do it. Cut. Print. That's a wrap!

The Hollywood Brown Derby Lounge

DDP: No / Cost: $
Type: American; Lounge; Snacks, Drinks

Couldn't get a reservation at the Brown Derby? No worries. You can try some of the same flavors here. It's a great chance to sit at one of the outdoor umbrella-covered tables, watch the people-parade go by, order a couple of small plates to share, and sample some of the specialty drinks this place excels at making. The artisanal cheeses and charcuterie board will surely amuse your taste buds. Ah, now *here* you can still get the Wagyu beef in slider form, but it's on a plate that also includes smoked cheese and bacon with an avocado and duck confit, chipotle-veggie slaw, sweet onion-orange conserve, and crispy leeks. Braised beef arepas (corn cakes), cochinita pibil steamed buns (habañero sauce—hot!), the famous Cobb salad, and tamarind-glazed pork belly with plantain and sweet potato hash are other delightful alternatives. Those great Derby desserts are offered, too, but here they come as a mini-trio sampler. The drink menu is outstanding. Specialty cocktails and martinis, premium ales and beers galore, flights (martinis and Margaritas), and red and white wines by the glass offer you a veritable wealth of beverage possibilities. They also do a mighty good non-alcoholic Shirley Temple, Pink Palace, or Maliblue Beach for the kids.

The Trolley Car Café

DDP: One credit (Q) / Cost: $
Type: American Bakery Cuisine; Quick Service; Snacks, Drinks

Across the street from the Brown Derby, look for this quaint café on the corner of Hollywood and Sunset Boulevards. It's a veritable Starbucks heaven, from the two dozen varieties of blended frappuccinos to the almost two dozen espressos. Refreshers, coffees, teas, and seasonal offerings galore round out this extremely robust drink menu. You can find delightful pastries from La Boulangerie to pair with your beverage. If you're hungrier than that, select from a roster of other choices available seasonally: breakfast sandwiches, roast beef, pastrami, or turkey sandwiches, blueberry and cheddar salad, the infamous Darth Vader cupcake, a fruit tart, chocolate-covered brownie, cookies, and other goodies. Covered seating is available outdoors. This little café might be just what you're looking for. Save me a seat!

Echo Lake

Echo Lake is a man-made lake in southern California, the backdrop you might recognize from many early silent films. An aerial view of Hollywood Studios shows that its original design, later abandoned, incorporated the lake as one of Mickey Mouse's ears. It's still possible to see Mickey's two eyes and the suggestion of where a second ear would have gone from high above the park on Google Earth. Gertie, the dinosaur who stands in Echo Lake, was a vaudeville favorite, the animated subject of hand-painted films that influenced a young Walt Disney. Many of the buildings ringing the lake are similar to those once found in Los Angeles.

Echo Lake Kiosks, Wagons, and Carts

- The Echo Lake **Ice Cream Cart**, in addition to all the usual items, sells frozen bananas covered in chocolate and nuts, an Olaf strawberry lemonade bar, and frozen lemonade.

- **Dinosaur Gertie's Ice Cream of Extinction** looks like a big, green brontosaurus, an architectural nod to the many southern California buildings shaped like something unusual in the early to mid-twentieth century. Big oranges and donuts, many abandoned, still decorate the landscape. At Gertie's, you'll find soft-serve vanilla, chocolate, and twist...when it's open, that is. (It's only open during busy times.) Get it in a cup or a waffle cone.

Mickey ice-cream bars and ice-cream sandwiches are sold here, too.

- **Peevy's Polar Pipeline** is on Hollywood Boulevard near Echo Lake. Check out the refreshing frozen concoctions like Bacardi superior rum, Tito's handmade vodka, and others that rotate. Non-alcoholic frozen drinks are Coke, blue raspberry, raspberry lemonade, and wild cherry. Peevy's isn't serving snacks currently, but it is sometimes a spot for health-conscious snacks like carrot and celery sticks with lite ranch dip, whole pieces of fruit, pickles, grapes, and apple slices. The offerings change seasonally.

- Funnel cake fans, get ready! Next to the Indiana Jones Stunt Spectacular is the little **Epic Eats** where you'll find funnel cakes topped with soft-serve ice cream and strawberries, cinnamon sugar, or powdered sugar. It's selling ice cream waffle cones, root beer floats, dreamsicle floats (with Stoli vanilla vodka), beer, and soft drinks.

50's Prime Time Café

DDP: One credit (T) / Cost: $$ (TiW)
Type: American; Unique/Themed; Lunch, Dinner

Another of the "don't miss" restaurants here at Hollywood Studies is this 1950's unique café. Find it near Indiana Jones and right across from Gertie, the dinosaur on Echo Lake. You'll feel like you've stepped into a black-and-white television program—and that's how you'll be treated. Oh, and by the way, you'll want to request being seated at one of the tables with a TV screen to experience the full 1950s effect. If being told to "eat your vegetables" or "get those elbows off the table, dear" doesn't bother you, jump into the spirit of the place and have a blast from the past! The décor is authentic mid-century modern, down to the last flying brass duck on the wall. With TV sets turned on and kitchen tables set, you'll find good, old-fashioned food prepared in traditional American style served by friendly wait staff who are part of the experience.

Start with beer-battered onion rings, a wedge of iceberg lettuce salad, or chicken noodle soup. Many items are called Dad's, Mom's, Cousin's, Grandpa's, or Grandma's famous or favorite recipe. Stuffed pork chops, fried chicken and mashed potatoes, meat loaf, pot roast, veggie lasagna, chicken pot pie, fish of the day, and salmon Caesar salad are just some of the entrées. If you've been good, think about rewarding yourself with warm apple crisp, Dad's brownie sundae, (Walt's favorite) pineapple upside down cake, or maybe a big slice of Mom's famous chocolate-peanut butter cake for dessert—with ice cream, of course. Kids will be just as happy as adults with their menu: four choose-your-own-entrées (salmon, grilled chicken, chicken tenders, or mac and cheese). Sides like fruit salad, corn, mashed potatoes and a seasonal cupcake will satisfy most children.

Just as intriguing as the food are the drinks. A PBJ milkshake (it's amazing), Ariel or Buzz punch, and Mickey's Bee Bop drink with glowing ice cubes in a souvenir cup are just a few. The adult beverages are equally enticing. Many red, white, and blush wines are available, along with craft and draft beers, but it's the crazy cocktails "from Dad's liquor cabinet" that take center stage here in the 1950s. A Mowie Wowie, Dad's Electric Lemonade (it's neon blue!), or Grandma's Picnic Punch (that literally packs a wallop) will open your eyes.

Prime Time Café is one of those special dining experiences that Disney does so well. Don't miss out on this homage to 50s fun!

Backlot Express

DDP: One credit (Q) / Cost: $
Type: American; Quick Service; Mobile Orders; Lunch, Dinner

Made to resemble a studio backlot, compete with movie props, this quick stop is perfect for healthy alternatives to the usual park fare—although you'll find some of those here, too. Look for Backlot Express between Star Tours and Indiana Jones. It's huge, open-air, but covered from the elements. The former Star Wars menu at Backlot has been replaced since Star Wars: Galaxy's Edge has come to Hollywood Studios. The backlot burger is served with fries or carrot sticks, an Angus 1/3 pound burger with bacon and cheese, chicken and biscuits with county gravy and strawberry glaze, a tasty and traditional Cuban sandwich with roasted pulled pork, sliced ham,

Swiss cheese, pickles, and mustard is hearty and satisfying. A Caprese sandwich (fresh mozzarella and vine-ripe tomatoes) and carrot sticks or a Southwest salad won't destroy your diet. Disney check meal is an uncrustable, but children can also choose mac and cheese or chicken tenders. For dessert, indulge with the sinfully delicious peanut butter brownie or a key lime verrine (layers of key lime custard and graham cracker topped with whipped cream and white chocolate garnish). Drinks are widely varied and include seasonal slushies, juices, fountain beverages, beers, wines, and margaritas. Quick service, shady seating, good options, and reasonable prices make for a nice break in the day.

Dockside Diner

DDP: One credit (Q) / Cost: $
Type: American; Quick Service; Lunch, Dinner

This dockside diner, a modified steam tramper, is permanently docked on Echo Lake. Originally, this diner paid tribute to the classic 1931 film Min and Bill, starring Marjorie Dressler (who won the Best Actress Oscar for her performance) and Wallace Beery in the title roles. Now, it's simply called the Dockside Diner. It won't offer some of the specialty dining experiences you can enjoy elsewhere in the park, and the menu is pretty limited, but the food is plentiful and reasonably priced, with all-beef chili-cheese dogs, foot long dogs, chili-cheese nachos, and barbecued pulled pork sandwiches. Kids can grab an uncrustable Disney check meal or mac and cheese. The S'mores brownie or shakes are simple but decent desserts. Margaritas, a milkshake with Kahlúa and Baileys Irish Cream, fountain beverages, wines, and beers, or a frozen lemonade with a shot of Bacardi rum or Tito's vodka, are available.

Hollywood & Vine

DDP: One credit (T) / Cost: $$ (breakfast), $$$ (lunch and dinner) (TiW)
Type: American; Character Buffet; Breakfast, Lunch, Dinner

Breakfast at 8:00 a.m. means getting into the park early provided you are seated on time. Remember, you are guaranteed the next *available* table, not a table reserved for you and you alone at 8:00 a.m. This charming, old-fashioned diner is on the corner across from Echo Lake. Meet Princess Sofia, Jake from the Neverland Pirates, Handy Manny, Doc McStuffins, and other Disney Jr. regulars at breakfast and lunch. At dinner, Minnie and the whole gang will be here hosting themed holiday buffets.

Breakfast has serve-yourself American favorites like pancakes, Mickey waffles, eggs, potatoes, fruit, bakery treats, breakfast meats, hot and cold cereals, biscuits and sausage gravy, yogurt, and omelettes made to order. Lunch and dinner have rotating combinations of create-your-own salads, soup, seasonal pork, fish, chicken, pasta, salmon, and a mac and cheese. There is also a buffet area just for children. Soft-serve ice cream and an array of desserts are available. There are special holiday events with expanded menus—and prices. You'll sometimes find peel-and-eat shrimp, turkey and stuffing, marinated flank steak with garlic mashed potatoes, seafood mac and cheese, ham, and holiday desserts.

If you aren't able to get a reservation for Cinderella's Royal Table, you may be able to get one here. The food is adequate, pretty similar to most buffets anywhere else, but the characters themselves are always delightful. Breakfast is especially nice because you can spend the whole day in park afterwards, and the big menu appeals to just about anyone.

Tune-In Lounge

DDP: No / Cost: $
Type: American; Lounge; Snacks, Beverages

Maybe you couldn't manage to score a reservation at the 50's Prime Time Café, but cool your jets, Daddy o. You can order from the menu here at this sweet lounge right next door. If you like mid-century modern, you'll be in heaven. Everything is retro-chic, right down to the 1950s television programs playing on the televisions. All those rockin' cocktails from Dad's liquor cabinet are available plus a bunch of apps and the same main courses and desserts from the main café. This lounge is waaaay cool in *every* way! It's the kind of place that would make Annette, Sandy, Danny, Ritchie, and the Fonz feel right at home—hey, get ya' feet off the coffee table!

Muppet Courtyard

PizzaRizzo

DDP: One credit (Q) / Cost: $
Type: Italian/American; Quick Service; Lunch, Dinner

Remember Rizzo the Rat, a Muppet character? (You might even remember the 1969 *Midnight Cowboy* character Ratso Rizzo played by Dustin Hoffman who was Muppet Rizzo's inspiration.) He's the proprietor of this pizza establishment. Dine inside or out on the deck. If your kids crave mainstream-type Italian/American food, they'll find it here. It's no Via Napoli at Epcot's World Showcase, not by a long shot, but it will fill up the troops in a hurry with very little fuss. Meatball subs, pizzas, antipasto salads, and Disney check meals for the kids (mini-chicken sub or a yogurt Power Pack) are the main features. Kids can order a small cheese pizza or mac and cheese, too, both sided with applesauce, a Cutie, and choice a milk or water. A limited beer selection and limoncello lemonade plus many non-alcoholic beverages fill out the drinks list. For dessert, there's cannoli and tiramisù.

Mama Melrose's Ristorante Italiano

DDP: One credit (T) / Cost: $$ (TiW)
Type: Italian/American; Casual; Lunch, Dinner

Mama's is one of the better options for dining in Hollywood Studios. It's tucked behind the Muppet*Vision 3D Theatre in the Muppet Courtyard. The vibe is fun and old-time casual with plastic grapes and vines twined around the rafters filled with tiny lights. Book the VIP section for dinner and watch Fantasmic! over dessert and coffee. The menu is extensive enough to please nearly everyone's palate.

Appetizers are a big cut above average. Crispy calamari, vine-ripened tomatoes with fresh mozzarella, oak-fired mussels, and vegetarian minestrone are just some of the starters. Four crowd-pleasing flatbreads are great to share. Entrées range from standard Italian fare like spaghetti and meatballs, seafood cioppino, and chicken Parmesan to the more adventurous saltimbocca, polenta cake with mushrooms and herbed cauliflower, or shrimp campanelle. Desserts are the Italian classics tiramisù, cannoli, and gelato, plus a few American favorites like strawberry cheesecake and Ghirardelli chocolate cherry torte. If you simply can't decide, order the dessert sampler for mini-versions of several.

Kids will find their own create-your-own entrées: spaghetti, fish, and chicken. They can also order pasta dishes or chicken Parm, or cheese pizza. There are plenty of sides to including a cute "spaghetti and meatball" cupcake. The wine list featuring Italian and California wines is extensive and pairs well with the food. Try the liqueurs like limoncello, disaronno originale, sambuca Romano, or Angelico with 2 oz. pours. Beers are also available. Non-alcoholic beverages are inventive. Specialty and dessert cocktails (Italian Surfer, Double Espresso Martini, and many more) are sure to please. There is a lot to like at Mama's.

Toy Story Land

This area will remind you of Andy's backyard from the *Toy Story* films. Everything is gigantic so that you will feel like you're the size of a toy yourself! Slinky Dog Dash, Toy Story Mania!, and Alien Swirling Saucers are the main attractions. You'll see larger-than-life figures like Woody, Jesse, Buzz, and Rex throughout the land, as well as other familiar toys you'll recognize. Things are definitely kid-friendly including the choices of things to eat, but adults will find plenty to enjoy as well.

Toy Story Land Kiosks, Wagons, and Carts

- If you're looking for warm churros with chocolate sauce or Mickey Pretzels with cheese sauce, the **Market** has you covered. It also stocks a wide selection of both alcoholic and non-alcoholic beverages. Coke products, strawberry lemonade, and tropical fruit punch in addition to Margaritas, piña coladas, and several kinds of beer are available.

- **Neighborhood Bakery** can fix you up with an Incredible Hero Sandwich (cold cuts, cheese, and olive tapenade on a "hero" roll with chips), a Mrs. Incredible mask-shaped pretzel, Num Num cookies (do not pass these up—warm, soft inside, crunchy outside, chocolate chip, big enough to share—a favorite of young Jack-Jack Parr), popcorn, slushies, and specialty items inspired by the Incredibles make stopping here a fun surprise...and again, think Num Num!

Disney's Early Morning Magic—Toy Story Land
DDP: No/ Cost: $$$$
Type: American; Quick Service Continental Breakfast

Sure, it's pricey, but if you want to get to the popular attractions here early, have a nice meal, and get to meet Woody, Buzz, and Jessie, this might be the way to go. Yogurt, fruit, pastries, cereals, and a main course like avocado toast or fried chicken and a cronut with beverages is set up just outside Toy Story Land. At this time, it's being offered on Monday, Wednesday, and Friday from 7:30 a.m. until 8:45 a.m. with breakfast served until 10:00 a.m. Call to see if days coincide with your visit. The price of $79 for adults and $69 for kids 3-9 does not include admission to the park. Early admission is only to the Toy Story Land attractions and at 9:00, the exclusive access ends as other guests are admitted. Attendance is limited and you must reserve and pay in advance.

Woody's Lunch Box
DDP: One credit (Q) / Cost: $
Type: American; Quick Service; Breakfast, Lunch, Dinner

Find Woody's oversized lunch box (look for a big Thermos) and be sure to try the wildly popular pop tarts-style goodies sold here. Breakfast is just what the Toy Story gang would enjoy. S'mores French toast sandwich, banana split yogurt parfait, a hearty breakfast bowl, or the smoked turkey sandwich will fill up tummies of any age, but that chocolate-hazelnut lunch box tart or the raspberry lunch box tart (both with candied bacon sprinkles on top) are absolutely not to be missed!

Lunch and dinner entrées are equally appealing to most guests, and guess what? You can still get those crave-worthy "lunch box tarts" at *any* meal here—or just for a snack! The beef brisket sandwich melt, the three-cheese grilled cheese sandwich, the smoked turkey sandwich, and the novel "totchos" (tots covered in beefy chili, cheese, sour cream, and green onions) are yummy indulgences. Add to these a vegetable macaroni salad, tots (called "potato barrels" here), a Mandarin orange, and some tomato basil soup and you've got yourself a nice little meal! This adorable lunch box has plenty tucked inside for kids of any age.

You've seen half of Disney's Hollywood Studios. Now, let's find out what the other half has to offer. As the second smallest theme park at the resort, it's relatively easy to see it all in a day, but the recent additions, Toy Story Land and Star Wars: Galaxy's Edge, certainly merit a visit and have significantly added to public interest in this park!

Disney's Hollywood Studios, Part 2

Pixar Place, Commissary Lane, Animation Courtyard, Sunset Boulevard, Star Wars: Galaxy's Edge

Pixar Place

The Pixar Animation Studios area in Disney Hollywood Studios is a smaller, representative model of Pixar's own studio in Emeryville, California. Pixar began in 1979 as the computer division of Lucasfilm. Back when the park opened and actually functioned as a production studio, the sound stages here were used in those productions. Now, they've been repurposed. It's a small area where you'll find Toy Story Mania! and not much in the way of dining options, aside from a few snacks.

Pixar Place Kiosks, Wagons, and Carts

- While you won't find any full-service restaurants in Pixar Place, you won't go hungry, either. **Joffrey's Coffee and Tea Company** is a familiar façade at Walt Disney World and can be reliably counted on for good coffee, espresso, pastries, and tea. Seasonal beverages are usually available at Joffrey's.

- If ice cream is what you want, and it's open during busy seasons, there's an **Ice Cream Cart** selling Mickey ice cream bars, ice cream sandwiches, and frozen lemonade. Adults will find beer sold here.

Market

DDP: One credit (S) / Cost: $
Type: American; Quick Service; Snack

 Pretzels with cheese and churros with chocolate sauce are the snacks here. Fountain beverages, lemonade, punch, and Margaritas, beers, piña coladas, a wild strawberry lemonade with vodka are the current beverages.

Commissary Lane

In addition to a lounge, there are two eateries on Commissary Lane. The first is intended to closely resemble the actual ABC TV Studio cafeteria where actors, directors, and crew members rubbed elbows years ago. Its Deco style is authentic to the period. The second is a unique/themed dining experience, one you won't want to miss if you can help it. It's a trip back in time to an era when convertibles with enormous fins roamed the earth and drive-ins weren't yet extinct in southern California.

ABC Commissary

DDP: One credit (Q) / Cost: $
Type: American; Quick Service; Fast Casual; Mobile Orders; Lunch, Dinner

Enter though a palm-lined promenade and step back into the golden age of television. Don't expect a lot of creative menu entries—it's old school. Watch vintage show trailers and see posters highlighting hit shows of the past. Props and wardrobe items are also on display.

The commissary has different menus for lunch and dinner. At lunch, a BBQ rib platter, a land and sea platter, a fish and shrimp platter, chicken strips, and a 1/3 pound Angus beef burger come with various sides like steak fries, coleslaw, and veggies or apple slices. Mediterranean salad, a vegan burger, and a chicken club sandwich are other options. Disney Check meals have the kids covered with a turkey sandwich, an uncrustable, or the Power Pack with yogurt. The kids menu features a cheeseburger, mac and cheese, or chicken strips as well.

Dinner has some of the same choices as lunch, but it adds braised beef and enchilada, shrimp teriyaki bowl, a Southwest

BBQ burger, and a teriyaki veggie bowl. Desserts will vary, but they are currently serving an apple almond tart or a chocolate banana cream almond crisp at dinner. There are many fountain beverages and a couple of nice Robert Mondavi wines.

While the food may not be the pinnacle of park dining, it's just right if you're looking for something reasonably priced, fast, and reliably decent. There are many allergy-friendly choices, so be sure to check the menu if that's something you'd appreciate.

Baseline Tap House

DDP: No / Cost: $
Type: American; Lounge; Snacks, Drinks

To wet your whistle and grab a little something to nosh, Baseline might be exactly what you're looking for at this point in your day. A big, fresh Bavarian pretzel with beer-cheese fondue and spicy mustard, coffee-rubbed rib-eye steak puff with olive salad, California cheese and charcuterie plate, or some spiced almonds are the nibbles. Get specialty non-alcoholic drinks or beers, ciders, and wines on tap—and lots of them! There are a couple of cocktails, too: Exotic Margarita and California Sunset.

Sci-Fi Dine-In Theater Restaurant

DDP: One credit (T) / Cost: $$ (TiW)
Type: American; Unique/Themed; Lunch, Dinner

If you've made a reservation, this is such a cool place to eat; if not, maybe you'll get lucky with a cancellation. Sci-Fi Dine-In is popular for a reason. It's one of those special venues you and your group won't soon forget. Sit in modified 1950s convertible cars under the "stars" (the little lights-in-the-ceiling variety) and watch great trailers of those famous old sci-fi and horror thrillers on the big screen that you may remember watching on late-night cable television during your childhood. The atmosphere is unique and the food is pretty good, too.

Start with the fried dill pickles for a taste sensation. Shrimp and crab fondue is another tasty appetizer, as are the onion rings and crispy chicken tenders. You can try the classic wedge salad with blue cheese if you'd like something cool. Better yet, share the Sci-Fi Appetizer Sampler to taste several!

The menu here is as "jumbo" as the fins on some of those classic cars. Just about anything your heart desires can be found on this menu. A drive-in BBQ burger, flame-broiled New York strip steak, buffalo chicken salad, shrimp pasta, cheese steak sandwich, a big barbecue platter with smoked pulled pork, ribs, chicken, and sausage—you name it, Sci-Fi probably has it. Vegetarian falafel burger or vegan tofu lettuce wraps are other choices. Disney Check meals are a beef skewer, chicken and cheese quesadilla, and wheat penne pasta. Kids menu items also offer chicken tenders, cheeseburger, and mac and cheese.

Hope you saved room for dessert because they are definitely galactic! The house-made candy bar is heavenly—white and dark chocolate mousse with crispy pearls between layers of sponge cake covered with chocolate ganache. The S'mores brownie and ice cream is equally delicious. What about a warm, glazed donut with cinnamon apples, vanilla-bean ice cream, and caramel sauce? If you have any will power left, there's always the fresh fruit salad or the no-sugar added brownie and ice cream dessert.

Beverages are as imaginative and playful as the menu. Crazy cocktails with names like Magical Star Cocktail, Orbiting Oreos, Godiva Chocolate Martini, or Long Island Lunar Tea might intrigue the adults. No? Then how about a list as long as a drag race of specialty draft, craft, and bottled beers? There are plenty of California wines and sangria, too. Joffrey's coffee and lots of non-alcoholic beverages are available.

Don't miss out on a chance to visit a drive-in movie under the stars and sit in a vintage convertible, all the while dining on delicious menu selections. Be sure to have your photo taken out front sitting in the stretch convertible. This is a very special Disney experience!

Animation Courtyard

When you see a large arch, you'll know you've arrived at Animation Courtyard, an area dedicated to the Disney animated films. Years ago, in the early days of the park, this is where the backlot tours began. Now, you can see Disney Junior Live Onstage! with puppet characters from the Disney Junior Channel or a really fantastic live stage version of The Little Mermaid.

Animation Courtyard Kiosks, Wagons, and Carts

- You won't find much in the way of food items in Animation Courtyard, so either eat up beforehand or wait until the next area, but during busy seasons, there is usually an **Ice Cream Cart** serving the ever-present Mickey ice cream bars, ice-cream sandwiches, Nestle's orange cream bars, strawberry fruit bars, frozen bananas covered in chocolate and nuts, frozen lemonade, and Coke products.

Star Wars: A Galactic Spectacular Dessert Party at Disney's Hollywood Studios

DDP: No / $$$$
Type: American; Dessert

Some of your favorite Star Wars characters like Kylo Ren, Chewbacca, and BB-8 show up. The Storm Troopers march by. You'll have reserved seating while enjoying Star Wars-themed dessert treats, charcuterie and cheeses, and beverages. Cost is $79 for adults and $45 for kids 3-9. Some of the latest offerings have included Luke Skywalker's favorite blue milk panna cotta with crispy pearls, freeze-dried chocolate hazelnut mousse raspberry mousse domes, and warm bread pudding. Roasted red pepper hummus, black been dip, smoked sea-salted flatbread are some of the recent savories. Light-speed Margaritas, beers and wines, plus lots of non-alcoholic drink choices are available. After enjoying the treats inside the Star Wars Launch Bay, you are escorted to a reserved area to watch Disney Movie Magic and Star Wars: A Galactic Spectacular. Guests also take home a souvenir.

Sunset Boulevard

"All right, Mr. DeMille, I'm ready for my close-up," is the most famous line to come from the classic 1950 film *Sunset Boulevard,* directed by Billy Wilder and starring Gloria Swanson and William Holden. It was made into a Tony-winning musical in 1991 by Andrew Lloyd Weber. This area, a fond tribute to the famous street in California of the same name, represents the first major expansion of Hollywood Studios, in 1994. It's home to the incredible Tower of Terror, symbol of this park,

Beauty and the Beast Musical, and that wild ride known as Aerosmith's Rock 'n' Roller Coaster. It's also home to several places offering quick meals and snacks.

Sunset Boulevard Kiosks, Wagons, and Carts

- A well-supplied **Coffee, Espresso, and Pastries** kiosk can be found at the exit from Tower of Terror. It'll meet your caffeinated pick-me-up needs, and maybe tempt you with some pastries as well. There are also a couple of frozen beverages. Add a shot of Baileys, Kailua, or Jameson to a coffee or latte, if you're so inclined.

- **Hollywood Scoops** is located in front of the Tower of Terror. Homey and quaint with its striped awning, it looks just like those little places you'd have seen all over Southern California in the 1930s and 1940s. Order hand-scooped ice cream (lots of flavors including sugar-free) served in a cone or a cup. Try warm apple crisp a la mode, a brownie sundae, fresh-baked cookie ice cream sandwiches, ice cream sundaes, or an alcoholic root beer float. The name is a nod to Hedda Hopper and Louella Parsons, the original gossip column queens of Hollywood scoops.

- In front of Fantasmic! is an **Ice Cream Cart** with those well-known Mickey ice cream bars, ice cream sandwiches, frozen lemonade, Coke products, plus three kinds of beer.

- Next to the Rock 'n' Roller Coaster, look for a food truck called **KRNR The Rock Station**. Get an all-beef hot dog with chips or with chili and cheese, nachos with cheese, chocolate chip cookies, waffle cones, frozen Coke or lemonade, root beer floats, lots of Coca-Cola fountain beverages, some specialty drinks with alcohol, beer, and a Jack Daniel's with Coke. Probably a good idea not to fill up on hot dogs before climbing on the roller coaster, though.

The following venues, taken together, are much like the famous Los Angeles Farmers Market. Hollywood Studios has just a few of these little stands, while the big Farmers Market boasts over one hundred, but the vibe is similar.

Anaheim Produce

DDP: No / Cost: $
Type: American; Quick Service; Snacks

Sure, you can get Mickey pretzels and the ubiquitous churros and chips here, but this little produce stand specializes in healthy snacks. Rotating selections of fresh whole fruit, granola, hummus, carrot and celery sticks, Babybel cheese, Mandarin oranges, fruit cups, tomatoes, grapes, pineapple, pickles, sweet potato chips, dried cranberries, trail mix, and more will give you an energy boost. Frozen lemonade, frozen margaritas, and frozen seasonal coladas will keep you cool. Three kinds of ice-cold beer and the many fountain beverages made by Coke are also sold at this modest little marketplace here on Sunset.

Catalina Eddie's

DDP: One credit (Q) / Cost: $
Type: American;. Quick Service; Mobile Orders; Lunch, Dinner

The real "Catalina eddy" is a weather phenomena that causes thick clouds and dropping temperatures after dark. It's most prevalent from April to September, often centered around Catalina Island off the southern California coast, a playground of vintage Hollywood movie stars. This place is much nicer than the weather that inspires its name. Look for it on Sunset near the Tower of Terror and the Rock 'n' Roller Coaster. The offerings are simple: pizza (cheese, pepperoni, or meat lovers) and Caesar salads (one of them with chicken). House-made seasonal cupcakes will satisfy your sweet tooth, as will chocolate mousse or lemon cheesecake verrine (a verrine means small glass in French, and you'll notice they're popular this season at Walt Disney World). There's also vanilla cake with chocolate custard. Disney Check meals for the kids are Smucker's Uncrustables or the Power Pack with yogurt. There is also a cheese pizza on the children's menu. For drinks, Eddie serves up Coke beverages, apple and orange juice, a slushy, hot cocoa, tea, or coffee, sangria, and various beers.

Fairfax Fare

DDP: One credit (Q) / Cost: $
Type: American/Mexican; Quick Service; Mobile Orders; Lunch, Dinner

If you haven't yet tried tasty empanadas (a half-moon shaped pastry enclosing a filling; the empanada has Argentinian origins), here's your chance. Order the beef empanadas with cilantro rice, black beans, and corn/tomato salsa. Equally good is the mojo pulled pork sandwich with sweet plantains (a different kind of banana). If you're really hungry, get the generous fajita combo platter with chicken and pork. There's a 7-layer rice bowl with either vegan chili, pulled pork, or grilled chicken. The Fairfax salad is definitely hearty with pulled pork, roasted corn, tortilla strips, and cheddar cheese topped with jalapeño ranch dressing. So is the foot-long, chili-cheese, all-beef hot dog. Kids Disney check meals are turkey sandwiches or Smucker's Uncrustables. Chocolate mousse, tres leches verrine, and seasonal cupcakes are for dessert, and as you may already know, cupcakes at Disney are seriously out of this world. There's a wild Captain Morgan Fruit Punch Cocktail, a red stag black cherry bourbon lemonade, and a Smirnoff raspberry vodka lemonade. Coke products and three kinds of beer, along with the usual coffee, tea, and cocoa complete the drinks menu. The food at Fairfax is different, a cut above, and will give you an idea of what authentic Hollywood flavors really are.

Fantasmic! Dessert and VIP Viewing Experience

DDP: No / Cost: $$$
Type: American; Quick Service; Dessert, Beverage

You must have a valid park admission to take advantage of this package. The cost is $39 for adults and $19 for children (3-9), which includes tax, and no gratuity is expected. You pick up a pre-made snack pack of salty and sweet treats like chocolate-dipped strawberries, cheese and crackers, a make your own "worms and dirt" pudding, dried fruits and nuts, and various drinks (alcoholic options for adults) in a souvenir cup. After you have your dessert, you are shown to a reserved VIP area to watch the show and enjoy your snacks. Make reservations online or by calling (407) 939-3463. This package is only available for the first nightly showing of Fantasmic! Should the show be cancelled for any reason, you will be given the opportunity to be admitted to VIP seating for an alternative showing up to 5 days after the cancellation. This is true at many of the special experiences.

Fantasmic! Dining and VIP Viewing Experience: Mama Melrose's / Hollywood & Vine / The Hollywood Brown Derby

DDP: One credit (T), Two credits at Brown Derby (T) / Cost: Varies
Type: Varies; Table Service; Varies

Cost at Mama Melrose's is $46 for adults, $28 for children 3-9, but you must also have a valid park admission for the park. Cost does not include tax or tip at the restaurants. One Table Service credit (T) may be used per package purchased. Each package includes an entrée, dessert, and nonalcoholic beverage or one full buffet where applicable. Each package includes one voucher for reserved seating at Fantasmic! At Hollywood & Vine, cost per adult is $46 at breakfast and $28 for children, $60 per adult at lunch or dinner and $36 for children and one Table Service credit (T) may be used. At the Hollywood Brown Derby, lunch or dinner for adults costs $63, children's meals are $22. Two Table Service credits (T) may be used. The meal packages do not include alcohol. Make reservations 180 days before your visit. These packages are available on all show days, but if the show is cancelled, guaranteed seating is available for an alternative performance within 5 days of your original reservation. Again, you must have a valid park admission to watch Fantasmic! Even if the show is cancelled due to weather, your dining reservation will still take place.

Rosie's All American Café

DDP: One credit (Q) / Cost: $
Type: American; Quick Service; Lunch, Dinner

Rosie's claim to fame is the fried green tomato sandwich. Cheeseburgers, a foot-long hot dog, and nuggets are also on Rosie's menu. Kids can get Disney Check turkey sandwiches or the Power Pack with yogurt. The children's menu has nuggets, seasonal fruit, and a beverage. Desserts are seasonal cupcakes, strawberry shortcake, or chocolate mousse. Coke products, several beers, a sangria, coffee, tea, cocoa, juices, and milk are served. Other than the fried green tomato sandwich, most of the menu items here are much like those found throughout the parks.

Sunshine Day Bar

DDP: No / Cost: $
Type: American; Quick Service; Lounge

The sun only shines on very busy days, the only time you'll find this counter open. It replaced Toluca Turkey Legs. These days, you'll find blackberry moonshine lemonade, cherry blossom, Southside fizz, assorted beers, and other alcoholic beverages. Look for it on Sunset near the Tower of Terror and Rockin' Roller Coaster.

Star Wars: Galaxy's Edge

There's a full-scale replica of Han Solo's Millennium Falcon, the Smuggler's Run flight simulator, and the jaw-dropping Rise of the Resistance where you'll engage in combat with Kylo Ren (arrange to meet this character at his Meet-and-Greet if you can because it's truly a spectacular in-person experience) in the largest set ever built for a "dark ride" attraction that includes several hundred animated objects immersing riders in a battle between the Order and the Resistance fighters. It's all set on the planet Batuu, a realistic recreation that will make guests feel like they've dropped into an alien world. The area itself represents a trading port during the time of the rise of both the First Order and the Resistance. A lot of typical park foods or snacks will replaced in this land by other worldly goodies and treats in order to maintain the illusion of actually being on Batuu.

Bob Iger announced that the new land would be "occupied by many inhabitants: humanoids, aliens, and droids...the attractions, the entertainment, everything we create will be part of our storytelling. Nothing will be out of character or stray from the mythology." Since Lukasfilm had a hand in the design, rest assured the results are amazing!

Guests can drink and dine in Oga's famous cantina, complete with music by the droid R-3X who acts as DJ. A costumed cast member portraying Oga Garda will be strategically placed behind the bar to give the impression that he is running the establishment. Snack on a roasted ronto beast from Tatooine cooked over the engine of a podracer. The music for this newest land was composed by John Williams and recorded at Abbey Road Studios by the London Symphony Orchestra. Prepare to be immersed in a fantasy fictional realm that feels very real indeed. If you plan to visit shortly after it opens to the public, you will need to make reservations. The number of guests admitted initially will be strictly limited. Some of the experiences will likely be restricted or even unavailable in the opening few weeks, depending on guest demand (which you may safely assume will be sky-high) and other unforeseen circumstances.

StarWars: Galaxy's Edge Kiosks, Wagons, and Carts

- In a few of the films, you've noticed Luke Skywalker sipping blue or green milk. Here, it's served frozen. Get yours at the **Milk Stand** and join the Resistance. Good it is.

Docking Bay 7 Food and Cargo

ADP: No;Cost: $
TYPE: American, Vegetarian, Quick Service

Everything looks "alien" at this large hangar serving galactic goodies. Sit indoors or outside, and you'll see evidence of the planet's crumbling infrastructure. Chef Strono "Cookie" Tuggs is the purveyor of fresh supplies at this big hangar. His food calls to mind some of the out-of-this-world offerings available at the Animal Kingdom's Avatar region at Walt Disney world. Nothing will seem familiar, but that doesn't mean it won't be delicious.

Kat Saka's Kettle

ADP: No; Cost: $
TYPE: American; Quick Service; Snack

The grain merchant Kat Saka offers grains from across the galaxy including good old popcorn as you've never had it before, so you can munch while exploring Black Spire Outpost.

Outpost Mix is at once sweet and savory—not to mention colorful. Drinks are also available.

Oga's Cantina

ADP: No, Cost: $

TYPE: American, Table Service, Unique/Theme Dining, Bars and Lounges; Lunch, Dinner

Just about anyone who has seen the Star Wars films has dreamed of stopping in at Oga's for a bite to eat and a refreshing libation. Try one of the brightly colored concoctions like the Jedi Mind Trick cocktail, Bad Motivator IPA, or Toniray wine, but if you order an alcoholic beverage, be sure you have your valid planet Earth ID available. Some drinks have boba balls, a fun addition that adds interest and color.

Ronto Roasters

ADP: No, Cost: $

TYPE: American, Quick Service; Snack

See the pitmaster droid turning a spit of meat as it's being roasted by the engine of a podracer. The meat is "ronto," a beast from the planet Tatooine. The savory smells of grilled sausage and roasted pork wrap will have you drooling like Jabba the Hut.

The unique snacks at the theme parks are part of what makes the Disney experience so special. Make sure to try some while you are here because you won't find them back home. The unique meals will linger in everyone's memories long after the vacation comes to an end.

Way to go! You've successfully managed to navigate the many food options in all four of the Walt Disney World theme parks. If you made reservations six months ahead of time and got a table at the most popular places, great. If you didn't, there's always next time. Not only that, there are plenty of great places to eat, whether you have reservations or not. Eating earlier or later than average will allow you to take advantage of the less busy off-hours. Don't forget to check for same-day reservation cancellations, too. There are still more areas on Disney property you'll want to visit because the dining options there are so appealing. Next up—the BoardWalk.

Disney's BoardWalk
Disney Dining Off-the-Beaten Path

On July 1, 1996, Walt Disney World's BoardWalk Resort and entertainment area opened. It was designed by Robert A.M. Stern, former head of the Yale School of Architecture, to evoke the feeling of turn-of-the-last-century Coney Island in Brooklyn, New York, and Atlantic City, New Jersey. "BoardWalk,"as it's used here, is not a figure of speech; the walkway is constructed of boards just like the originals on which it is based.

As the sun goes down, the lights and colorful façades of the buildings reflected in the water turn this place into a nostalgic, shimmering dream. If you have childhood memories of playing games of chance at the midway of your local amusement park or fair, they will come back to you on the Board-Walk. Share them with the next generation. Street musicians, balloon artists, magicians, and other friendly performers rotate through the area and add to the excitement and old-time ambience.

Guests promenade along the quarter-mile long, U-shaped boardwalk by the shores of Crescent Lake to shop, be entertained, or just people-watch. To do all of that, of course, they need something to sustain them. The dining possibilities here have expanded over the last twenty-odd years, making this charming district a destination in itself.

AbracadaBar

DDP: No / Cost: $
Type: Lounge
Such a clever venue, especially if you happen to be a magic

afficionado. The place is filled with vintage posters and props from those golden-olden days of prestidigitation and sleight of hand. The bar menu is lengthy with hand-crafted cocktails like The Conjurita, Magic Hattan, Sour Assistant, Parlor Trick, Magic Mirror, Pepper's Ghost (that's the name of one of the illusions used in the Haunted Mansion), and more. A few nibbles are certain to appear as if by magic like cones of popcorn and nuts, some spicy fries, fish bites and fries, Kurobuta pork belly, or an old fashioned shrimp cocktail. You'll that find sparkling and white wines will pop up right before your eyes, wines from California, Italy, and France. Beers in bottles, cans, and draft multiply like rabbits out of a hat. Just about any sort of drink you wish to conjure is right at your fingertips—hey, presto!

Ample Hills Creamery

DDP: No / Cost: $
Type: American; Quick Service, Bakery Cuisine; Snacks

This is the first time you can visit Ample Hills outside of New York City. Take a peek through the window on the Promenade to watch the preparation. Ample Hills is a great name for this sweet shop selling a variety of the very coolest of ice cream flavors around (Sally Sells Seashells, Malty Salty Pretzel Punch, Red Velvet Ooey Gooey Butter Cake, Nona D's Oatmeal Lace… and that's just the beginning). The dozen-and-a-half flavors can be had in cones large or small (waffle, sugar, or cake) with M & Ms, chocolate chip, cookies, or pretzel toppings. You can also order a milkshake and chose your ice cream flavor, but it won't be easy. Every day is sundae here!

Big River Grill and Brewing Works

DDP: One credit (T) / Cost: $$ (TiW)
Type: American; Casual; Lunch, Dinner

If you are someone who appreciates microbreweries that produce craft beers, Big River is the only one located on Disney property. Dine inside or under an umbrella table on the Boardwalk overlooking Crescent Lake. Prices are relatively affordable, especially when compared to a premier dining establishment like Flying Fish.

The beer-cheese soup comes highly recommended by the cup or bowl. A nice variety of quesadillas, nachos, or salads with chicken or salmon are offered as appetizers. On the entrée menu, you'll find plenty of great choices: casual sandwiches with kettle chips, chicken, pastas, steaks, a ribeye steak, ribs, blackened fish tacos, flame-grilled meatloaf, four burgers (including a Kobe beef burger and the black and blue), blackened mahi mahi, and salmon. The meals are hearty and satisfying, and most are meant to go well with the beers on tap. The kids menu is intended to please most young diners: mac and cheese, hot dog, hamburger, grilled cheese, grilled chicken and choice of nice sides like cheddar mashed potatoes or fresh fruit, veggies, and kettle chips. What's for dessert? Chocolate confusion or New York-style cheesecake, both OMG!

Drinks include the usual array of non-alcoholic beverage choices. Cocktails are just about anything you can think of: mojitos, margaritas, and a long list of martinis. Sangria and red or white wines are available, as well as red and white alternatives. There's a Southern Flier Light Lager beer, low in carbs and calories. Beer is taken very seriously here. Offerings may vary seasonally and go and come over time. Try the Gadzooks Pilsner, Steamboat Pale Ale, Summer Wheat, Rocket Red Ale, or Sweet Magnolia American Brown Ale. Each one is lovingly described. For example, the Steamboat Pale Ale is "a classic American-style Pale Ale with the distinctive pine and citrus character of its signature Cascade hops. Original gravity: 13.0 degrees, Plato Alcohol by volume: 5.5 percent, Bitterness units: 36." For beer and ale devotees, or anyone who just wants a tasty, filling meal that won't break the bank, look no further than Big River Brewery.

BoardWalk Bakery

DDP: One credit (Q) / Cost: $
Type: American; Quick Service; Snacks, Breakfast, Lunch, and Dinner

This pretty bakery on the BoardWalk features items different from those you'll find in the theme parks. Some menu selections would be right at home in Atlantic City! How does a breakfast "Everything Everything Bagel Sandwich" with a fried egg and Tillamook Cheddar Cheese (so good!) and fruit sound? There's a "Butter Butter Sandwich" on brioche and an "Ooey Gooey Sandwich," too. You can count on breakfast pastries like a jazzy crumb cake (do try it), muffins, and croissants. Lunch and dinner are the same and feature a big and beefy sandwich or the roasty toasty sandwich (remember the little Roasty Toasty man who turned the tiny wheel in the old popcorn carts in days of yore?) that's vegetarian. Caesar with chicken or an herb-grilled chicken and apple salad are filling. (Maybe that Maine lobster on a split-top roll with chive butter will return at some point.) Kids will find ham and cheese on a bun or a Disney check turkey sandwich on their menu. Muffins, brioche, Jersey crumb cake (save some for me!), croissants, key lime tart, or a pretty variety of specialty cupcakes should make those taste buds of yours sing like the Jersey Boys.

BoardWalk Joe's Marvelous Margaritas

DDP: No /Cost: $
Type: American/Mexican Cuisine; Quick Service; Snacks

Joe not only has many flavors of Margaritas (watermelon, sunshine, strawberry, Grand Mariner, Patrón Añejo), he can also fix you up with a delightful Dole whip smoothie (with or without Captain Morgan Original Spiced Run), a strawberry smoothie, a piña colada, several kinds of wine, and assorted beers. You can also get bottled drinks here. Sit and sip while enjoying nachos, roasted almonds, a jalapeño-stuffed pretzel, a Mickey Pretzel with jalapeño sauce, or roasted pecans. Watch the people parade and enjoy the Florida sunset as the cooling breeze over the water ruffles your hair.

ESPN Club

DDP: One credit (T) / Cost. $$ (TiW)
Type: American; Unique/Themed; Lunch, Dinner

A 90-foot square HD television is always tuned to the sports channel at this bar and grill. In fact, there are close to 100 video monitors with satellite feeds from around the world. Choose from 30 different programs. If you make a rest room stop, you'll discover TVs over all the stalls—home was never like this! ESPN is a full 13,000 square feet but seating fills quickly. You might want to make a reservation ahead of time to be sure you'll have a table when you arrive.

Start with an eclectic collection of chowder, chili, nachos (ahi tuna or club), crispy pink Florida shrimp, seasonally inspired soups, salads (the "bacon and blue" wedge is great), club fries, and hot, medium, or mild ESPN wings. Burgers are the specialty here, and there are several appealing kinds to choose from. Both hearty and lighter entrées dot this extensive menu. Steak, cowboy mac and cheese, turkey sandwich, fish and chips, hot fried chicken, Reuben sandwich, Baja fish tacos, Southwest seasoned fish, and lots more should fill even the emptiest stomach. Kids have lots to select from, too, with the Disney check grilled fish or chicken or a turkey pinwheel, or they might rather go for a cheeseburger or hot dog on the regular kids menu. They can get the fruit salad or that hilarious and yummy "worms and dirt" cupcake—the one that used to be available in the Animal Kingdom but isn't any longer, so here's your chance.

S'mores bread pudding, seasonal fruit crumble, no-sugar chocolate gelato, chocolate hat trick, or the are-you-*kidding*-me Boston trifle (layers of vanilla bean custard, chocolate midnight cake, roasted almonds, and hot fudge sauce) will surely sweeten the deal.

The list of non-alcoholic specialty drinks is imaginative and inventive, fun for the young and young at heart. Wines, many from California, are available as well as several kinds of draft beers. An intriguing part of the ESPN menu is the very long list of "Championship Spirits" such as The Jockey Julep, Three Point Martini, Cage Match Collins, or Tee Time. Draft beers are plentiful, as are "Home Run" brews from all over the world. There's a "White vs. Red" match-up on the wine list, with California, Italy, Germany, New Zealand, and Spain on the roster. ESPN is all about sports, so if *you* happen to be sports-minded, stop in and prepare to be impressed.

Flying Fish

DDP: Two credits (T) / Cost: $$$
Type: American, Seafood Cuisine; Fine/Signature Dining; Dinner

A table at Flying Fish is a hot ticket on the BoardWalk. Call at the earliest possible moment to secure a reservation. They are sometimes difficult to obtain. A dress code is enforced. If you want to dine here, follow these attire guidelines: "Men may wear khakis, slacks, jeans or dress shorts and collared shirts. Sport coats are optional. Women may wear Capri pants, skirts, dresses, jeans or dress shorts. Not permitted are tank tops, swimsuits, swimsuit cover-ups, hats for gentlemen, cut-offs, torn clothing and t-shirts with offensive language and/or graphics." Prices are relatively steep but, judging from FF's popularity, many people think it's worth the price for a true gastronomic splurge. The updated decor is as breathtaking as the dining. Look for the blown-glass bubbles suspended from the ceiling, the school of tiny glass flying fish, and graceful banquettes curved like waves.

You can watch your food being prepared on the kitchen stage from some seating areas. The current appetizers are knockouts. Try the lobster bisque, Wisconsin burrata with heirloom figs and a walnut vinaigrette, grilled baby Romaine salad, local soft-shell crab, artisan cheeses, crispy oysters, PEI mussels, jumbo shrimp, or Kurobuta pork belly. The freshest of seafood is the star of the show. Salmon, Hokkaido scallops, swordfish, and sea bass are joined on the menu by free-range young chicken, seafood pasta, Wagyu filet mignon, and a jaw-dropping Tomahawk rib-eye for two priced at the princely sum of $150. As if that weren't enough, the enhancements add a whole new level of indulgence. Add Hokkaido scallops, shrimp scampi, or a cold water lobster tail to any of the main courses. Desserts are unusual and exciting. Try "Florida Sunset," "Blueberries, Limes and Seashells," or "Cocoa Breach" for some surprisingly delicious, masterful flavor combinations. All of the desserts are uniquely different from what you'll find elsewhere, so save room!

The kids aren't forgotten. Appetizers for the small fry include free range chicken noodle soup, veggies and greens, or seasonal fruit. They can create their own fabulous entrees such as seared sea bass, grilled Wagyu steak, shrimp scampi, or Mickey pasta, sided by eight yummy options sure to fill up their plates and their tummies. The specialty cocktails and coffees are befitting of this heady culinary experience.

The French press coffee pot for two would go very nicely with any of the phenomenal desserts. Sommelier wine selections are international and thoughtfully chosen to complement the outstanding food. You won't go wrong dining at Flying Fish—providing you can get a reservation, that is.

Funnel Cakes

DDP: No / Cost: $
Type: American; Quick Service; Snacks

Find the funnel cake vendor on the water side of the Board-Walk between Flying Fish and Big River. Get them fresh and hot! You can top yours with ice cream, powdered sugar, or chocolate sauce. It's the perfect treat to savor while strolling along the lake. There is cotton candy, too, so get ready to feel like a kid again.

Pizza Window

DDP: One credit (S) /Cost: $
Type: American/Italian; Quick Service; Snacks

Sit indoors or dine alfresco at this lake-side spot. Pizza many ways is the order of the day. The personal pizza with garden salad and fountain beverage combo is a good value. Cheese, pepperoni, veggie, white pizza with bacon and mushrooms, or sausage and mushroom are your options. The Italian hoagie or meatball subs come with chips. Salads like garden, Caprese, or antipasto pair well with the pizzas. Mini cannolis are for dessert, and beverages include fountain drinks, sangria, or beer.

The To-Go Cart

DDP: No /Cost: $
Type: American; Quick Service; Snacks

For a little place, there's a long menu at this cart. Hot dogs are the main event: foot longs, cheese dogs, chili dogs, corn dogs, and dogs in a basket with fries and a drink will see you though until your next meal. You can also order a hamburger, grilled chicken sandwich, pulled pork sliders, or mozzarella sticks, alone or in a basket with fries. Chicken fingers are only available as the combo. Buffalo wings, fries, nachos with cheese, onion rings, a PB&J, chili fries, cheese fries, and all kinds of combinations of the above plus beverages, both fountain and bottled, make this a good stop. It's right on the water in front of the AbracadaBar.

Trattoria al Forno

DDP: One credit (T) / Cost: $$-$$$ (TiW)
Type: Italian; Casual; Character Kids Breakfast; Breakfast, Dinner

While the cuisine is Italian, there are plenty of menu items that most American palates will find just delightful. It's a popular spot (replacing celebrity Chef Cat Cora's Kouzinna in 2014).

Breakfast offers the usual fare with unusual names inspired by *The Little Mermaid*. If you come for breakfast, you'll encounter Ariel, Prince Eric, Rapunzel and Flynn Rider who will sign autographs and pose for pictures with your party. (They only visit during breakfast, and characters may change without notice.) The tower of pancakes with an apple compote and bacon or sausage, eggs your way, potatoes and bacon, ham, or sausage, calzone with scrambled eggs, poached eggs, oak-grilled steak asparagus, cheesy-egg torte, or the simple fruit, Greek yogurt, honey and house-made granola are just some of the choices this season. The Disney check kids option is an egg-white spinach and tomato omelette with potatoes or a steak, scrambled egg substitute, and fresh fruit. The kids menu also has pancakes or a character waffle with sides. Get a platter of breakfast pastries for the table.

No lunch is served, but come back at dinner for an immersion in the cuisine of Italy. Even the wine list is 100% Italian here. Antipasti offers PEI mussels, a nice salad with fresh pears, porchetta, goat cheese, candied walnuts and vanilla vinaigrette, fried calamari, Caprese salad, or charcuterie. Four appealing pizzas are served. Next comes the main course, and the choices are extensive. Steak, chicken parm, house-made pasta, lasagne, veal osso buco, whole roasted fish, littleneck clams, seared sea scallops, herbed veal, pork, and beef meatballs will please most. Disney check meals for the children at dinner are grilled chicken or seasonal fish.

Desserts are a bit on the "mini" side (unusual for Disney) like "a spoonful of gelato" (and even if you assume they're talking about a quenelle, that's still pretty skimpy) or "a lady finger" tiramisù or white chocolate custard and "an amaretti cookie." You may rather skip it or get dessert elsewhere.

After cruising the dining possibilities on the BoardWalk, your next stop is Disney Springs. Restaurants there come and go over the years, so what you found on your last vacation to Walt Disney World may very well have been replaced this time around. Some of the most exciting new restaurants in the entire resort have opened recently at Disney Springs. Sure, the shopping has always been special, but now the eating establishments are just as special. Try to make time for a visit! You won't regret it.

Disney Springs, Part One
The Marketplace

Many places and attractions at the resort have undergone several iterations and have managed to successfully reinvent themselves. Disney Springs is no exception. On March 22, 1975, during the resort's fourth year, this shopping and entertainment area opened as the relatively modest Lake Buena Vista Shopping Village. Lake Buena Vista is the mailing address for Florida's Disney operations. Before the land was bought by the Disney organization in the 1960s, it was known as Black Lake. Buena Vista Distribution Company was founded in 1953 by The Walt Disney Company after the release of *Peter Pan*. The Walt Disney Studios in Burbank, California, are located on Buena Vista Street. You'll notice the Buena Vista name used by Disney again and again. It means "good view."

By 1977, the area was renamed Walt Disney World Village. Another name change came in 1989: Disney Village Marketplace. Early names put the focus squarely on shopping. That's no longer true. In 1989, the name was more reflective of the multi-use nature of the venue: Downtown Disney. What is now The Landing was then Pleasure Island, an adult-centered bar and entertainment center. Yet again, in 2015 after considerable expansion that added two parking structures and 150 new tenants, the area is now called Disney Springs. It is currently comprised of four areas with over 100 shops and stores and almost 70 places to eat and drink.

Shops

The Ganachery Chocolate Shop

Find "sophisticated" chocolate, ganache, and spirits at this attractive shop filled with every kind of chocolate imaginable. You can even discuss the merits of each with one of the resident chocolatiers on the scene. You'll be assisted in selecting something specially suited just to your taste. Watch the in-house magic happen in the kitchen where things are freshly prepared. Before you even arrive or after you're back home again, you can now order select sweets on the Shop Disney Parks app. They are pricey. Right now, there are seven different gifts including salted caramels and those fancy chocolates you can only find at Ganachery. At the store, Disney character-themed chocolate lollipops are available, along with a wide assortment of many people's favorite kind of candy—chocolate!

Goofy's Candy Company

You can design your own individually prepared sweet treat or select from those already on tempting display in the cases and on the shelves. The candy apples are giant, adorably decorated, and sure to please. They resemble a rotating cast of characters like Olaf the Snowman, the Cheshire Cat, Mickey in Fantasia, Mike from Monsters, Inc., Maleficent with horns in her dragon form, and of course, Goofy. The Goofy's Glaciers section has frozen slushy drinks you can blend to suit. They're not only beautiful and bright but the perfect cooler on a hot day. Candy galore in many gorgeous forms is what this store is all about. Even if you don't have a sweet tooth, you'll enjoy seeing the artistic culinary creativity on display. There's a large cut-out Goofy figure saying "Gawrsh, Thanks!"as you exit. No, Goofy, thank YOU!

Dining

4 Rivers Cantina Barbados Food Truck

DDP: No / Cost: $
Type: Latin, Mexican Cuisine; Quick Service; Lunch, Dinner

Step right up and choose your filling—brisket barbacoa (barbecue), Nana's pork sofrito, chicken tinga, grilled tri-tip steak, or black beans and rice. You can get them in a taco cone like a big ice cream cone made of tortilla, in tres tacos (3 tacos—so different fillings are fine), a burrito bowl, or over nachos. There's also a traditional squash blossom quesadilla with queso fresco (fresh cheese) and a side a black beans and cilantro rice. A cheese quesadilla is on the kids menu. For dessert, try the dulce de leche churro balls or the chocolate hazelnut spread nachos. Assorted Coke beverages and beers are sold. This is the authentic type of street food so popular today

Aristocrepes

DDP: One credit (S) / Cost: $
Type: American; Quick Service; Snacks

You'll find sweet (banana chocolate hazelnut, strawberries and cream, or S'mores) and savory (beef or ham and cheese) crêpes and a selection of wines, beers, alcoholic sodas, and non-alcoholic beverages at this kiosk. They've recently added "bubble waffles" in salted caramel or strawberries—both amazing! This is a treat popular in Hong Kong, Macau, and Taiwan, and now, you can sample it, too, right here in Florida.

B.B. Wolf's Sausage Co.

DDP: One credit (S) / Cost: $
Type: American; Quick Service; Snacks

Get it? The Big Bad Wolf is selling sausages! Brat, Hawaiian, pastrami/Reuben, Italian, veggie, and Texas chili-cheese versions come with chips. Try the "Three Little Pigs" for a trio of three mini-versions of favorite flavors. The little house with its walk-up counter looks like it could have come straight out of the old story. Draft beer and fountain beverages are sold and a frozen sweet tea lemonade. For dessert, what else but chocolate chip cookie dough with candied maple bacon? Little pig, little pig, let me come in!

Dockside Margaritas

DDP: No / Cost: $
Type: American; Quick Service; Drinks

Many varieties of margaritas on the rocks (Sunset, Orange Grove Rum Runner, Habañero Lime, and more) or frozen (strawberry or lime), beer, wine, hard cider, and a limited selection of non-alcoholic drinks are available. With views of Buena Vista Cove, you'll feel like you've made a stop in old Florida where the flavors are fresh and the vibe is cool.

Earl of Sandwich

DDP: One credit (Q) / Cost: $
Type: American; Quick Service; Breakfast, Lunch, and Dinner

The fourth Earl of Sandwich, busy at the card table and reluctant to leave for a meal, slapped a piece of meat between two pieces of bread and invented the menu item that's been popular ever since. This extremely busy and highly popular restaurant was founded by the eleventh Earl of Sandwich, John Montagu, his younger son also named John Montagu, and businessman Robert Earl, who was the founder of the Planet Hollywood franchise. You'll find the restaurant near the Once Upon a Toy shop.

Breakfast sandwiches, fresh fruit yogurt, oatmeal, muffins, fruit cups, and made-to-order omelettes are served until 11:00 a.m. Lunch and dinner feature lots of familiar sandwiches as well as some original creations like the Full Montagu (beef, Swiss, turkey, and cheddar), Holiday Turkey (turkey, stuffing, gravy, and cranberry sauce), and Chipotle Chicken Avocado. Freshly tossed salads (Cobb, chicken Caesar, Greek, Thai chicken, and a healthful berry, chicken, and almond salad with balsamic vinaigrette) are available, with many add-ons. Try the hand-crafted wraps and artisanal soups, too, that vary seasonally. There are enough choices to suit most people. Sides are mac and cheese, coleslaw, chips, potato wedges or potato salad, and pasta salad. Kids have a long menu of their own with plenty of appealing choices like pizza bread, grilled cheese, a house salad, and turkey and Swiss. Smoothies, fountain beverages, and sweets like cookies, brownies, strawberry shortcake, cupcakes, and frozen bananas are available. The Earl has something for everyone, including "lite" menu choices called the Skinny Earl.

Florida Snow Company

DDP: No / Cost: $
Type: American; Quick Service; Snacks

This little kiosk is located between The Landing and the Marketplace. You can order shaved ice (snow cones) in lot of sweet flavors/neon colors and two sizes. You'll also find fresh roasted cinnamon glazed or salted nuts, and bottled beverages. What a perfectly cool snack for a hot day.

Ghirardelli Soda Fountain and Chocolate Shop

DDP: One credit (S) / Cost: $
Type: American; Quick Service; Snacks

Your sense of smell might lead you to Ghirardelli's, but if not, it's next to the World of Disney shop. Sundaes like you've never had them before are the order of the day. They come with toppings galore and have imaginative names: Earthquake, Cressy Field, Ocean Beach, Presidio Passion, Golden Gate, Treasure Island, Strike it Rich, and others. Try one of the Painted Ladies for an intensely dark sundae: Midnight Reverie, Espresso Escape, or Mint Bliss. Shakes and floats, scoops and cones, and sweet treats will leave everyone loosening their belts a notch or two. Hot chocolates, hot, cold, and frozen beverages, and classic coffee drinks are on the menu. Want to take something home? Check out the well-stocked shop filled to the rafters with Ghirardelli chocolate goodies and souvenirs.

Joffrey's Handcrafted Smoothies Kiosk

DDP: No / Cost: $
Type: American; Quick Service; Snacks

The popular Joffrey's may be found in many locales at Walt Disney World. This little stand serves a tremendous variety of smoothies like the Flyin' Hawaiian, Razzy Jazzy, Purple Piñata, Mango Tango, Flamingo Frost, or Tropical Sunset. Juices, coffee, tea or alcoholic beverages with Kahlua, Baileys, or Jameson are also sold here. The quality at Jeffrey's is consistently high.

Rainforest Café

DDP: One credit (T) / Cost: $$
Type: American; Unique/Themed; Lunch and Dinner

Find this themed restaurant next to the Art of Disney shop. Other than not serving breakfast, it's similar to the one at Animal Kingdom. Refer to chapter 7 for a full description.

Rainforest Café Lava Lounge

DDP: One credit (Q) / Cost: $
Type: American; Casual; Lounge; Snacks, Drinks

The Rainforest Café Lava Lounge is situated in a gorgeous, peaceful spot on the water at the far end of the Marketplace. You'll access the outdoor covered seating area (right on the lake) through what appears to be flowing magma inside a "lava tube" near the entrance. Water cascades down the rocks outside, a croc is poised to snap, and there's a tall volcano that belches fire.

Order the Awesome Appetizer Adventure for three (or more), crustacean crab dip, ahi poke tower, mozzarella/arugula flatbread, or lava nachos for two. There are many creative specialty cocktails for your pleasure. Try a special cocktail like the Blue Nile, Tropical Getaway, or a Mongoose Mai Tai, some served in souvenir glasses. If you were unable to get a table in the actual Rainforest Café itself, always busy, you can still order from the regular Rainforest menu here at the Lava Lounge. This is a cool place (plenty of fans blowing) to sip a drink, share an appetizer, and relax from your busy day at the parks or shopping at Disney Springs.

Starbucks

DDP: One credit (S) / Cost: $
Type: American; Quick service; Snacks

Starbuck's favorites like frappuchino, espresso, latte, smoothies, iced coffee, tea, refreshers, and hot chocolate are on the menu at this walk-up counter, in sizes grande (16 oz.), venti (24 oz.), or trenta (30 oz.). Try the addition of a flavor or shot of espresso. There are seasonal specialty drinks. Breakfast sandwiches, steel-cut oatmeal, and a tremendous choice of pastries pairs well with anything Starbucks.

T-Rex Café

DDP: One credit (T) / Cost: $$
Type: American; Unique/Themed; Lunch and Dinner

One of two locations, the other in Kansas City, your dino-happy kids will think they've landed in prehistoric times as they enter this themed café. It's an exciting, educational restaurant with interactive, hands-on activities and lots of life-sized dinosaurs that seem almost alive. The themed dining rooms are incredible. Check out the ice cavern with its frozen mastodon, Jurassic fern forest with huge buzzing wasps, and a gigantic, moving octopus in the "underwater" bar. Watch for the meteor shower that happens every twenty minutes. Be sure this isn't going to frighten your youngest party members because the illusion is oh-so-real. In addition to the restaurant, there's also an attached shop stocked with dino-themed merchandise.

For appetizers, start off with nachos, mozzarella sticks, bruschetta, flatbread, or a "Supersaurus Sampler" (serves four) if you can't decide. The menu items, natch, have dinosaur names, but you'll recognize the food. Plenty of soups, salads, and pastas will appeal to both grown-ups and children. (Don't think you need to have kids in tow to thoroughly enjoy this fascinating venue.) Add onion rings, shrimp, or St. Louis-style spare ribs to your entrées. Good old burgers and sandwiches with names like Megasaurus, Bronto burger, Paleozoic chicken sandwich, and Pork-asaurus are available. For the carnivores among your party, try NY strip steak, St. Louis ribs (Mega Mes-O-Bones), or chicken. Seafoods such as shrimp, fish and chips, and salmon can be supplemented with add-ons. Red-skin potatoes, waffle fries, coleslaw, French onion or tomato-basil soup, seasonal vegetables, chips, or "raptor" rice will all help fill up the ravenous raptors in your pack. The menu is as enormous as a brachiosaurus. Kids have lots to choose from, mostly smaller versions of the adult options but some things show up only on their menu. Their desserts are a chocolate tar pit or a saber-tooth sundae, both adorable.

As you might imagine, even the desserts here are dino-sized. The dessert section is called The End is Near! How about a Chocolate Pudding Cake (with raspberry sauce), Sorbet

Sampler, Cosmic Key Lime Pie, Chocolate Extinction (enough for four or more), or meteor bites for two (donut holes with sauces for dipping)? That will surely sweeten the meal deal at T-Rex. This is a very popular venue, so don't neglect making those key reservations!

Wetzel's Pretzels

DDP: No / Cost: $
Type: American; Quick Service; Snacks

Across from World of Disney is a little stand where you can find delicious, fresh, warm pretzels. Get "sinful cinnamon," "sour cream and onion," "almond crunch," or try the baked cheese and pepperoni pretzel. For dipping, Wetzel's provides jalapeño or cheddar cheese, pizza, sweet glaze, and caramel sauce. If you're still hungry, order a Wetzel's hot dog, cheese dog or "dog bites" with lemonade, frozen lemonade, or frozen granita.

Wolfgang Puck Bar & Grill

DDP: One credit (T) / Cost: $$$
Type: Mediterranean, American; Fine/Signature Dining; Lunch, Dinner

After undergoing a complete renovation and reimagining, Wolfgang Puck's has returned. Lunch menu is more casual than dinner, and prices are a bit more wallet-friendly. This is an excellent place to dine when you have time to relax and savor—not when you're in a hurry. If you've got a limited time to dine, try the Express.

There are items to share for the table like artisanal salumi (artisanal pork cold cuts and cheeses with marinated vegetables), house-made rosemary focaccia, bruschetta, or roasted meatballs. For appetizers and salads, tortilla soup with lime cream, tempura calamari and shrimp, wood-grilled shrimp, local burrata, and some sweet little baby gem lettuce salads with chicken or shrimp should get you started. Half a dozen kinds of pizza will ably demonstrate the dish that made the chef famous. Sandwiches include a grilled chicken, Italian salumi (not a typo) and provolone, and a shaved beef panini. Fries, broccolini (with Parm and lemon breadcrumbs!), and potato purée are the sides. Wolfgang doesn't skimp on delectable desserts. An apple pie sundae, key lime pie, a cookie plate, crème brûlée, carrot cake, chocolate lava cake, and more will suit most. The kids menu is filled with appealing options from the healthful (grilled chicken breast, roasted potatoes, sautéed carrots) to the indulgent (bacon wrapped meatloaf). There's also a gelato bar—a long list of flavors with another long list of favorite toppings. In addition, there's a convenient grab-and-go section with lots of portable fare to take for later.

Dinner has some of the same entrées as lunch like pizza and pasta but adds to it a whole grilled sea bass, Heritage Farm pork chop, roasted half chicken, grilled New York strip, seared Florida red snapper, chicken, wienerschnitzel, braised beef short ribs, and a nice 32 oz. Porterhouse for two at $88.

Handcrafted cocktails abound: Show Me Love, Lilly Belle (after Walt's wife Lilian), Gitty Up..., Devil in Disguise, Warm and Fuzzy, and many more fun surprises. You can always count on an international selection of wine by the glass from noted vineyards including Wolfgang Puck's own Cabernet Sauvignon from California. Beer, more than two dozen varieties, will suit the preferences of most guests. There is also an extensive non-alcoholic beverage list including some fun mocktails like Pomegranate Delight, Raspberry Velvet, and Peach-Passion-fruit Smash. Come eat at Wolfgang's when you fancy a special lunch or dinner where much thought, skill, and care has gone into the menu and food preparation. It's a pleasant interlude that should leave you very satisfied.

Wolfgang Puck Express

DDP: One credit (Q) / Cost: $
Type: American; Quick Service; Breakfast, Lunch, Dinner

Located beside Disney's Days of Christmas shop, Wolfgang Puck will gladly satisfy your need for a quick meal. You'll find modern, clean lines, and the illusion of eating in a chef's kitchen that just so happens to be well-equipped with plenty of tables. This places makes a point of using fresh, locally sourced ingredients, and the menu reflects a commitment to tasty, good food choices.

At breakfast, order a spinach and mushroom omelette, breakfast pizza, breakfast sandwich, Belgian waffles, corn-flake-crusted French toast with fresh fruit, or the "classic": scrambled eggs, bacon or sausage, crispy potatoes, and sourdough or wheat toast.

The lunch and dinner menus substantially expand the possibilities. Soups vary with the season and are currently butternut squash with cardamom cream or chicken noodle with carrots and chives. Salads, sandwiches (how about one made from that bacon-wrapped meatloaf with garlic aioli, crispy onion rings, and house-made chips?), and of course, plenty of pizzas and pasta will make nearly everyone happy. If you want more choices, consider entrées like chicken, crispy chicken tenders, more of that bacon-wrapped meatloaf sitting on mashed potatoes and topped with crispy onion rings, or roasted salmon with veggies. Desserts are a fresh fruit cup, brownies, cookies, cheesecake, and frozen yogurt. Kids can select from spaghetti, grilled chicken and mashed potatoes, cheese or pepperoni pizza, mac and cheese, or crispy chicken tenders. The food is certainly a cut above average.

Disney Springs, Part Two

The Landing

Shops

Erin McKenna's Bakery NYC

DDP: No / Cost: $
Type: American; Quick Service; Snacks

Known as the world's premier gluten-free bakery, Erin's is an excellent example of how you can successfully combine both good taste and vegan and gluten-free treats. She makes cupcakes, tea cakes sold by the slice or loaf, cookies, donuts, and more. You can also get just cupcake tops, a frosting shot, or cake bites if all you want is a taste. Look for Erin's cookbooks and other merchandise sold here as well.

Restaurants

The Basket at Wine Bar George

DDP: One credit (Q) / Cost: $
Type: American/Italian; Quick Service; Lunch, Dinner

Sometimes, you'd rather have a picnic outdoors or even in your own hotel room, and if that's your plan, this place can help. If you want an entire picnic basket, make your selections of sandwiches, cookies, wine, and nibbles. Spend $60 or more and you'll even receive the basket! Sandwiches are goat cheese, fig, and arugula, ham and cheese on ciabatta, or prosciutto, brie and olive salad on a baguette. Choose olives and hummus, crispy mac and cheese bits, a chicken skewer, and lots more. Chocolate chip cookies and seasonal offerings provide dessert.

Beverages include beer, cider, and non-alcoholic drinks are also available. Some 130 wines by the glass, bottle or ounce are sure to complement your charcuterie or sandwich. Great idea, by George!

The BOATHOUSE

DDP: Two credits (T) / Cost: $$-$$$
Type: American/Seafood; Fine/Signature; Lunch, Dinner

Dine dockside in this popular venue surrounded by beautiful "dreamboats" from the 40s, 50s, and 60s. You can also take an Italian water taxi and tour the lake and waterfront. Make a splash in a vintage amphicar (amphibious automobile— yes, these were real vehicles, and they didn't belong to James Bond) or ride the nineteenth-century Lady Rose while sipping champagne and nibbling daintily on chocolate strawberries. As you might well imagine, none of these experiences comes cheap. In fact, quite the reverse.

The food at the BOATHOUSE is described as "Florida Surf and Turf" or more recently "Sea and Shore." Like the boat rides, eating here doesn't come cheap. The Captain's Raw Bar has oysters on the half shell, lobster cocktail, yellowfin tuna poke (a raw fish salad of Hawaiian origin), jumbo lump crab, and wild Gulf shrimp. There are two more bars, the Admiral's Club Bar and Dock Bar. Chopped, wedge, Caesar, and garden salads are served. "Buckets" with fried fish, clam strips, or coconut Baja jumbo shrimp and fries are another option. Entrées of the sea (lobster, salmon, swordfish, ahi tuna), the sea and shore (lump crab, ribs, chicken, seafood mac and cheese, baked and stuffed lobster, pasta), sandwiches (lobster roll with a full Maine lobster, burgers, filet mignon sliders), and steaks (certified USDA blue-star heritage Angus), chops, and provisions provide practically anything you might want for lunch or dinner. The filet mignon Oscar-style is a 12 oz. steak with jumbo lump crab, asparagus, and sauce Béarnaise. There are more sides than you can shake a stick at—truffle fries, broccoli, roasted corn on the cob, asparagus, and more. If you can find room, try the key lime pie in a Mason jar, whiskey/caramel cornbread cake with stone fruits, a S'mores baked Alaska, and several others to tempt you. This is not only first-class dining, the setting is also a stand-out.

Chef Art Smith's Homecomin'

DDP: One credit (T) / Cost: $$ (TiW)
Type: Southern/American; Casual; Brunch, Lunch, Dinner

The point of this delightful restaurant is to make you feel like you've somehow stumbled upon a church supper in full swing or maybe wandered into Grandma's cozy kitchen. Look for it between STK Orlando and Morimoto Asia. It's "down home" cooking with a definite Floridan flair. There's an emphasis on fresh, local, and satisfying in every sense of the word.

Brunch is pure comfort food. Biscuits, house-made doughnuts, Bee Haven fried green tomatoes, eggs and ham, hush puppy Benedict, French toast (Texas toast on the griddle), shrimp and grits, short rib hash, and the eye-widening fried chicken and doughnuts with choice of side will surely hold you until suppertime. "Kiddos" have French toast or a junior farmer plate. The Rise 'n Shine cocktails include Garden, Proud, Whiskey, Southern, and Bloody Marys. Mimosas, sangrias and sweet tea 'shine join the usual breakfast beverages.

The menu is highly descriptive. Church lady deviled eggs, bunch of puppies (hush puppies, that is), thigh-high chicken biscuits drizzled with hot honey, and Bee Haven Bay fried green tomatoes are just a few of the delightful starters. Pork (in a great Cuban sandwich), chicken, and fish sandwiches are served with barbecue chips drizzled with ice box dressing. One entire menu section is devoted to "salads and dumplings"! For entrées, chicken and doughnuts, pork barbecue, fried catfish, shrimp and grits, Florida grouper, and several others will remind you of home—assuming you had a fabulous chef in the family...and lived in the South. Art's signature fried chicken (brined in buttermilk for 24 hours) comes "served with creamy mashed potatoes, cheddar biscuits, and love." Sides are likewise plentiful.

You can't leave without trying a real Southern dessert like hummingbird cake (said to be so sweet it attracts those pretty little birds), pecan pie (sometimes chocolate pecan pie), key lime pie, or Art's own famous 'shine cake—moonshine, that is. You'll be glad you came!

Cookes of Dublin

DDP: One credit (Q) / Cost: $
Type: American; Quick Service; Breakfast, Lunch, and Dinner

In years past, Ireland wasn't famous for its cooking, but that has all changed—and for the better. Cookes, located near Raglan Road Pub and Restaurant, is well known for its excellent food and hospitable service. Enjoy your meal indoors or outside under the umbrellas bearing the Cookes name.

Light, crispy "day boat" selections make a fun lunch choice. Battered fish, shrimp, and even Irish-style sausages are served with chips—chips, in this case, means hand-cut fries. The savory pies are something different and delicious, either the beef and lamb or the chicken with field mushrooms. Burgers with chips (fries) and fresh salads will appeal to most American palates. Anyone in your group game to try the "Hog in a Box" for supper? It's slow-roasted pork shoulder with baby potatoes, sage and sweet onion stuffing, and apple sauce. A nice selection of side orders is offered including delicious Irish vintage cheese and bacon dip, mushy peas now renamed "crushed garden peas" (you might find yourself pleasantly surprised), and double battered onion rings. Desserts are fresh and light, like the (seasonal) strawberry roll or the baked meringue with strawberries, or dense and sinfully rich, like the Jammy Dodger cookie or orange chocolate pillow cookie, or peanut butter and chocolate chip cookie. The food here is a big cut above average. So is the Irish-style live entertainment. Bring on the shamrocks!

The Edison

DDP: One credit (T) / Cost: $$
Type: American; Casual; Lunch, Dinner

It's designed to make guests feel like they are being served in an old 1920s electric factory, hence the name. Ceilings are soaring and there is a wide choice of themed areas like the Ember Parlour, Telegraph Lounge, the Patent Office, Waterfront Patio, the Lab, or the Tesla Lounge. Lots of variety acts entertain here: live cabaret, DJs, aerialists, contortionists, and more.

Appetizers, called shares and nibbles, are candied bacon, fried calamari, shrimp cocktail, deviled eggs with crisp potatoes and sliced speck, fries with bacon, crumbled blue cheese and chopped green onion, and Mediterranean dips with pita chips. There are half a dozen fresh salads: Greek, Caesar, chopped, and more with enhancements available. Sandwiches are typical favorites like burgers, French dip, buffalo chicken, pulled pork, a great organic tomato soup with gooey grilled cheese, turkey club, fish tacos, and a veggie burger (the "impossible" one).

Eight desserts are currently on the menu, but expect them to vary with the season. Shakes, apple cobbler, banana split, gelato, and a couple of wows like the triple chocolate voltage cake with chocolate mousse topped with espresso ganache, raspberry sauce, whipped cream and chocolate pearls, or the fun lollipop tree dessert for two with cheesecake pops, bubble gum, and whipped cream. Kids will doubtless enjoy the atmosphere at Edison's as much as the adults, and can choose from burgers, tomato soup and grilled cheese, or chicken tenders on their own menu with either gelato or a chocolate chip cookie for dessert.

There is an enormous selection of draft, bottled, or canned beer and cider (more than 20 kinds), and wines by the glass (more than 16 kinds) or Edison Classic or Signature Cocktails (more than 30) make the drinks menu here nothing short of electrifying! It's one of the newest places at Disney Springs and designed with fun in mind. Edison's a real jolt!

Enzo's Hideaway

DDP: One credit (T) / Cost: $$
Type: Italian; Table Service; Special and Unique Dining; Lounge, Lunch, Dinner

It calls to mind a 1920s speakeasy, which is where the "hideaway" part comes into play. Meal periods are slightly atypical. Supper is only served from 5 pm-10 pm on Sunday. It's like Mama used to make with a big antipasto board and salad, meats (chicken, meatballs, braised Wagyu short rib, sweet and spicy sausage) served with fingerling potatoes and seasonal vegetables. You are invited to bring your own wine—no corkage fee. There's plenty of rigatoni pasta, too, and a variety of sweets and ice cream.

Lunch has charcuterie and small plates of salads, soups, roasted potatoes. Main courses are many kinds of pasta, eggplant or chicken Parm, burgers, sirloin steak, or sea bass. The items here are authentic like "sheep's milk ricotta" in the cannoli, pistachio torte with olive oil cake, roasted strawberry jam, and whipped mascarpone, and a tiramisù or hazelnut gelato with caramel sauce. Things lean more to the genuine Italian than to American-Italian at Enzo's. You won't find "thin squid ink pasta" just anywhere, but you'll find it here. Alcoholic and non-alcoholic drinks abound in this rustic little "tunnel bar" with lots of exposed brick and arches.

Jock Lindsey's Hangar Bar

DDP: No / Cost: $
Type: American; Table Service; Lounge, Snacks

This place looks like a plane hanger turned dive, but it's got a fantastically cool vibe. Who's Jock Lindsey? He's a friend of Indiana Jones, and the pilot who gets Indy out of some close shaves. He has a pet snake named Reggie and two planes, OB1 and OB-CPO, in a not-so-veiled reference to George Lucas' other famous franchise. You can sit on the proprietor's boat docked outside named the Reggie in honor of said snake. You can even sit in an actual diving bell. The bar's decorated with memorabilia from Jock's many travels and adventures. Pull up a seat, get some tasty apps, and order something tall and cold.

The names of the snacks are as creative as can be: Tanis Tuna, Air Pirate's Pretzels, Satipo's Empanadas, Snakebite Sliders, Lao Che's Peppers, Doctor Astorga's Queso Fundido, to name just a few. Try a "Jocktail" at happy hour or order one of the numerous signature alcoholic libations with descriptive and colorful appellations. Here are a few: Cool-headed Monkey, German Mechanic, Bedtime Story, Wrong Islandl, and German Mechanic. Non-alcoholic beverages include the Poisonless Dart, Diving Bell, Antidote, and Teddy's Tea. Look for wines galore, beers and hard cider, a flight of whiskey and one of beer, and even bubbly Prosecco. There's something here for you—and for Jock's old pal, Indy!

Joffrey's Coffee and Tea Company

DDP: No / Cost: $
Type: American; Quick Service; Snacks

Premium iced teas, frozen tea or lemonade, spirited beverages hot or cold, black teas, loose leaf teas sold by the 2-ounce bag, a pu'erh chocolate-flavor tea, oolong teas, green teas, herbal and rooibos teas, and white teas will surely be enough to put tea lovers in a tizzy trying to decide among the many options. Then, of course, there's the decision about what to have with your cuppa. Several kinds of cookies (some tea flavored), cheesecake, and brownies are available. The talented baristas here can add Disney character art atop your latte on request.

Maria and Enzo's Ristorante

DDP: One credit (T) / Cost: $$
Type: Italian; Table Service; Brunch, Lunch, Dinner

If you're looking for a new Sunday brunch locale, you might want to drop by Maria and Enzo's new place. The *prix fixe* meal starts off with a pastry basket and antipasti. Salads are Caesar, Caprese, orange and fennel, and Norwegian smoked salmon (by way of Italy). Choose smoked bacon, frittatas, roasted potatoes, scrambled eggs, Italian sausage, and a really special Brioche French Toast (fresh berries, vanilla mascarpone whipped cream, maple syrup). There's a carving station and two kinds of pasta. The brunch dessert is a chocolate fountain with all kinds of goodies that benefit from being dunked. It's a special experience, Sunday's only.

At lunch and dinner, there are lots of antipasti choices and soup: meatballs, fried rice balls stuffed with meat and mozzarella, seasonal veggies and bean soup, charcuterie, fried Sicilian cheese fritters, and calamari. Lunch offers several Italian sandwiches. The salads are all popular and a bit different from what you'll find elsewhere. The roasted baby beets with toasted walnuts and a citrus Dijon dressing, misticanza with rainbow carrots, apple, and fennel, and the burrata Caprese are good choices. The pasta includes many favorites—spaghetti and meatballs, three cheese ravioli, potato gnocchi—but also less common entrées like a roasted eggplant with zucchini and Parm, chicken sausage ragu with Parm cream sauce, and a Sicilian baked pasta with peas and Caciocavallo cheese. Main dishes include chicken Parm, grilled mahi mahi, sea bass, and a grilled Angus rib-eye with roasted forest mushrooms. Kids can choose from spaghetti and meatball, slice of pizza, penne and butter, or chicken tenders. Come check out one of the newer places to dine Italian-style at Disney Springs.

Morimoto Asia

DDP: One credit, lunch (T), Two credits, dinner (T) / Cost: $$-$$$ (TiW)
Type: Pan-Asian; Fine/Signature; Lunch, Dinner

Iron Chef Masaharu Morimoto works his brand of culinary magic here at The Landing, not far from Raglan Road. His newest restaurant is popular and packed, so if you hope to dine here, make a reservation in advance, although it's certainly possible to squeeze in at the last minute if you're feeling lucky and can scoop up someone's cancellation. The soaring, two-story ceilings with their twenty-foot-long sparkling chandeliers are breathtaking. There's a kitchen stage where you can watch the dishes being prepared, intimate dining spaces, a lounge, and a sushi bar on the second story with its own entrance. The chef creates stunning and clever flavor combinations with foods from China, Japan, and Korea. Regardless of your personal preferences, if you enjoy Asian food, you'll find something delightful here.

The lunch menu is slightly less extensive than dinner, but it's similar. For starters, try edamame with sea salt, rock shrimp tempura, hamachi tacos, or tuna pizza, among others. Dim sum is a small plate of something wonderful. Egg rolls, pork or chicken bao, pork or chicken dumplings, and many others are available. Sushi rolls range from the usual California to the unusual "spider" or barbecued eel and avocado rolls. Soups and salads, noodles and rice, spare ribs, and entrées featuring seafood, chicken, pork, veggies, Morimoto Peking Duck (for two) and beef will leave you wondering how to pare down all those tempting choices.

If you really want to impress your dining partner(s), there are a couple of towers to consider. Sushi and Sashimi Pagoda at $100 serves 2–3 and includes a whole lobster, oysters on the half shell, shrimp cocktail, 5 pieces of nigiri (edible sea weed, 10 pieces of sashimi (raw fish), and 1 roll. The Sushi and Sashimi at $200 is similar but adds King crab and serves 4–6.

From non-alcoholic drinks like the Blushing Dragon or Morimoto Punch to wine by the glass, cocktails like a Morimotini or Dim Sum Bloody Mary, beers, and sake, you'll find plenty of fantastic beverages to accompany any meal selection. Desserts are available and range from the prosaic (churros) to the sublime (MM parfait for two—chocolate cream puff, vanilla gelato, hazelnut chocolate crunchies, sesame mochi), providing you have room for anything more. Morimoto Asia has been such a welcome addition to Disney Springs!

Morimoto Asia Street Food

DDP: One credit (Q) / Cost: $ (lunch)-$$ (dinner)
Type: Pan-Asian; Quick Service; Lunch, Dinner

Want to sample the famous flavors of a real Morimoto meal without the reservation or substantial investment? Grab some quick and savory snacks, noodle dishes, sushi, yummy bao tacos (pork, chicken teriyaki, or short rib in a soft, steamed bun), and plenty of signature drinks. It's Asian street food, yes, but it's prepared in high style and tastes amazing.

Paddlefish

DDP: Two credits (T) / Cost: $$ (TiW)
Type: Seafood/American; Casual; Lounge, Brunch, Lunch, Dinner

Climb aboard an old-fashioned paddle-wheeler and dine right on the water. This restaurant was formerly Fulton's Crab House, and now it's named after a freshwater fish only a mother could love—the homely, humble paddlefish.

Sunday brunch has come aboard recently at the Paddlefish. It's great, too! The King Meets the Captain is peanut butter and banana-stuffed French toast coated with Cap'n Crunch and sided with a fresh berry compote. The much-loved Monte Cristo is a welcome guest, here served with bacon and a fried egg. The crab and asparagus Benedict has two poached eggs, jumbo lump crab, grilled Nueske (it's the best!) bacon slab, under Hollandaise—oh, man!

Appetizers are fun here. Dinner has a wider selection than lunch. Try crab fries, a lobster corn dog, littleneck clams, charred octopus, crab cakes, calamari, beef skewers, or friend green tomatoes. Lobster bisque with sherry cream (oh, yes) and New England clam chowder are the soups, or you can try green, Caesar, or wedge salads. There are chilled, raw seafoods including ahi poke, crab ceviche, tableside lobster guacamole (serves 4), or fresh oysters, Dutch Harbor king crab, jumbo shrimp, lump crab ceviche, and ahi tuna poke piled high in an impressive $70 tower (serves 4). Crab and lobster entrées come with farmer's market corn and new potatoes. Bass, salmon, scallops, catfish, jambalaya, swordfish, shrimp pasta, cioppino, fish and chips, and lots of other tempting treats "from the port" are available. Steaks, burgers, filet mignon, and Kurobuta pork join the seafoods. If you want something different, consider a specialty Low Country boil, a New England boil, an Alaska boil, or a Cracker boil. Various seafoods come with sweet corn on the cob, red potatoes, and cornbread. The list of sides is immense. Crispy Brussels sprouts, blistered green beans (good!), skin-on fries, mac and cheese, asparagus, and lots more big enough to share will go very nicely with the entrées. Desserts are "down home" delicious: New York cheesecake cake, a brownie milkshake, flourless chocolate cake, key lime pie, strawberry shortcake (in season), chocolate crème brûlée, and a truly killer spiced apple bread pudding with vanilla ice cream and caramel. Need I say more? I can't—my mouth's full!

Paradiso 37, Taste of the Americas

DDP: One credit (T) / Cost: $$ (TiW)
Type: North, Central, and South American Street Food, Casual, Lunch and Dinner

Paradiso 37 is adjacent to the Hangar Bar, right on the water. Dine inside and prepare to gasp at the impressive Tequila Tower or watch the boats go by outside while you sit under an umbrella on the deck and enjoy a cool breeze off the lake. Keep in mind that this place is loud and lively! The popular bar is sure to be hopping at night.

The eats span the Western Hemisphere. South American "crazy corn" comes fire-roasted with cheese. Barbecued beef quesadillas, Santa Fe chicken tortilla soup, or loaded nachos will start the party off right. Platters of the Americas include cedar plank roasted salmon, Baja fish tacos, South Carolina ribs, pork, chicken, and many more. Salads with chicken, shrimp, or steak might be just what you want for lunch. There are also all kinds of burgers and sandwiches, imaginatively different sides (arepas, wasabi fries, truffle fries, cilantro rice), and desserts like the house special chocolate stack, tres leches cake, churros, or seasonal fruit sorbet. There are plenty of non-alcoholic beverages and beers, but don't forget the tremendous tequila selection.

Pizza Ponte

DDP: One credit (Q) / Cost: $
Type: Italian; Quick Service; Lunch, Dinner

Sometimes, you're simply too busy to sit still for a leisurely meal. Pizza Ponte has you covered with pizza by the slice—tomato and basil, forest mushroom, porchetta, 4-cheese, spicy salami, and the Big Roman are currently on offer. Grab a prosciutto di Parma sandwich or Parma ham and cheese. There are pomodoro, muffuletta, and tonno (Sicilian tuna) sandwiches, too. Quite a few desserts can be yours here, mostly Italian specialties. Cannoli, orange olive oil cake, pistachio and mascarpone parfait, Italian cookies, tiramisù, biscotti, baba, Nutella parfait, and more will taste great with one of the many kinds of espresso, macchiato, cappuccino, or ciccolata (hot chocolate). Beer and wine are also served. This is one of the newer places at Disney Springs.

Raglan Road Irish Pub and Restaurant

DDP: One credit (T) / Cost: $$ (TiW)
Type: Irish Cuisine; Unique/Themed; Brunch, Lunch, Dinner, Late Night Dining

Look for Raglan Road right next to Cookes of Dublin. In fact, they share a kitchen. This place is simply chockablock with cozy atmosphere. The new Rhythms of Raglan Dance show is an hour and a half of Irish music and dance on Saturday and Sunday from 10:00 a.m. until 3.00 p.m. Every night of the week there's live entertainment with singers and bands playing

Irish classics from 4:30 p.m. to 1:00 a.m. and on the patio stage outside daily from 8:00 p.m. to 12:30 a.m. You could be forgiven for thinking you'd wandered into a delightful Dublin pub. There's even a song about Raglan Road recorded by the Dubliners, a group of Celtic singers:

> On Raglan Road on an Autumn Day,
> I saw her first and knew
> That her dark hair would weave a snare
> That I may one day rue...

Prices are slightly less expensive at lunch. Dinner starts at 3:00 p.m., and "pub grub" is served late nights from 11:00 p.m. "until late." There's a dynamite weekend brunch. An Irish egg, soul soup (ask about it), slow-roasted Guinness glazed baby back ribs, scallops from Georges Bank, shrimp, cheeses, and the famous Dalkey duo described below will get your brunch started. You might want to try the full Irish breakfast, just like in the old county. The Anglo Irish is more suited to American expectations. Salmon, waffles, pancakes, braised short rib, pork hash, crab Benedict, and several other enticing main courses are surprisingly tasty.

Start with an Irish egg, mighty mussels, or smoked salmon with crème fraiche and capers. Appetizers to share include baby back ribs, pan-seared shrimp, Georges Bank scallops, Dalkey duo (battered cocktail sausages and Dublin's famous Irish Dalkey mustard for dipping), and more. Wonderfully fresh salads like Go(at) Fig(ure) or Salmon Diner Squared with creatively combined ingredients are a meal in themselves. Entrées run the gamut from a special shepherd's pie, stuffed leg of lamb, and beef stew with Guinness, to burgers, seafood, heavenly ham, fried chicken, bangers (sausages), and lots more. Sides are unique and imaginative—garlic Parmesan truffle chips, crushed garden peas (aka mushy peas), smokey bacon and almond-roasted Brussels sprouts, and beer-battered onion rings are just a few of them. If you still have room, don't neglect the amazing desserts: fluffy lemon clouds (lemon and meringue), chocolate heaven, bread and butter pudding, Raglan delight (a light raspberry Pavlova), trifle sinful, apple crumble, and more. It will be difficult to pick one, so pick several and share with the table.

As you might imagine, Raglan Road has you well covered with its drink menu. Bottled and draft beers (Guinness, naturally), non-alcoholic beverages, specialty libations (how about a Dublin donkey or a Baileys shake?), wines, and bubbly should perfectly accompany all that Irish deliciousness. The staff is extremely friendly and helpful—and I'm not just saying that because I'm half Irish. Don't overlook this place—it will be a delightful memory of your visit to the auld sod of Ireland, even though you never left Orlando!

STK Orlando

DDP: One credit, lunch (T), Two credits, dinner (T) / Cost: $$-$$$$ (TiW) **Type:** Steaks/Seafood; Fine/Signature; Lunch, Dinner

Anniversary, birthday, or just a fantastic dinner to remember—think STK. Your meal will be something special. The venue is modern, sleek, and oh-so-chic. The food is fantastic. It's hard to go wrong with anything on the menu, but remember that such a beautiful meal will not come cheaply. You'll pay handsomely for the privilege of dining here. A 28-ounce dry-aged porterhouse for two will set you back $98, but share it and celebrate! The menu isn't lengthy—it doesn't need to be. What's here is absolute perfection. As with any good steakhouse, however, you must make your preference for doneness very clear. Be explicit.

Salads and appetizers (try the Wagyu burger called Lil' BRGs or order the shellfish platter for the table) are imaginative and luxurious. Salads are interesting. Hearts of palm and Asian pear, heirloom tomato and burrata cheese, baby gem lettuce Caesar, blue iceberg, and shaved Brussels Sprouts with apples, cranberries, and Marcona almonds should please most diners. There's also a well-stocked raw bar. Entrées include chicken, seafood (grilled Maine lobster, Chilean sea bass, seared tuna, and market fish), but the star of the show is steak. That whopping porterhouse, a petite filet mignon, sirloin, Delmonico, bone-in ribeye steak, or the 34-ounce dry-aged Tomahawk (long bone rib steak for two at the princely price point of $128) will quell any carnivore's craving for red meat. Again, you need to be perfectly specific when expressing your preference and expectation for doneness. Add truffle butter, a peppercorn crust, a couple of shrimp, or a lobster if you just can't get enough surf and turf. Eight delightful sauces like STK, Bernáise, au poivre, blue butter, and four others will complement the meat beautifully. Sides are every bit as sinfully indulgent as the main courses. Think creamy Yukon potatoes, Parmesan truffle fries, wild mushrooms, and Brussels sprouts with bacon.

Dessert, too? Well, if you must, there are many on hand to end your meal with something irresistible (caramelito bar, orange dream cheesecake, an insanely decadent warm bag o' donuts, warm baked cookie with chocolate sauce, caramel, and vanilla ice cream, or a berry parfait), but as I mentioned, there's no doubt that at STK, steak is the main event. The drink menu is as impressive as the food. Look for creative specialty cocktails (Green Intensity, ...Not Your Daddy's Manhattan, Poisoned Apple), a dozen lovely bottled beers, and a great many wonderful wines (mostly from California and France). Raise a glass of Moët & Chandon with your special someone and enjoy the evening! Cheers!

Terralina Crafted Italian

DDP: One credit (T) / Cost: $$
Type: Italian; Table Service; Lunch, Dinner

This restaurant, formerly Portobello County Italian Trattoria, has been completely remodeled and redesigned, so if you haven't been lately, you won't recognize it. Chef Tony Mantuano and Executive Chef Justin Plank capture the flavors of Italy's Lake District. Everything has been completely refreshed.

Antipasti is just right. There's the popular tower that serves 4, crispy eggplant fries, crab crostini, carpaccio (baby arugula, shaved Parm, fried capers, and grilled crostini), burrata, crispy Italian chicken bites, fried calamari, or meatballs are satisfying and tasty. There are many salads like Caprese, Caesar, or baby greens, and seasonal soups.

Pizza here is wood-fired. Artisan pepperoni, mushroom, sausage, calzone, margherita, and a rotating pizza of the week are available. Entrées for the table are a citrus-herb brick chicken, slow-roasted beef short rib, or house-made porchetta. As you might imagine, pasta choices are many. Ravioli, capellini with crab, spaghetti pomodoro and meatballs, rigatoni with sausage, spaghetti Bolognese, bucatini with clams, gnocchi, penne and shrimp, and a house-made lasagne will please most fans of Italian cuisine. If you'd prefer a crispy parm burger, swordfish, a ribeye steak, a center-cut pork chop, or the catch of the day, that can be arranged. Sides are currently broccolini, Yukon gold mashed potatoes, green beans, seasonal grilled veggies, polenta fries, and potato planks. Enhancements include grilled chicken, salmon, or shrimp.

Eight desserts of Italian origin will bring a sweet end to your visit to Italy's Lake District. The cappuccino crème brûlée, chocolate paradise, or a chocolate-dipped gelato sandwich are wonderful choices, but there are also lots of gelato flavors and even a gelato sundae with toffee crumbles and whipped cream. Cocktails with an Italian flair, beers from all over the world including Italy, and some unusual Italian non-alcoholic beverages make the drinks menu here interesting. The atmosphere is pleasant, the menu is new and inventive, and there's a table just waiting for you and your friends to come see what the buzz is all about.

Wine Bar George

DDP: One credit (T) / Cost: $$
Type: American; Table Service; Casual; Lunch, Dinner

For some easy-going bites and beverages, George has a few things that might be perfect for you. At lunch, there's a chicken salad sandwich, BLT + C (cheese), and steak fries with caramelized onion aïoli, each paired with a wine to suit. Small plates are hummus, grilled romaine, spiced olives, jicama-kohlrabi salad, crispy mac and cheese bites, burrata, chicken skewers, housemade meatballs and more. You might like one of the "boards" of cheeses, meats, and grilled breads; if you have a large party, try that "big board" filled with some great charcuterie. Family-style plates that serve 2-4 people: skirt steak, whole grilled Greek sea bass, or wine-braised chicken. The olive oil cake, key lime pie, or chocolate experience (pairing of three wines with three chocolates) are your dessert choices. The choices of wines, beers and ciders, sparkling wines and champagnes, and cocktails is one of the most complete and exciting you'll find anywhere.

Vivoli il Gelato

DDP: No / Cost: $
Type: American; Quick Service; Snacks

Choose gelato or sorbetto from a delightful list of flavors that vary seasonally. Try a "Nutella brownie sundae" or a "spaghetti sundae." How about a gelato or sorbetto float or milk shake? The tiramisù shake, cannoli shake, or creamsicle float are full of Italian flavor. The paninis are petite and the flavors rotate, so you can buy one, two, or three of them. Lots of biscotti for dipping into drinks are made fresh daily, as are tortine (tarts) that come filled with a variety of Italian ingredients. Coffees like Americano, macchiato, cappuccino, latte, espresso, and doppio (a double espresso), iced tea, Coke products, and Italian sodas are available here as well.

Next, we'll explore eating options offered in Disney Springs, Town Center. While you won't encounter quite as many upscale restaurants, there are some unique eating venues to explore, like a Sprinkles Cupcake ATM for any after-hours cravings that might strike, Frontera Cocina, Amorette's Patisserie, The Polite Pig, and several quick stops for grab-and-go snacks. It's difficult to imagine that there are more dining choices yet to come, but dust off that imagination of yours because you're only halfway through the culinary cornucopia better known as Disney Springs.

Disney Springs, Part Three

Town Center

Shops

Candy Cauldron

If you see someone walking around Disney Springs eating a "poisoned" apple that looks exactly like the one the Wicked Queen prepared for Snow White, don't be concerned. That's just one of the many kinds of candy and caramel apples you'll find at this sweet shop. Order one just the way you want it and then watch yours being made!

Restaurants

Amorette's Patisserie

DDP: One credit (S) / Cost: $
Type: American; Quick Service; Snacks, Lunch, Dinner

Located next to Levi's in Town Center, Amorette's is known for "sophisticated" snacks; this bakery will have items you won't find just anywhere. These signature pastries are guaranteed to make your eyes light up, your tummy rumble, and your mouth water. They are as delectable as they are gorgeous, and their names are as fun as the treats themselves. 49th and Broadway/NY Cheesecake, Dancing with Pavlova/Light Meringue Crisp, Avant-Garde, and Sunset on Mile Marker 0/Key Lime Tart will give you just a hint of what's on the menu.

Amorette's dome cakes are truly inspired. They've become an instant park classic! Order a Mickey, Minnie, Donald, Goofy, or Pluto. They're sure to make any dinner special! Call

Amorette's at 407-934-3500 at least 72 hours in advance. The option to order a cake on the Shop Parks app has just been added. The sweet masterpiece can be delivered to your table following a meal at a Disney restaurant. It will delight your whole gang, while other diners look on in envy. You can choose small cakes or large. An eleven-layer red velvet and chocolate number filled with chocolate mousse and cherry mousse and frosted with Italian buttercream just amazes! There is a lovely peach-colored blossom resting lightly on top, as a scattering of real gold leaf cascades across the top and down the side. You can get it full sized or petite.

If you'd like to find out how the magic is made here, sign up (well in advance) for a 90 minute interactive decorating class where you'll "make and take" a signature dome cake of your very own. This event happens before the bakery even opens and class sizes are small. Beverages, alcoholic or non, are served and you also receive a little gift. They can hold your creation while you visit Disney Springs, so you can pick it up later in the day. How thoughtful!

As you might imagine, there are lots of additional kinds of seasonal specialties and fancy pastries, absolutely beautiful to look at, and lots of champagne and sparkling wines to go with them. There's coffee and ganache hot chocolate, too.

Sandwiches are once again being offered, so you can have a light meal here before selecting a magnificent treat. Try turkey or ham on focaccia, veggie croissant. If you're feeling French, order one of the scrumptious crêpes like Caprese, ham and cheese, strawberry and crème, or banana and hazelnut with salted caramel. Amorette, darling, where have you been all my life?

Blaze Fast Fire'd Pizza

DDP: No / Cost: $
Type: American; Quick Service; Snacks, Lunch, and Dinner

Fired pizza cooks quickly, and you can expect yours done in 180 seconds! The ingredients are artisanal while the dough is made from scratch. Choose original, higher rising, or gluten free dough to build your own pizza. The specialty pizzas are inventive and satisfying with just about every topping you can imagine: red vine, BBQ chicken, meat eater, art (artichokes) lover, green stripe (pesto), veg out, link in, and white top. Get a simple salad to go with your pizza. Plenty of beers, wines, and non-alcoholic beverages are available at Blaze, and desserts, too. Try the S'more pie or other assorted sweets. It's a great place for a quick yet delicious meal or snack. Find it next to D-Luxe burger on the water that surrounds The Landing.

Chicken Guy!

DDP: No / Cost: $
Type: American; Quick Service; Lunch, Dinner

This isn't just *ANY* Chicken Guy—it's Guy Fieri who's selling this chicken. It's next to Planet Hollywood. Signature Sandwiches come with two chicken tenders (fried or grilled) to which you can add sauces (cheddar, bourbon, brown sugar, or BBQ) smoked bacon, or a Southwest with pepper jack, avocado cream, charred corn, roasted peppers, black beans, lettuce, tomatoes, and crispy tortilla strips. Make any sandwich a "combo" and you'll get it made with three chicken tenders, fries, and a fountain beverage. Guy is known for being "saucy" so look for plenty of them to try—Guy's favorites, classics, or hot 'n' spicy. Sides here are fries with special seasonings, American slaw, fried pickle chips, Mac Daddy mac and cheese, loaded fries, and more. Thinking something a little lighter? Go with salad bowls. Try chopped chicken Caesar, Southwest sweet corn, or BBQ chopped chicken. Kids have their own menu with tenders, grilled cheese, or mac and cheese. There are frozen treats on hand which may vary. Currently, you'll find a Triple Double Mint with crushed Oreos, mint chocolate soft serve, chocolate mints, whipped cream, and chocolate sauce or a Cinnamon Apple version with vanilla soft serve, Cinnamon Toast Crunch and Apple Jacks cereals, and whipped cream. Too much is never enough with this Guy!

City Works Eatery and Pour House

DDP: No / Cost: $
Type: American; Casual Dining; Table Service; Lunch, Dinner

Coming soon!

Coca-Cola Store Rooftop Beverage Bar

DDP: No / Cost: $
Type: American/Global; Quick Service; Drinks

Coca-Cola started way back in 1886 when Dr. John Pemberton, an Atlanta pharmacist, wanted to concoct an good-tasting non-alcoholic beverage that could be sold at soda fountains. The rest, as they say, is history. That first Coke was five cents a glass. Today, nearly two billion Cokes are served daily, many of them right here at Walt Disney World. Cokes, cocktails, alcoholic smoothies, and mocktails—they're all here waiting for you to try. You'll also find water, coffee, energy drinks, floats, icees, and icee floats. For an international treat, try the Cokes of the World tray or the combo tray. You'll be surprised at how the rest of the world likes its Coca-Cola to taste. There's a "freestyle experience" offering you five refills within an hour. There's no doubt about it—Coke is king here. Have a beverage and enjoy the panoramic view of Disney Springs from your rooftop vantage point. Things do go better with Coke!

The Daily Poutine

DDP: One credit (S) / Cost: $
Type: American; Quick Service; Snacks

What's poutine, you may be excused from wondering? It's a homey dish that originated in Québec Provence in Canada. Fries are the base, topped with cheese curds and a light brown gravy. Although popular in Canada and sold in some northern areas of the U.S., it's still an uncommon treat, especially south of the Mason-Dixon Line. Classic, Latin, Italian, Oktoberfest, and French versions of poutine are offered, along with beer, sangria, and fountain beverages.

D-Luxe Burger

DDP: No / Cost: $
Type: American; Quick Service; Fast Casual; Breakfast, Lunch, Dinner

While it might look like a cute little farmhouse with the requisite white picket fence from the outside, step inside and you'll find burgers galore on this ranch. It's located right across from Blaze along the small water channel that surrounds The Landing and divides it from Town Center.

D-Luxe has recently added breakfast during busy times of the year, and there are lots of very nice options here. Get a classic breakfast burger with bacon, egg, hash browns and a hamburger patty on a Parker House roll. Lighter choices are a Greek yogurt parfait or the egg white frittata sandwich with spinach and avocado crème. There's a crispy chicken biscuit, the spicy El Diablo breakfast burger, and fries with either sausage gravy or sauce Béarnaise.

For lunch and dinner, find classic (you can get a duo or an ultimate duo with fries and two fountain beverages if you've got a yen to share), barbecue, El Diablo (chorizo, fried banana peppers, pepper jack cheese, chipotle mayo), a seasonal burger, a classic cheeseburger, the "cluck" chicken burger, and the veggie with all kinds of toppings and fresh-cut fries that come with free dipping sauces. When it's available, the kids will have fun ordering a "hamburger" red velvet macaroon for dessert that looks just like the big one. Their menu has a grilled chicken sandwich Disney check meal, a cheeseburger, or chicken nuggets. Get shakes or malts made with gelato, alcoholic or not, to go with that burger. There are plenty of Coke products, iced tea, and milk. Find wines, draft beer, and hard cider plus alcoholic floats with root beer or orange soda. You'll get a burger cooked to order, so tell 'em to make yours just the way you like it!

Frontera Cocina

DDP: One credit (T) / Cost: $$
Type: Mexican; Casual; Lunch, Dinner

Take the small bridge, the one just in front of Morimoto Asia, across the water and you'll find Frontera Cocina. If you've watched Chef Rick Bayless, six-time winner of the James Beard Foundation Award, on television, you'll know just what to expect here—fantastic, delicious, and authentic Mexican cuisine. Frontera means "border," but there is nothing borderline at this place. It's all simply fantastic. The restaurant from outside appears fairly standard, but the cuisine in this kitchen is a big cut above average, and it boasts a huge menu. If you have a favorite Mexican dish, you'll very likely be able to enjoy it here.

Chef Rick didn't get where he is by playing it safe. Sure, chips and salsa are available, but so is Sikal Pak, a creamy Yucatán pumpkin seed-habañero dip with crispy cucumber and jicama slices served with warm tortilla chips. Tired of regular guacamole? Try either the verde (green), bacon, or atomic version (with hot habañero sauce). Tortilla soup or queso fundito (melted cheese and chorizo sausage) with warm corn tortillas are perfect starters. There are salads, tacos (try the succulent carne asada with soft tortillas), and tortas. Entrées include delectably prepared chicken, shrimp mojo de ajo (pan-roasted Mazatlan blue shrimp with slow-cooked chicken broth, lime, chipotle), carne asada (steak), carnitas (pork shoulder), and shrimp enchiladas suizas (Swiss style). Even the sides are a twist on the traditional. Yes, there is rice, but the rice comes studded with plantains and cilantro. You'll find beans refritos with cortina cheese, grilled Mexican squash, and more for sides.

Desserts are a warm pecan pie bar, platano (banana) sundae with Mexican vanilla ice cream and toasted pecans, and a coconut-lime quatro leches cake (that's right, four kinds of milk, not the standard three). The drink menu is as extensive as the food menu. Cocktails are plentiful: All the Pretty Girls, Cinco de Mayo, Frontera Old Fashioned, plus plenty of others. Sparkling wines, sangria, an international wine list, tequila flights, beers galore, or a wide array of cool non-alcoholic beverages will help if you've had one too many habañero peppers! This is the perfect opportunity for you to enjoy real Mexican cuisine prepared beautifully, thoughtfully, and inventively! Bayless hits all the right gastronomic notes in his Mexican symphony of flavors.

Frontera Cocina Quick Window

DDP: One Credit (Q) / Cost: $
Type: Mexican; Quick Service; Snacks, Lunch, and Dinner

No time to stop for a full, sit-down meal but still craving some truly awesome Mexican food? Stop at the quick-service window and pick up some chips and guac with three tacos— either beef barbacoa (chipotle braised beef) or cochinita pibil (achiote braised pork shoulder). There are also margaritas, either a signature Frontera or a blood orange jalapeño.

A couple of Mexican beers and Coke products are available in addition to a Fiesta Mexicano Iced Tea with melon, mango, and papaya. If you like Mexican food, you can't go wrong at this little window.

Häagen Dazs

DDP: No / Cost: $
Type: American; Quick Service; Snacks

Hot, tired, and in need of a cool pick-me-up? Then look for this kiosk between YeSake and Wetzel's, right on the water. You can order a "dazzler" sundae like a banana split, mint chip, rocky road, or dulce split in small or regular sizes. There are sundaes in three sizes starting with "kiddie" and going up from there. Check out those shakes with toppings or without, and don't forget the frappes in coffee, mocha, and caramel. There are several ways to dress up your cone, so step up to the counter, decide on your favorite flavor, and place your order.

Joffrey's Handcrafted Smoothies Kiosk

DDP: Snack (S) / Cost: $
Type: American; Quick Service; Snacks

In addition to its Marketplace location, there's a Joffrey's Smoothies in Town Center as well, adjacent to YeSake and Wetzel's. As you've no doubt noticed, Joffrey's is found in many locales at Walt Disney World. The Purple Piñata, Mango Tango, Flamingo Frost, Frozen Sun Drop, and several other concoctions are on the menu. This kiosk serves a tremendous variety of smoothies blended with Dippin' Dots vanilla yogurt and Minute Maid juice. Coffee with Kahlúa, Baileys, or Jameson, tea with vodka and lemon, and juices are also sold.

Planet Hollywood

DDP: One credit (T) / Cost: $$
Type: American; Casual; Table Service; Unique/Themed Dining; Lunch, Dinner

Planet Hollywood, the franchise that began in 1991 as an answer to the Hard Rock Café's wild popularity, just underwent a Hollywood-style face lift in Orlando, reopening in January 2017. The globe has morphed into an observatory dome with outside balcony seating at Stargazer Lounge. You'll find some twenty craft beers on tap and ten signature cocktails. Four dining levels inside have a view of the 4,500 square-foot video wall with projections that look absolutely real, due to a high-def, three dimensional visual effect. An interesting museum's worth of Hollywood memorabilia is displayed inside.

The menu has lots of popular items with some new names plus some delightful newcomers, like chicken crunch, five cheese dip, hummus trio, and a "high roller sampler" to start (serves 4). The list of choices is lengthy. Salads are spinach and berries, chicken or shrimp Caesar, Hollywood Bowl (turkey, bacon, Swiss, hard boiled egg, cheese, and more), and steak-house salad. Four great pastas join a crowd of Guy Fieri's "big bite burgers" (including a Morgan's veggie or—on the opposite end of the caloric spectrum—one topped with bacon mac and cheese), and "signature sandwiches." Try the house-roasted turkey, Swiss, cranberry sauce, BBQ chips, LTOP (lettuce, tomatoes, onions, pickles), and "donkey sauce" (celebrity chef Guy Fieri's phenomenal invention, consisting of mayo, garlic, Worcester, and mustard; Fieri, in fact, created the burger and sandwich menu here) on a garlic-buttered pretzel roll called the Turkey Pic-A-Nik. Pulled pork, crispy fried chicken, and pimento grilled cheese round out the sandwich menu.

Entrées range from steaks, ribs, and chicken, to salmon and mahi mahi. Add a side salad, baked potato, triple fries, fresh fruit, roasted garlic mashed potatoes, cilantro rice, or a green bean blend to create your perfect combo. The addition of freshly cut fruit is a nice change from the usual. Healthy choices are possible here, but you have to look closely to find them.

Single-serving desserts are as expected, except for the different and fab British sticky toffee pudding, but there are some eye-popping shareable sweet treats like the Planet Melt-down or an asteroid-sized Brownie Sundae Martini. Drinks includes shakes (with starry names) galore, many appeal-ing non-alcoholic specialty drinks, and a wide assortment of wines, hard cider, and beers. Check out the three specialty beverages for children if you have them in your party. The drinks come with signature cups, adorable names, and appeal-ing ingredients. Kids will have no trouble choosing from their own menu (spaghetti with meatballs, mac and cheese, cheese pizza, and chicken fingers or a salad with a special dessert of the day) and there's so much to see here that they'll be kept busy watching all the action, which includes some live entertainment. This place is awesome. What a Guy!

The Polite Pig

DDP: One credit (Q) / Cost: $
Type: American/Barbecue; Quick Service; Lunch, Dinner

Adjacent to the big water tower is a newer arrival at Town Center; it's the latest restaurant venture of the Petrakis family. They already have two successful venues in the Orlando area, the Ravenous Pig and Cask & Larder. Expect to find locally sourced seasonal ingredients and a modern twist on traditional Southern barbecue. There's an open kitchen where you can see all the food preparation in action.

Snacks here are unusual. You'll find barbecue "burnt ends" meatballs with cheddar grits, a hop salt pretzel with beer cheese fondue and IPA mustard, polite rub chicken wings, and a yummy slider trio that includes Southern pig, brisket, and fried chicken. If you're partial to bourbon, they have an eye-popping fifty kinds of it available at the Bourbon Bar! Try one of whiskey flights to sample several. There is a multitude of small-batch cocktails, some wines, and beers, too. Caesar, BBQ Cobb, and a simple greens salads pair nicely with the barbecue selections. Sandwiches come with a pickle spear, but you may want to add one or more of the many appealing sides like Southern potato salad, baked beans, sweet potato tots, crispy Brussels sprouts, or BBQ waffle fries and more. Check out the "low and slow" brisket sandwich, yummy onion straws, pickled peppers, and pimento cheese. Cedar plank salmon, baby-back ribs, pork shoulder, smoked turkey, brisket, and chicken are available "from the smoker," accompanied by slaw, Texas toast, and choice of one additional side like tomato and watermelon salad, crispy Brussels sprouts, charred broccoli, sweet potato tots, and lots more. Kids menu items are smoked pork slider, mac and cheese, BBQ meatballs, sliced smoked turkey breast, and chicken tenders. Orange blossom honey cake is a house specialty, and red velvet cake or an old-fashioned buttermilk chess pie are also on the menu.

Sprinkles Cupcakes

DDP: No / Cost: $
Type: American; Quick Service; Bakery; Snacks

Located opposite Frontera Cocina on the water surrounding The Landing, you'll encounter "Cupcake Central." If you see a large crowd of excited and hungry guests milling around a glass door, you've very likely found Sprinkles Cupcakes. Famous Sprinkles is credited with starting the nation's cupcake craze, which, as you've no doubt discovered, is still going strong, especially here at Walt Disney World.

There are four kinds of red velvet cupcakes—regular, gluten-free, sugar-free, or vegan. With sixteen cupcake flavor options like chocolate marshmallow, salty caramel, or carrot, you're sure to find one, or several, that will suit you just perfectly. Ask about special and seasonal flavors, too. There are half a dozen cookie flavors, from traditional chocolate chip to salted oatmeal cornflake, and you'll also see a dozen regular (chocolate, vanilla, etc.) to wild (Cap'n Crunch) ice cream flavors to make the party complete. If you're being seriously decadent, order a cookie sandwich with your choice of ice cream filling or a Sprinkles cupcake sandwich in your choice of flavors. There are brownie sundaes, cookie sundaes, triple scoops, and just about every sort of float, milkshake, or malt you can imagine. Beverages are also available, including tea, juice, coffee, espresso, and latte.

If you get a Sprinkles craving and the shop is closed, there's an ATM cupcake machine that dispenses cupcakes for you 24/7. All the cupcakes are baked and frosted fresh every day. Use the easy touchscreen to select your flavor. Swipe your credit card (no cash). A robotic arm puts your choice into a little box and loads the dispenser which swivels open to reveal the treat. *Et voila*—instant Sprinkles!

Stargazer's Bar

DDP: No / Cost: $
Type: American; Quick Service; Lounge; Snacks

Sit outside under the stars and sip on something delicious. If you're wondering where all the astronomy comes into some of the names in this corner of Disney Springs, it's because Planet Hollywood was dubbed Planet Hollywood *Observatory* after its most recent remodel. Now, the observatory part has been dropped, but some of the celestial names still hang on— like Stargazer's, for instance. The cocktails here have names like the stellar Margarita, sparkling Sputnik, Halley's comet, space monkey, planetary punch, moonwalk, and more. This bar specializes in a huge variety of Florida craft beers, some dozen and a half of them. There's also plenty of bottled beer and a few rotating wine selections. The venue is really pretty and the atmosphere is definitely out of this world.

Wetzel's Pretzels

DDP: No / Cost: $
Type: American; Quick Service; Snacks

Wetzel's is part of the cluster of snack kiosks at the far end of Town Center that includes YeSake, Häagen Dazs, and Joffrey's. Just as in the Marketplace, Wetzel's is a little stand where you can find delicious, fresh, warm pretzels. Get "sinful cinnamon" or "almond crunch," or try the baked cheese and pepperoni pretzel. For dipping, Wetzel's provides jalapeño or cheddar cheese, pizza, and sweet caramel sauce. If you're still hungry, order a hot dog or cheese dog with lemonade, frozen lemonade, or frozen granita.

Disney Springs, Part Four:
West Side

AMC Movies at Disney Springs 24

DDP: No / Cost: $
Type: American; Casual; Lunch, Dinner

You will find this unusual theatre opposite the Planet Hollywood. We're not just talking Milk Duds, popcorn, or Junior Mints here—not by a long shot. The theatre seats are comfy, and there's a counter or tray in front of them to hold your lunch or dinner.

Wings, nachos, pretzel bites, loaded tots, crispy Brussels sprouts, filled wedge lettuce cups, or a "Big Bite" sampler will get your started. There are some great sushi rolls, or maybe you'd like to try the Korean BBQ Bacon Buns. Fries, three kinds of flatbreads, and many kinds of burgers are available, too. Bowls include Asian steak and shrimp, two kinds of chicken,BBQ brisket with mac and cheese, and bacon/chicken mac and cheese, each loaded with enough goodies to make a complete meal. Caesar salad, chicken Caesar wrap, Cobb salad, or chopped Cobb wraps are other choices.

In addition, there's a substantial kids menu tailored just for younger tastes. Molten chocolate churros, a triple chocolate brownie sundae, or chocolate, vanilla, or Oreo milkshakes are sweet distractions. Still craving those Milk Duds? No worries. You can also order any of the traditional favorite movie candies, popcorn, Coke beverages, coffee, tea, and more to your heart's content. A full menu of alcoholic beverages is available, too, at MacGUFFINS Bar in the lobby. All you have to do is press a button to order your food. Gosh, going to the movies was never like this!

Bongos Cuban Café

DDP: One credit (T) / Cost: $$
Type: Cuban Cuisine; Casual; Table Service; Unique/Themed Dining; Lunch, Dinner

Gloria Estefan is the visionary behind Bongos, a café that recreates the vibe of Havana, Cuba, in the 1950s. It's adjacent to Wolfgang Puck on the water. Bar stools are giant, colorful conga drums. Bamboo lines the walls and bright glass light fixtures add to the festive ambience here. Enormous potted palms and plants bring the tropics indoors.

Soups and salads are available with classic Cuban garlic toast. Appetizers are hearty, spicy, and delicious. The Estefan Kitchen Cuban Combo serves two and might be the way to go if you're not sure what to pick. Cuban empanadas, ham croquettes, fried calamari, loaded baked potatoes, bacon-wrapped plantains (maduros), Cuban empanadas, black bean hummus, and many more will start off your taste-of-Cuba meal with flair. Beef many savory ways, pork, ribs, chicken, and seafood of almost every type imaginable should please just about everyone in your group. There's also a helpful section called the "Calorie Conscious Cuban" for those watching their waistlines. Those items are gluten-free and grilled.

Traditional Latin desserts like flan, rice pudding, churros, and tres leches cake are joined on the dessert menu by chocolate mousse, chocolate mousse cake, tres leches cake, and guava New York-style cheesecake. To quench your thirst, you'll discover a lovely array of inventive cocktails, wines from California and South America, and plenty of beers. Many non-alcoholic choices are available, too. The lively décor is almost as great as the Cuban cuisine at Bongos.

Bongos Cuban Café Express

DDP: No / Cost: $
Type: Cuban Cuisine; Quick Service; Snacks, Lunch, Dinner

Several of the menu items at Bongos can be found here, too, and it's right next door. Portions are smaller, so you could try a couple of different items and share among the group. The Cuban sandwich made from slow-roasted pork, Swiss, pickles, and mustard is a sure-fire winner. Soups, salads, appetizers, and wraps make a great, quick meal or snack. There are entrées as well, but no substitutions: chicken bites or Cuban Criolla beef bites. Side orders like plantain chips, sweet plantains, or black beans can be added to your order. Plenty of children's items are also on the menu. Desserts are chocolate chip cookies, flan, cheese pastry, or guava pastry. Coffee, tea, fountain beverages, beers and wines, and more will go well with any of the Cuban food at Bongos. Muy delicioso, no matter where you're from.

City Works Eatery and Pour House

DDP: No / Cost: $
Type: American; Casual Dining; Lunch, Dinner

For sports fans or just fans of some tasty snacks, you'll find a huge variety of beers. Coming soon!

Fantasy Fare Food Truck

DDP: One credit (S) / Cost: $
Type: American; Quick Service; Snacks

The bright red food truck carries good things to eat from the Magic Kingdom, and since it's on wheels, it moves around sometimes. You'll generally find it with other food trucks next to the water between Bongos and Starbucks. It's usually only open during dinner, except at very busy times when it's also open for lunch. You might find things like shrimp and lobster mac and cheese, chicken and waffles, chicken strips with waffle fries, or a hand-dipped corn dog with waffle fries. Coke beverages are available. Items on the menu will vary seasonally.

Springs Street Tacos Food Truck

DDP: One credit (S) / Cost: $
Type: Mexican; Quick Service; Snacks

Try those street tacos you've heard so much about and see why they've become so popular. Steak, fish, rice and bean, chicken tacos or a taco combo and chips and dip are available at this truck. What you'll find on the menu here at any given time is subject to change without notice. Currently, a variety of ice cream bars and assorted Coke beverages and signature cocktails and beers are available, but the trucks move around and are not always on site. There are often musical performances in the evenings near the food trucks at Exposition Park. A new **Mac & Cheese Food Truck** has just joined the mobile fleet.

Front Porch

DDP: No / Cost: $
Type: American Cuisine; Lounge; Drinks

You'll find the welcoming al fresco porch between House of Blues and the concert hall. There's an outdoor stage that features live entertainment every night of the week (cancelled in case of inclement weather). An extensive bar menu with beers and wines offers something for just about every guest.

House of Blues Restaurant and Bar

DDP: One credit (T) / Cost: $$ (TiW)
Type: Southern/American/Global; Casual; Lunch, Dinner

The cuisine at House of Blues is Southern and global, and the music is cool—and there are a lot more styles than just the blues. You might hear R and B, hip hop, reggae, or something entirely different. Fantastic regional and national bands play here while you dine in style. There's a popular Happy Hour every day.

Sunday brunch is an all-you-care-to-enjoy meal, with gospel performers who will sing out the "good news." It's loud and down-home style, so don't expect to carry on a quiet conversation. You can expect the usual breakfast items like pastries, eggs, ham, sausage, eggs, made-to-order omelettes, and biscuits and gravy, but there is also Creole chicken jambalaya, smoked BBQ chicken, carving stations, chicken and waffles, and other special items like white chocolate banana bread pudding with crème anglaise. Call to book a reservation.

Lunch and dinner menus are the same. Start with hand-stretched, grilled flatbreads, each using fresh, inventive combinations of ingredients. Appetizers range from traditional Southern, Voodoo Shrimp, Carolina "mess," and gumbo to more trendy like wings three ways, BBQ brisket nachos, and house specialty dips with tortilla chips. Three kinds of flatbreads are featured, BBQ chicken, mushroom, or Margherita. Cool salads like wedge, Cobb, or Southern can be enhanced with chicken, salmon, or Cajun shrimp. American classics abound:

ribs, Cajun pasta, jambalaya, shrimp and grits, chicken fried steak, salmon, NY strip steak, and lots more. There are build-your-own burgers and signature sandwiches, and don't forget the many varieties of sides such as house-made coleslaw, BBQ beans, sweet corn, root veggies, and mac and cheese. The sides and entrées are seasonal and will vary. The bourbon bread pudding is jaw-dropping. Key lime pie, a Georgia sundae, and a skillet cookie are on the dessert menu as well. Kids will find plenty to make them smile on their special menu with pepperoni pizza, mini cheeseburgers, hot dogs, pasta, chicken tenders, grilled cheese, or mac and cheese. There is a greater-than-usual variety of non-alcoholic specialty beverages and Coke products, coffee, and tea. Sparkling wines, red and white, and a large listing of beers and hard cider are served. Don't expect to find peace and quiet because this joint is jumpin'! You *can* expect to find down-home favorite foods.

House of Blues, The Smokehouse

DDP: One credit (Q) / Cost: $
Type: American; Quick Service; Snacks, Lunch, and Dinner

A little building in front of the House of Blues specializes in smoked meats. For a quick meal or snack, it's a satisfying option. You'll find slow-smoked brisket on a brioche bun with coleslaw, baby back ribs, pulled pork, pulled chicken, smoked turkey legs, hot dogs, and a huge platter of Smokehouse nachos to which you can add meat(s) of your choice. Sides go well with the main dishes: coleslaw, baked beans, or chips. A kids menu is available with an all-beef hot dog or a pulled pork slider. Sweets are stocked here (cookies, candies, brownies) along with Coke beverages, juices, wine, and beer.

Jaleo by José Andrés

DDP: Two credits (T) / Cost: $$-$$$
Type: Spanish Cuisine; Table Service; Dinner

What's Jaleo? Well, there are lots of words that describe it: fuss, din, racket, commotion, pandemonium, to-do, shouting, jumble…and the list goes on, but you get the idea. This is one of the very latest of the upscale dining establishments to come to Disney Springs, accompanied by a great deal of fanfare and excitement. Read the current menu very carefully to be sure this is what you're looking for in a meal. Chef José Andrés, internationally renowned, was a big "get" for Disney Springs. He is the one usually credited with introducing tapas (a meal made up of various "small plates") to United States diners.

Starters are definitely not your average wings and things. "Pan de cristal con tomatoe" is slices of bread brushed with fresh tomato. There's an Iberian ham cured 36-48 months that's hand-carved at your table. A creamy, raw sheep's milk cheese with toasted bread, quince paste, and fig jam serves two. There are many ham or pork dishes, again not the way you may be used to having them. Spreadable cured sausage with honey-comb and toasted bread, cured acorn-fed pork sausage, and other kinds of cured meats will be a true culinary adventure. There are cheeses, many made from raw milk. "Rey silo rojo" is served with almonds and bitter orange jam. A soft, semi-sweet goat cheese comes with a rosemary cracker and fig jam. You can choose from three cheeses or five (serves 2 or more). Taco with caviar, liquid olives stuffed with pepper and anchovy, oysters with lemon, gin, and tonic, heads-on shrimp, or a Spanish tapa—potato salad with tuna conserve, carrots, peas, mayo, and Spanish trout roe (eggs) are a virtual culinary tour of Spain.

Ready for a cup of soup or salad? There are half a dozen, none of them common. Read the list of ingredients carefully before ordering to avoid any unwanted surprises. Some are great like warm Brussels sprouts salad with apricots, apples, and Serrano ham. Others may be more exotic than what you had in mind.

Chicken fritters, mushroom and goat cheese fritters, fried bacon-wrapped dates, a pressed sandwich of Spanish ham and Manchego cheese, a mini-burger made from Iberian pigs, lots of fish and seafood in the Spanish style, meats like grilled pork sausage with sautéed white beans, Canary Island-style marinated rabbit confit, and more are examples of the small plates. José also makes large plates that serve two: skirt steak made from those "legendary black-footed Ibérico pigs" for $69, Jasper-grilled lamb chops, a grilled whole sea bass, or the grilled 45-day aged ribeye for $75. There are five kinds of paella—read ingredients carefully unless you want both rabbit *and* chicken in yours. What you'll find here is very definitely *not* an American-type meal. The style of preparation is classically Spanish and very authentic. There's no other place quite like this one at Disney Springs. If you're up for a gastronomic adventure, you'll find it here.

Joffrey's Handcrafted Smoothies Kiosk

DDP: No / Cost: $
Type: American; Quick Service; Snacks

The popular Joffrey's may be found in many locales at Walt Disney World. This little stand serves a tremendous variety of smoothies like the Flyin' Hawaiian, Razzy Jazzy, Purple Piñata, Mango Tango, Flamingo Frost, or Tropical Sunset. Juices, coffee, tea or alcoholic beverages with Kahlúa, Baileys, or Jameson are also sold here. The quality at Jeffrey's is consistently high.

MacGUFFINS

DDP: No / Cost: $
Type: American; Casual Dining; Lounge; Snacks

This lounge is in the AMC Movies lobby. You can take your snacks and drinks inside with you if you want to catch a movie after ordering. Check out the first listing in this chapter to get an idea of the wide variety of tempting treats you can find on MacGUFFINS menu. The options include some fun surprises like Chesapeake crab cakes, crab Rangoon dip with hot white cheddar, a seafood sampler, Parm fries, Thai coconut chicken tenders, a prime rib grilled, lobster carbonara pizzetta, and for dessert a divine carrot cake, cinnamon apple crumble, or a Belgium waffle sundae. All your movie favorite candy and popcorn, a huge variety of cocktails, and plenty more will keep you satisfied at this cool, modern lounge. You might even decide to skip the flick and just chill.

Pepe by José Andrés

DDP: One credit (Q) / Cost: $
Type: Spanish Cuisine; Quick Service; Fast Casual; Lunch, Dinner

The chef knows his stuff, but before you eat at Jaleo, his other restaurant, you might want to try a quick bite here. Sandwiches on pan de cristal (crystal bread) are B.E.L.T. (bacon, egg, lettuce. and tomato), flat iron steak with caramelized onion and cheese, or veggie with roasted peppers, onion, asparagus, eggplant, spinach, and Manchego cheese. Instead of pressed panini, chef has pressed Bikini sandwiches like Bikini with ham, cheese, and mustard, or one with four cheeses and a side of honey mustard. Never heard of the Bikini? It comes from from the Bikini Concert Hall in Barcelona, Spain. There, vendors have been selling the pressed ham and cheese sandwiches to late-night concert-goers for many decades. Take a bite and the sandwich crackles as it gives way to the gooey, melted cheese center. They are a treat! Sandwiches served on a roll are fried chicken, an all-beef hot dog, Spanish sausage, or Serrano ham and Manchego cheese. Cold sandwiches are a Barcelona club, a "rusa" (salad) of beet, pea, carrot, egg, and cornichon (tiny sweet pickles), or tuna. Sides like seasonal fruit, chips, gazpacho, and more pair with the sandwiches. In addition, you'll find a tuna salad with hard-boiled egg, peppers, tomato, and olives or a green salad, both with sherry dressing. Sangria, wines, and beer are sold by the glass. Juice, tea, milk, or bottled Coke products are available. If you'd like something cool, there's soft serve (in favorite Spanish flavors of sweetened milk, cinnamon, or lemon), swirl soft serve, or seasonal sorbet. As for me, make mine one of those ham and cheese Bikini sandwiches every time. Thanks, Chef!

Starbucks

DDP: No / Cost: $
Type: American; Quick Service; Snacks

Starbucks favorites like frappuchino, espresso, latte, smoothie, iced coffee, tea, refreshers, or hot chocolate are on the menu at this walk-up counter in sizes grande (16 oz.), venti (24 oz.), or trenta (30 oz.). Try adding a flavor or a shot of espresso. You'll find fruit cups, frozen bananas, and frozen lemonade, too.

Splitsville Dining Room

DDP: One credit (T) / Cost: $-$$ (TiW)
Type: American; Casual; Lunch, Dinner

Eating in a bowling alley was never like this! The luxury lanes and upscale modern décor make this an entirely different experience. Find it across from the AMC Movies on one side and across from Wolfgang Puck on the other. It's 50,000 square feet filled with bowling, billiards, bars, and dining—plus live entertainment. As they say in their advertising literature, "Not your typical bowling alley menu. Hope you don't mind." Oh, you *won't*.

Appetizers ought to please most. Macho nachos, filet sliders, Parmesan chicken tenders, dynamite shrimp, ahi tuna and avocado, and more will start off your meal with a strike. Sushi rolls such as California, California crunch, ninja crunch, super tuna, crouching tiger, and volcano roll are a pleasant change of pace. There are pizzas, of course, in all your favorite flavors: margherita, meat lovers, veggie, firehouse, Hawaiian, and gluten free, to name a few. Tacos in many varieties and bowls with an Asian flair come next, followed by burgers and sandwiches. All that and we haven't even touched on the entrées. You'll find main courses like pulled pork, mahi mahi and voodoo shrimp, steak Alfredo, salmon, chicken, and fish and chips. Splitsville also serves entrée salads with chicken, ahi tuna, or turkey.

As you'd expect, desserts here are equally fun. Try a Ghirardelli brownie with ice cream, an ice-cream sundae, a cupcake, float, or a "giant cake" with layers stacked so tall that "you just might need a ladder," the menu jokingly advises patrons. There is an extensive list of frozen cocktails, bowl drinks to share, classic cocktails, draft and bottled beers, red and white wines, and non-alcoholic beverages. Younger guests in your party will appreciate the kid-pleasing children's menu. This is an inspired way to mix games and goodies in Disney Springs, with choices to spare!

Wetzel's Pretzels

DDP: No / Cost: $
Type: American; Quick Service; Snacks

Just like other Wetzel's kiosks, here is a little stand where you can find delicious, fresh, warm pretzels. Get "sinful cinnamon," the newer "sour cream and onion," "almond crunch," or try the baked cheese and pepperoni pretzel. For dipping, Wetzel's provides jalapeño or cheddar cheese, pizza, sweet glaze, and caramel sauce. If you're still hungry, get yourself a Wetzel's hot dog or cheese dog or "dog bites" with lemonade, frozen lemonade, or frozen granita.

YeSake Kiosk

DDP: No / Cost: $
Type: Global; Asian/Japanese; Quick Service; Snacks

The small, brick, stand-alone building near Wetzel's Pretzels holds a surprising amount of international goodies. World Flavors Tamaki (a Japanese wrap, but these aren't made with dried seaweed) gives you a flour tortilla wrapped around white rice and a main ingredient like Chinese-style pulled pork and veggies, fresh ahi tuna, fresh salmon, cooked shrimp, grilled chicken, yakiniku grilled beef, and a veggie lover's option. Dress it up with add-ons such as shredded cheese, sour cream, walnuts, tempura crunch, avocado, sour cream, or pico de gallo and more. There are six kinds of sauce including aioli yuzu (Japanese citrus sauce), Korean BBQ, sesame ginger, spicy poke, wasabi ponzu, or sweet teriyaki. If you've never tried a sake slush, this is your opportunity, but there are lots of drinks to choose from, both alcoholic or not. There's a sake-bourbon, sake-cosmo, and sake-blue coconut frozen punch. Coke products and four kinds of canned beer are also on the menu. Quick food with an international twist makes a filling snack.

Unique and Signature Dining
The Best of the Disney Resort Hotels

All of the Disney resort hotels will have on-site restaurants and places to buy snacks for the convenience of guests. There are a combination of more than 400 places to eat and food-related special experiences at the resort, and that number has tic-tic-ticked up by about 25% since I began writing dining guides several years ago. Not *all* of them are included in this guide. Some of Disney Resort Hotel places to eat are just okay, pretty hum-drum, and nothing that you won't find back home. Poolside snack counters aren't included. The water parks aren't, either. The number of places to find eats at Disney is like watching one of those world population or national debt digital displays—it just keeps going up!

A handful of the dining establishments located at the resort hotels, however, *are* truly exceptional. They offer special Unique/Themed experiences and Fine/Signature dining fare that measure up with the best anywhere on Disney property—or anywhere else, for that matter. Regardless of where you might be staying, you can take advantage of eating at any of the following restaurants, but many if not most will require advance dining reservations if you hope to get a table. It has been said before, but it is worth repeating: Even with an ADR, you *don't* have a table waiting for you at, say, 8:00 p.m. Rather, you have a reservation for the *next available table* that opens up after you arrive at 8:00 p.m. This simple fact eludes a large number of guests who vociferously complain that "their" table wasn't available on time.

There aren't many fine dining establishments in the country that follow Disney's rather unusual reservation policy, so people should be forgiven for being upset when they show up for a table they reserved a full six months in advance and then must wait for up to an hour to be seated, or even longer. It doesn't happen all the time, but it does happen sometimes. Be forewarned. Be aware that prices and menus change frequently without notice. The entries in this guide will give you a good idea of what *kinds* of foods you may expect at a particular restaurant. Specific menu items are never guaranteed. The best chefs used fresh, seasonal ingredients, and they like to keep their menus as fresh as the food they serve. Expect change and you won't be disappointed.

Guests occasionally report being poorly treated by a member of the wait staff, even at some of these luxury dining establishments. Should this happen to you, don't hesitate to discreetly bring it to the attention of the maître d'hôtel who should be able to rectify the situation immediately. Do not accept poor service or rudeness. There is no need to get into a protracted battle of wills with the wait staff. Neither should you suffer or seethe in silence and later post a scathing indictment of the entire restaurant. Be polite, be friendly, but be firm. When you are paying handsomely for excellent food and service, you have every right to expect it.

Meals at these places are not bargains. Eating at any of them is a moderate to major financial splurge; eating at one certainly won't be easy on your wallet, so don't expect to find any "good deals" here. If you have something special to celebrate or simply feel like indulging in a memorable meal, then consider the following restaurants, which are listed in alphabetical order by the name of the hotel where they are located.

Note: Some of the resort restaurants feature character buffets. Those are covered in the next chapter.

Animal Kingdom Lodge

Boma—Flavors of Africa
DDP: One credit (T) /Cost: $$ (TiW)
Type: African, American; Unique/Themed, Buffet/Family Style; Breakfast, Dinner

Just about everyone will find many offerings to their liking at this family-friendly buffet that looks like nothing so much as an open-air African marketplace. Even the carving stations are positioned under thatched roofs.

Breakfast entrées include American standards (pancakes, waffles, eggs, oatmeal, French toast bread pudding, and more) in addition to some African additions like sweet plantains and an African fruit fool (a mix of fruit and custard). Some unusual breakfast items are the oak-grilled asparagus and tomatoes, hand-carved turkey or ham, a create-your-own yogurt bar, quinoa, and corned beef hash. Try the Kenyan press coffee to accompany your breakfast buffet, but you'll find other beverages of every sort, too.

The dinner buffet is equally pleasing. A tremendous array of soups and salads, many you'll recognize and others more exotic, are on attractive display. There is a rotation among the many menu choices, so expect variety. Entrées include whole roasted salmon, pork ribs and shoulder, whole Durban-style roasted chicken, fish, turkey, or spice crusted beef sirloin, along with African pap (porridge made from softly ground maize), fufu (made with green plantain flour and cassava), and boboti (minced meat and an egg-based topping) to liven things up a bit. The same variety applies to the side dishes. Yes, there are familiar mashed potatoes and spiced sweet potatoes, but there is also peanut rice, kokonut rice, plantain crisps, Zulu cabbage, and geel rys—the name means yellow rice, and it often accompanies boboti.

Kids can find plenty of things that are familiar like fish or chicken nuggets, mac and cheese, or penne pasta and meatballs. As is usual at Disney buffets, desserts are plentiful and appealing: key lime cheesecake, a pretty zebra dome, apple cobbler, bread pudding, guava panna cotta, cookies and brownies, and a Kenyan coffee tart are just a few of them. The setting is exotic, and so is the food—but it's not so exotic that everyone in the party can't find something delicious at Boma. It's a good value; feel free to have "all you care to enjoy" here.

Jiko—The Cooking Place

DDP: Two credits (T) / Cost: $$$-$$$$ (TiW)
Type: Indian/Mediterranean/African/American; Fine/Signature; Dinner

The décor is beautiful with a wall that changes colors like the sunset. What appear to be birds in flight are suspended overhead. Window seats have a pretty view of the "savanna." Banquette seats are extremely close together. The food here is not necessarily for everyone. Jiko is more adventurous and different than typical Disney dining establishments.

Appetizers include grilled wild boar tenderloin, spice route-inspired squash bisque, North African-spiced scallops, and Jiko salad with greens grown in the Epcot Land Pavilion with heirloom tomatoes, goat cheese, and sweet-and-spicy pumpkin seeds. There is an artisanal cheese selection, most of which have nothing to do with Africa. They come, instead, from Utah, Vermont, and the Canadian border. Descriptions of the cheeses are quite specific. Five tasting portions come with accompaniments

Menu items from "the cooking place" are sometimes cryptic. What, you might be excused for wondering, are "inguday tibs in brik"? Don't fret. Everything including the ingredients is described. Entrées are equally eclectic and mix the usual with the very unusual. You'll find filet mignon, chicken, lamb, fish, and Botswana Setswaa-style beef short ribs alongside Bo Kapur Malay seafood curry or vegetarian West African Kori corn. Enhancements are coconut-curry shrimp, bobotie mac and cheese with elk and beef Wagyu, and Egyptian kushari (ancient grains, etc.). Desserts include African drum "beets" (coconut, strawberry and beet mousse with chocolate cake, candied beets, and balsamic strawberries), safari sunset carrot cake with lemon crémeux, and Kenyan coffee streusel with candied carrots, Tanzanian chocolate mousse with pink peppercorn meringue and coco nib crunch, a no-sugar angel cake with seasonal fruit, and malva pudding with melktart ice cream, kataifi, and Kanu tuile (luckily, the ingredients are listed; unluckily, the ingredients are sometimes even more indecipherable than the names of the desserts themselves). Everything is costly.

Disney check meals are shrimp with kushari, fish, and grilled chicken. Several more meals for children are offered as well like cheese pizza, grilled steak, or mac and cheese. Kids have a fun African shield dessert—a paint-your-own cookie shield served with vanilla ice cream.There are a great many specialty teas on the menu, some unusual after-dinner coffee drinks, a couple of South African wines, many brandies, ports, single malt whiskies, and liqueurs. Few non-alcoholic beverages are offered, so don't expect fountain beverages.

Be advised that guest reviews sometimes criticize the service at Jiko and other times praise it to the skies. That's true of almost any restaurant, but here the quality of the service would seem to be more uneven than at most of the other fine/signature-dining establishments. This has been true over the past several years. It's easier to get a last-minute or same-day reservation here that at most of Disney's better dining establishments. It's not everyone's cup of tea, but many guests rave.

Saana

DDP: One credit (T) / Cost: $$ (TiW)
Type: African/Indian; Unique/Themed; Breakfast, Lunch, Dinner

Saana is beautiful. Attention to detail makes dining here a treat. The colors are vibrant and cheerful. Look through the large picture windows to see African animals browsing just outside. Breakfast entrées have you covered with all kinds of familiar goodies, but you can also try new taste treats.

The Boere breakfast has eggs and bacon but also Tanzanian hash browns, tomato chutney, Boerewors sausages and a corn Johnny cake. The fruit sosataie has quinoa and dried fruit salad. Great grab-and-go items are numerous—oatmeal with brown sugar and raisins, sides of bacon, hash browns, eggs, banana bread, fruit, cereals, yogurt parfait, and more. The Indian-style bread sampler is a popular starter with five types of bread and three choices of dipping sauces. So is the artisan cheese selection and the salad sampler. Seasonal soups (including oxtail) and shellfish round out the appetizers. The lunch menu offers Tandoori chicken or shrimp and several appealing sandwiches (Kenya coffee/BBQ pulled pork) and burgers. At dinner, lamb, steak, duck, fish, and the highly regarded butter chicken (it's also on the kids menu—yay!) with basmati rice are just some of the entrées.

Finish with an African triple chocolate mousse, the inventive spice trade candy bar, or choose from puddings, tarts, and other seasonal favorites like the caramel n'dizi—banana financier with caramelized milk chocolate crémeux, hazelnut crunch, banana and white chocolate chantilly, and ginger raspberries. This is a place with wide appeal, good value, lovely atmosphere, and not-your-average park food.

Wanyama Safari

DDP: No / $$$$
Type: African; Fine/Signature Dining; Dinner

Wanyama means sunset, and that's when the safari and dinner happen. No more than 12 guests are booked per tour, and children must be at least 10 years old. Your guide provides a personalized tour with background on the animals and architecture of the Animal Kingdom. This is one of the few special dinners where you do NOT need a separate park admission. You will need to book reservations in advance, and if you cancel less than 24 hours before your scheduled safari, you'll be billed in full. There is a dress code at Jiko where the spectacular, multi-course, and utterly lavish dinner takes place following your safari. It is cancelled in case of inclement weather, but in that case, you would not be billed. The price is a bit of a mystery and isn't listed on the official website, but it's currently running $210 for one person. The Wanyama Safari is now open to anyone, although in the past it was only open to guests staying at the African Kingdom Lodge. It's certainly not a bargain, but it is a very memorable way to experience a personalized safari on the 46 acre savanna and a first-class African dinner in high style.

Contemporary Resort

California Grill

DDP: Two credits (T) / Cost: $$$-$$$$ (TiW)
Type: American/Seafood/Sushi; Fine/Signature; Brunch, Dinner

The Contemporary is one of the two original Walt Disney World hotels. It opened in 1971 and is still, after some refurbishment, going strong. The monorail runs right through the lobby on an elevated track. Dining here is every bit as gorgeous as you'd expect, and the view of the Magic Kingdom's Happily Ever After fireworks display is fantastic. During daylight, twilight, or at night, vistas of the Seven Seas Lagoon are gorgeous. In large part, this is what sets the California Grill above other restaurants—the view. The food is good and costly. Service varies. Some guests on the Disney Dining Plan have reported shabby treatment. Not every meal is going to be superlative, but the wait staff here has been criticized for being condescending, even rude, at times, which is never a pleasant experience—neither is it ever acceptable at any Disney restaurant. If you should experience something like this, bring it to the attention of a manager.

Brunch includes several items presented to the table. A selection of baked goods, cocktails for the adults and a non-alcoholic "sparkling Mimosa" for the children and non-drinkers, plus coffee come out out first. Then, you serve yourself from a buffet. Selections are not the same as you'll find at most Disney brunches. California rolls, shrimp tempura, (seasonal) strawberry salad, spicy tuna tekka maki rolls, hardwood smoked salmon, Greek yogurt, deviled eggs, salmon/tuna/shrimp nigiri (sushi made from thin strips of raw seafood over pressed, vinegared rice), house-made charcuterie, and more are on the menu. Entrées aren't the usual fare, either, and include shrimp and grits, pan-fried chicken cutlet and avocado toast, lemon-ricotta pancakes, brie and berries French toast, Shakshuka (Tunisian pepper and tomato sauce, house-made vegan meatball, organic egg, with house pita), steak and eggs, eggs Benedict, and blueberry pancakes. For dessert, try either "small minis," macaroons, or chocolate truffles. You may also order some of the excellent featured wines by the glass and cocktails.

Many people try to schedule their dinner around the fireworks, which occur pretty late during the summer months. That can lead to frustration. It's difficult to "fine tune" exactly when your table will actually be available or how long your meal may take. If you've eaten here earlier in the evening, however, just hold on to your receipt. Bring it back before the fireworks, and show it to be admitted to the outdoor viewing deck.

Dinner at the California Grill can be a great meal. It can also be so-so or sub-par, especially if your steak is sent out virtually raw when you ordered medium. Lots of problems can be avoided if you are as specific as possible about your preferences regarding exactly the way you'd like your food prepared.

Start with a tomato roasted flatbread in several appetizing flavors: pepperoni, porchetta, or veggie—all of them special. There is a wide selection of charcuterie like wild boar belly pancetta, venison terrine, and duck liver pâté. Lots of hand-rolled sushi rolls and sashimi are also offered, in common and uncommon varieties. The soups, salads, and appetizers are mouthwatering. How about delicious carrot-ginger soup with miso, carrot shortbread, and pickled petal onion, artisanal cheeses, or a house-made charcuterie? Fresh salads (strawberry in season), Sonoma goat cheese ravioli, or braised beef short rib wontons are all wonderful starters. The California Grill is renowned for creative dishes thoughtfully prepared. Other entrées are duck, Pacific sea bass, butter-poached lobster tail and jumbo sea scallop, bison, pork tenderloin, black grouper, filet of beef, half chicken, and Tonkotsu ramen with Chasu pork.

Cheeses, fruit-based desserts like an apple crostada, strawberry crème brûlée, a no-sugar carrot cheesecake, or a warm chocolate Valrhona (French chocolate) cake bring your meal to an end. Disney check meals are beef tenderloin, chicken, and wild salmon. Kids can also order cheese pizza or mac and cheese. Some nice Napa wines are available by the glass. Some of the cocktails have clever California names like the Monte Ray, Anaheim Mule, and Napa Blue Martini (the olives are stuffed with blue cheese). Classic beers and ciders are well represented and come from Ireland, California, Michigan, Florida, Scotland, Belgium, Colorado, Sweden and New York. Come for the view, but stay for the food.

Highway in the Sky Dine Around

DDP: No / $$$$
Type: Varies; Table Service; Dinner

This unique dining experience costs $170 per person including tax and tip. You have up to 24 hours before the event to cancel or you will be charged the full prince. Check in at The Wave... of American Flavors at the Contemporary Resort for an appetizer and specialty cocktail. Valet parking is included. Guests should be at least 12 years of age and older to attend and must be 21 or older to consume alcoholic beverages. The menu is seasonal, *prix fixe*. Dress code is the same as for Fine/Signature Dining venues. You'll ride the Monorail to the Polynesian for drinks and appetizers. Next, your trip takes you to Disney's Grand Floridian to sip champagne and enjoy a selection of artisanal cheeses and charcuterie. The main course is served at Cítricos. Board the monorail back to the Contemporary where an assortment of desserts, cordials, and coffee is served as you watch the Happily Ever After fireworks show from the patio. Make reservations in advance. Availability is limited.

The Wave...of American Flavors

DDP: One credit (T) / Cost: $$-$$$ (TiW)
Type: American; Unique/Themed; Breakfast (Buffet), Lunch, Dinner

What a funny name, ellipsis periods and all, but the emphasis is on good, healthful foods. The entrance is lit with blue and is meant to evoke diving into the tube of a breaking wave. The light fixtures inside look like jellyfish, and the wave motif is carried out on the ceiling and the backs of the chairs.

Breakfast is an all-you-care-to-enjoy buffet and is a reasonable value for the money. It includes all the favorite standbys. In addition, there's also an egg-white frittata, an omelette your way, the classic American, Floridian eggs Benedict, avocado toast, signature sweet potato pancakes, or glazed donut French toast. Lunch and dinner are non-buffet. Disney check kids meals are an egg white omelette, cheese omelette, oatmeal, or scrambled egg, but the kids menu also has Mickey waffles and those yummy sweet potato pancakes.

Lunch and dinner have soups, salads, PEI (Prince Edward Island in Canada) mussels, and crab cakes for appetizers, and sandwiches, salads, and burgers (including bison), seared King salmon, protein or noodle bowls, pasta, and a nice French dip. End with some sweetly different desserts like a seasonal flight trio, a trio of sorbet, artisanal cheeses, a chocolate flight, or the always-reliable crème brûlée.

Dinner appetizers are similar to lunch with a featured bacon and eggs with maple-lacquered pork belly, along with soups and salads. There are plenty of choices at Wave. Entrées include steak, fish, pork tenderloin, braised short ribs, cioppino, noodle bowl, scallops, chicken, and seared potato gnocchi. Desserts are seasonal. In cold months, you might see apple cobbler, German chocolate cake, bananas Foster, and more. In warmer seasons, look for lots of sorbet and those new tasting trios. Disney check meals are fish, chicken, or penne. Other kids meal choices are cheeseburger, beef kabob, or grilled cheese. There are loads of non-alcoholic beverages in addition to organic draft beers and cocktails. The prices are fairly reasonable especially when compared with other places on this list, the service ranks highly, and the food is very good.

Coronado Springs Resort

Maya Grill

DDP: One credit (T) / Cost: $$ (TiW)
Type: Mexican/American, Seafood/Steakhouse; Unique/Themed; Dinner

With representations of Mayan temples and paintings surrounding you, you'll dine in the style of Old Mexico, but the cuisine is definitely Nuevo Latino. Appetizers are inventive. You'll find the popular and delicious queso fundito (melted cheese topped with chorizo/sausage and served with tortillas), tacos Durango, Acapulco roasted beet salad, and many others equally appealing. Steaks, red snapper Veracruz, veggie tacos, shrimp tacos, fajitas, chicken, pork, and beef short ribs are spicy but friendly to American palates. Several seasonal signature dishes, higher in price, are available like a mixed grill, bone-in ribeye steak, or seafood grill platter. Desserts are typical south-of-the-border favorites like flan and fruit sorbet, but crème brûlée and a chocolate panna cotta Abuelita (that means like Grandma used to make) have been added. Non-alcoholic beverages as well as a huge variety of international wines and margaritas are available. Maya Grill is great if you're looking for something out of the ordinary.

The Grand Floridian Resort & Spa

Afternoon Tea at the Garden View Tea Room

DDP: No / **Cost:** $$$
Type: British; Table Service; Tea, Snacks

First, let's clarify something that throws most Americans for a loop. It might prevent you from sounding like an amateur. Afternoon tea is NOT called "high tea" in Britain. What you'll be served at the Floridian is not to be confused with the late-afternoon meal so cherished in the memories of English school children and hard-working laborers. Their "high tea" is what Americans know as supper. When they burst through the door all rosy-cheeked and peckish from a long day in the classroom, children are rewarded with foodstuffs such as bread and butter, something fried and savory, and perhaps baked beans with pickled salmon or herring. Men who work hard until 6:00 in the evening come home famished. A strong pot of tea, something of a costly luxury back in the day, helped revive them. They certainly didn't want finger sandwiches! Vegetables, perhaps steak and kidney pie, and grilled tomatoes would hit the spot. High tea is definitely a working-class tradition and has *nothing* to do with the afternoon tea service you'll find in the Garden View Tea Room.

The most famous locale for the upper-crust, those Downton Abbey denizens and their ilk, to indulge in the afternoon tea tradition remains the Ritz London; that's very much like the sort of tea experience you'll have if you take tea at the Garden View Tea Room. In fact, what many Americans think of as high tea is actually referred to as *low* tea by ladies who love to luxuriate in the ritual, and it *is* mostly the purview of ladies. One possible explanation for the nomenclature is that high and low refer to the tables upon which the tea was originally served. High tea, working-class tea, was served on the kitchen table, whereas low tea, leisure-class tea, was served on the low tables in front of sofas and chairs in the formal drawing rooms of elegant homes.

If you think prices at the Grand Floridian are steep, those at the London Ritz are positively heady. Basic tea service in the Garden View Tea Room ranges from $35 for tea and a few pastries, $50 if you add a few more goodies (and they *are* good!), and up to $150 for the works—tea for two with champagne. In London at the Ritz, expect to pay from £58 ($77 U.S.) for finger sandwiches, scones, and pastries with tea for *one* up to £87 ($115 U.S.), again that's for *one*, if you want the "celebration cake" included and a glass of "Reserve Ritz Champagne," and who *doesn't?*

There are picturesque glimpses of the gardens at the resort through the bright, airy windows. A strictly limited number of guests are accommodated, so make a reservation if you hope to try this quintessentially British treat. One issue some guests have noted is the occasionally snooty server or hostess, although that has never been my personal experience. Let me be perfectly clear about his: At Disney, you *never* need to accept shoddy service or rudeness. Politely but firmly ask to speak with a manager, and I can comfortably assure you the situation will be rectified immediately. Don't seethe in silence. Most servers are perfectly charming.

You'll get ONE pot of well-brewed tea per person (lots of signature blends, blacks, green and whites, oolongs, and herbals), kept hot by a darling tea cozy, not an unlimited supply as at the Ritz, but one pot is generally plenty. Choose among egg salad, chicken curry, cucumber and watercress, and other sorts of crustless sandwiches. You get to select those you want, which is helpful if you're not fond of something on offer. Children can have cheese or peanut butter finger sandwiches upon request. Small nibbles of cheeses and fresh fruit come beautifully prepared with an edible orchid. The tiny jam tarts are yummy; scones are fresh and feature Sultanas, golden raisins, a British must-have. (Ask for the recipe and it will be emailed to you. They are surprisingly simple to make.) If you're a fan of clotted cream or you've heard of it and simply wonder what all the fuss is about, use it on a scone. Chocolate-dipped strawberries are popular, but for most people, those delicate *pâte à choux* swans are the height of decadence. It's a splurge, but go ahead and be decadent for an afternoon—and don't forget to raise that pinky finger as you sip!

Cítricos

DDP: Two credits (T) / Cost: $$$ (TiW)
Type: Mediterranean/American;. Fine/Signature; Dinner

Cítricos is elegant and comfortable with a welcoming air. The focus is on high-quality fine dining. Children (they should be well-behaved and you ought to dine with them on the early side) will be very well taken care of by the friendly staff. Once, in desperation, I asked for a banana for a hungry grandson from a fabulous, decorative, fresh fruit display, and it was immediately presented to him without question.

Start with charcuterie—it's delicious, when available—or try a Cítricos cheese board. The cheese course has a nice selection of four cheeses. The first course has many options: tuna tartare, Florida shrimp and baby spinach, pork belly, arancini (smoked tomatoes and mozzarella), paté, and more. Entrées are beef short ribs, Berkshire pork, chicken, steaks, seafoods (tuna, red snapper, Maine lobster risotto), and vegetarian options. Foraged mushrooms sautéed with herbs, truffle fries, and Yukon gold mashed potatoes are the current enhancements.

Desserts are equally appealing. Tiramisù, profiteroles, strawberry-pomegranate mousse dome, warm chocolate banana torte, pistachio cheesecake, tropical fruit crème brûlée, seasonal sorbets, and other delectables will please just about anyone. Disney check meals are shrimp, beef, chicken, and pasta. Children can also choose from steak, pepperoni pizza, shrimp, mac and cheese, chicken, or a French-grilled ham and cheese sandwich. A large number of attractive specialty cocktails grace the menu, along with four international wines and a great many beers. Like Narcoossee's, Cítricos is a beautifully appointed dining location.

If you have any issues, the perfectly charming maître d'hôtel (trained on the Disney Magic cruise ship) will gladly and promptly rectify them. Cítricos is a perfect place to celebrate that special occasion or simply to enjoy a very pleasant meal. The chef here can also prepare a spectacularly decorated cake with advance notice. The last time we had this treat, the Chef who created the masterpiece was called Mickey—no relation. In fact, you can enjoy a $$$$ Chef's Domain experience

At Cítricos where you'll be given selections from the menu in a private dining room at a table for 8. Call at least a week in advance if you'd like to participate. Like the Hollywood Brown Derby, the Restaurant has added a Dine with an Imagineer experience, too. Call for details.

Narcoosee's

DDP: Two credits (T) / Cost: $$$ (TiW)
Type: Seafood/American; Fine/Signature; Dinner

The interior of Narcooseess's is lovely (and a little less formal than Cítricos) with a gorgeous, wrap-around view of the Seven Seas Lagoon. The unusual name is derived from the Creek word for "little bear." Brunch is no longer being offered here on Sunday.

There is a dress code, but it is "business casual" (and much less stuffy than the one imposed at the Victoria & Albert's): "Men may wear slacks, jeans or dress shorts and collared shirts. Jackets are optional. Women may wear dresses, skirts or dress shorts with blouses or sweaters. Not permitted in the dining room are tank tops, swimsuits, swimsuit cover-ups, hats for gentlemen, cut-offs, torn clothing and shirts with offensive language or graphics."

Dinner at Narcoossee's offers a selection of delicious soups and salads like butter-poached lobster bisque (wow), Caesar salad, or a really great seasonal mixed green salad with candied walnuts, house-made pickled blackberries, corn-bread croutons, and a Cabernet vinaigrette. Any of them will start your meal off beautifully. Starters are slow-poached chilled shrimp, mussels and cream, barbecue-grilled shrimp and grits, crispy calamari, shrimp and crab cake, or a selection of artisanal cheeses. Entrées are varied and appealing. Steak, halibut, salmon, chicken, pork, lobster, scallops, shrimp, and a Berkshire pork chop give most people something they will like. Those all-too-addictive "enhancements" are asparagus, potatoes, or roasted Brussels sprouts. Order whiskey butter or sauce Béarnaise to complement your steak, asparagus, or other selections. Cheesecake, sorbet, sugarless chocolate torte, banana cream tart, Narcoossee's candy bar, crème brûlée with coconut and chocolate, and other desserts will finish a delicious dinner. Disney check meals are chicken, veggie burger, shrimp or pasta. Other kids meals are steak, mac and cheese, chicken tenders, or a burger. Some attractive Napa wines and specialty coffee drinks are served. Narcoosee's is a gorgeous place to dine with beautifully prepared dinners and lovely water views, but while it's still expensive, you won't need to take out a second mortgage to eat here.

Victoria & Albert's

DDP: No / Cost: $$$$
Type: Modern/American; Fine/Signature; Dinner

First, a few words of caution: the V & A dining experience is not for everyone. Are dining plans accepted? No, and it is extremely expensive. No one under ten is admitted. It's not at all unusual for a couple to pay as much as $1,000 for their dinner, including enhancements, tax and gratuity. It's also not unusual for a multi-course dinner to last three-and-a-half to four-and-a-half hours. Many gush about the place and claim, perhaps to rationalize that kind of financial outlay for a single meal, that it is "worth every penny." For that kind of money, people tend to expect the very finest food and service, but it's impossible to meet everyone's lofty expectations. The vast majority of diners are quite satisfied, however.

Yes, of course, the strictest Disney dress code applies here. Don't worry if the gentleman has no sport coat, as they have many on hand to lend. For some, the stuffy atmosphere is off-putting. For others, the lengthy description and discussion about the food by the wait staff is inappropriately detailed and intrusive, even unintentionally humorous. If money is no object and you can manage to lower your expectations to a reasonable level, you might very well enjoy a special meal here. If not, you'd be wise to dine elsewhere. Reservations are highly recommended.

First course currently is amuse bouche, literally something to amuse the mouth—imperial caviar with ocean kiss oysters; second course is Maine lobster with celery root and finger limes; third course is "Glacier 51 Tooth Fish." If if it is unfamiliar to you, the website for this unusual fish notes: "...nothing can rival the story however, of Glacier 51 Toothfish, also known as Patagonian Toothfish. Isolated deep in the sub-Ant-arctic, a staggering 4,109 km from mainland Australia lies one of the most inhospitable islands in the world – Heard Island. On the southern tip of this spectacular geographical feature, the breathtaking Glacier 51 (fifty-one Glacier) pours into the surrounding treacherous icy waters creating the ideal envi-ronment for the highly prized toothfish found patrolling the underwater volcanic crevices 2,000 metres below sea level..." with a wild turbot enhancement, subject to availability; fourth course is honey-lacquered Rohan duck; fifth course is New Zealand elk tenderloin; sixth course is Australian Kobe-style beef; seventh course is Colton Bassett Stilton cheesecake with Burgundy pears; dessert course is a chocolate Bolivian tart. Last comes coffee. It will cost close to $185 for the seven-course meal, $235 for the ten-course meal in Queen Victoria's room, and another $65-105 for wine pairings, not including tax and gratuity. The menu changes seasonally and frequently, so this list gives you an idea of the kinds of things you might expect to find on the menu.

There are fourteen tables in the Dining Room, but only four in Queen Victoria's Room in a setting so intimate that some diners report feeling like they're eating in someone else's house, someone they don't actually know—a bit under the microscope, in other words. Every table in the QVR is assigned two waiters. If dining in the kitchen and interacting with the chef sounds like something you'd enjoy, book the Chef's Table ten-(and sometimes eleven)-course meal. There is only one seating for it per night. As many as ten or as few as two people may make a reservation. At press time, prices for dinner at the Chef's Table begin at $250 with wine pairings adding another $150, and that doesn't include tax or gratuity, but you do get a personalized signature menu of your dinner as a souvenir.

The V & A is an eighteen-year recipient of the AAA Five Diamond award. It is widely considered to be one of the top places to dine in the entire county. As long as you know exactly what you're signing on for ahead of time, you should enjoy your very special evening here.

Wilderness Lodge

Whispering Canyon Café

DDP: One credit (T) / Cost: $-$$ (TiW)
Type: American; Unique/Themed; Buffet/Family Style: Breakfast, Lunch, Dinner

Think rootin' and tootin,' definitely not high-falutin,' if you're planning to eat at the ironically named *Whispering* Canyon. It's buffet/family-style, with plenty of improvised "antics" from the wait staff and lots going on to keep the kids occupied— Lincoln logs, coloring, sing-alongs, and hobby-horse races.

At breakfast, starters are fresh fruit with yogurt and granola, the heavenly sticky-bun skillet, and a blueberry muffin. Practically any American breakfast favorite you might be craving ought to be available: several hearty skillets available, eggs Benedict traditionally made and vegetarian-style, egg-white omelette, ham-and-cheese frittata, buttermilk pancakes, Belgian waffle, steel-cut oatmeal, and a seasonal plate of fresh fruit. Lots of sides such as sausage gravy, toast, grits, bacon, and biscuits will fill up the whole posse. Order French press coffee, juices, and many non-alcoholic beverages, plus they'll be happy to whip up a Bloody Mary or mimosa for you.

Lunch offers some appetizers like a smoked beef and vegetable soup, burnt ends nachos (yum), and a house-made cornbread with honey butter (also yum). The all-you-care-to-enjoy skillet is a rancher's dream—ribs, pulled pork, chicken, sausage, Yukon potatoes, corn on the cob, charred corn, green beans, and baked beans. Sandwiches are plentiful: grilled chicken, applewood smoked turkey, pulled pork, and more. There's a bison burger, a house smoked-salmon salad, and a chopped salad with turkey and lots of fixin's. Could you still be hungry?

Upscale western fare like Whispering Canyon pioneer chocolate cake, apple pie a la mode, or a seasonal fruit cobbler might tempt you. Whatever happened to the popular Cowboy Hat Challenge? They took a ten-gallon "hat" (don't worry, it's plastic) and filled with scoops of ice cream (chocolate, vanilla, strawberry, mint-chip) and smother it in "every topping from the chuck wagon." Threw in a couple of brownies, cookies, a slice of apple pie, and top with toasted marshmallows on a skewer. It served four—but no more. Too many people ordered the hat and not much else to eat, so as of now, it's been taken off the menu. (If you're disappointed, you can still order the "Kitchen Sink" over at Beaches and Cream at the Disney Beach Club Resort.)

Dinner is every bit as down-home as breakfast and lunch. Appetizers are the same as at lunch. Entrées are a char-crusted NY strip steak, cedar plank salmon, skillet-fired red quinoa cakes, or one of those wowza cowboy skillets with everything a hard-workin' cowboy or cowgal desires. Desserts are the same as at lunch. Disney check meals are grilled chicken, fish, or chicken and cheese quesadilla. Red and white wines of the Pacific Northwest, draft and bottled beers, imaginative drinks like a Moonshine Flight, Magical Trail Cocktail, and a happy assortment of non-alcoholic beverages including that amazing French press coffee, any of which will accompany your meal to perfection.

Pull yourself up a chair (Cowboys or Native Americans are stenciled on the back), loosen your belt, and dig in. I guarantee you won't leave here hungry, partners!

Yacht Club Resort

Yachtsman Steakhouse
DDP: Two credits (T) / Cost: $$$
Type: American/Steakhouse; Fine/Signature; Dinner

Travel to New England without ever leaving Orlando. Some guests find the décor a bit plain, but the clean lines, knotty pine rafters, and maritime touches are appreciated by most. Although nautical, the entrée emphasis here is on steak.

Soups and salads include French onion, lobster bisque, Caesar, or a traditional steakhouse wedge. Start your dinner with jumbo shrimp, crab Louie, cheeses, or charcuterie. A true carnivore's delight, you'll find butcher's cuts on the menu and in a display window in case you'd like to select your own. Black Angus filet mignon, roasted prime rib, New York strip, and ribeye are currently featured. Something different? Try the King salmon, lobster pasta, chicken, or short rib Wellington. Something *really* different? There's a very special $120

Admiral's Platter for two: a tower of lobsters, chilled jumbo shrimp, mussels, oyster shooters, scallop ceviche, charred octopus salad, stone crab claws, and snow crab. There's also a 32 oz. Porterhouse for two (21-day aged) for $119.

Sides are truffle mac and cheese, creamed spinach, braised onions or mushrooms, Brussels and bacon, or twice-baked potatoes. If your sweet tooth remains unsatisfied, you must give the Admiral's Cake cake a try—truly scrumptious layers of Valrhona chocolate brownie, Carmel crunch, dark chocolate ganache, chocolate "springe" (for springform pan, it's German) cake, bananas Foster jam, and caramel ganache. There's also a Lexington sundae that's pretty amazing, a sorbet trio, sugarless carrot cake, lime semifreddo with meringue and guava, or crème brûlée. Disney check meals are grilled chicken or baked fish. Childrens menu items also include mac and cheese, pasta and meatballs, or a steak skewer. Kids are sure to love the Mickey puzzle dessert (it's incredible) and the frozen yogurt and berry push pop. Some good California wines are joined by La Garett's Amarone from Italy. Thurston Howell the Third would feel right at home at the Yachtsman—and so will you. Permission to come aboard!

There you have it, some of the best of the best. Don't come looking for bargains here. You'll pay quite a premium for a wonderful meal at any of these fine/signature or unique/themed restaurants, but if you're looking for something out of the ordinary, a dining experience that will be remembered long after your vacation is over, then select a favorite from among these stellar places, make an advance dining reservation, sit back, and enjoy!

Dinner Shows and Character Meals

More Fun at the Disney Resort Hotels

Menu items change frequently at Disney's character meals and dinner shows without notice, just as they do at almost any of the resort restaurants. Characters are always present at any character meal subject to availability, and that changes without notice, too. This chapter will give you a reasonable idea of the general kinds of foods and experiences to expect, but nothing is guaranteed. One of the two dinner shows, the Spirit of Aloha, is subject to weather issues and can be cancelled at the last minute. Mickey's Backyard BBQ Dinner Show has been canceled after a very long run.

Beach Club Resort and Villas

Cape May Café
DDP: One credit (T) / Cost: $$ (TiW)
Type: American; Character Buffet; Breakfast
Frequent Characters: Donald, Goofy, Minnie—in beach attire

Dining at this attractive and quaint café will take you back to the turn of the twentieth century on the Atlantic seaboard circa 1900. It's relaxing and a very simple way to be sure your party has a great opportunity to visit some of Disney's most popular characters. Meanwhile, you will enjoy a bountiful all-you-care-to-enjoy breakfast buffet before beginning your day's activities. Cold offerings might include salami, capicola (Corsican pork cold cuts), sliced meats and cheeses, hard boiled eggs, low-fat cottage cheese, Mickey waffles, apple sauce, fresh fruit, spinach salad, yogurt with house-made granola, bagels, assorted breads, and cold cereals. Hot offerings are items such as scrambled eggs, frittatas, ham, sausages, eggs with cheese and chorizo (spicy Mexican sausage), bacon, cheddar grits, hot quinoa cereal, and biscuits with sausage gravy. In addition, you'll find many assorted freshly baked pastries. There're are "sunrise sippers" like mimosas, sparkling wine, Bloody Marys, vodka and OJ, plus coffee, tea, and lots of juices. It's such fun to get a chance to visit with the Disney characters while enjoying a delicious breakfast buffet. Prices are reasonable, and you won't leave hungry.

Contemporary Resort

Chef Mickey's Fun Time Buffet
DDP: One credit (T) / Cost: $$$ (TiW)
Type: American; Character Buffet; Breakfast, Brunch, and Dinner
Frequent Characters: Mickey, Minnie, Donald, Goofy, Pluto

Chef Mickey's is one of the most difficult dining reservations to obtain. It's always popular and competition for a table is intense. You can't walk up and expect to get in. If you hope to dine here, you must start trying as early as you possibly can. The characters will lead guests in songs and dances as the monorails speed by. Each one comes to visit at every single table.

Breakfast has a first plate course: smoked salmon, seasonal melons and other fruits, yogurt and granola, and quinoa salad. The second plate course is frittata, breakfast potatoes, pancakes, Western scramble, ham, hash, tofu/spinach scramble, biscuits and bacon or sausage. For the young and young-at-heart Mouseketeers, there's a special buffet with scrambled eggs, tater tots, sausages, and Mickey waffles. Sweets may include Krispy Kreme donut holes, Rice Krispie treats, cheese blitzes with toppings, danishes, and Minnie's muffins.

The brunch menu is more extensive, with heartier choices. To the first plate, poached shrimp cocktail and seasonal salad selections are added. To the second plate, barbecue pork ribs and baked salmon join the menu, the hash changes from turkey to corned beef, and vegetables are added. The

Mouseketeers get chicken nuggets and mac and cheese. For the sweets and treats, those are a build-your-own sundae bar, a Mickey Mousse dome (it's amazing!), assorted pastries, brownies and blondies, and chocolate chip cookies.

At dinner, the first plate is fresh mixed fruit salad, shrimp cocktail, charcuterie, and seasonal salads. The second plate is pot roast, chicken, salmon, pot stickers, breads, seasonal vegetables, vegetarian options, seafood paella, and carving stations. The children will find a buffet stocked with nuggets, tots, and mac and cheese. Sweets and treats are currently key lime and seasonal fruit tarts, seasonal bread puddings, macaroons, cheesecake tarts, the build-your-own sundae bar, and chocolate chip cookies. Four non-alcoholic specialty drinks and about twenty classic cocktails (Moscow Mule, Bahama Mama, Ultimate Long Island Iced Tea, Pimm's Punch, and Rye Manhattan, to name just a few) are available at dinner, along with the usual variety of non-alcoholic beverages.

The place will be packed, noisy, and it can sometimes feel just a bit chaotic. Some guests have complained of chicken nuggets ground into the carpet and roving bands of excited children trailing in Mickey's wake. Don't expect to savor a relaxing, quiet dinner here. It's worth asking to be seated in the main dining room where the action seems to be centered (since it's the characters you came to see, after all). Chef Mickey's is lively and exciting, the choices are plentiful, but it's always very difficult to get a table.

Pirates & Pals Fireworks Dessert Voyage

DDP: No / Cost: $$$$
Type: American; Character Experience; Snacks/dessert
Characters: Peter Pan (at the end), Captain Hook, and Mister Smee

The cost per adult is *about* $75, but this experience is in need of some serious oversight. When it happens, it's great! Lots of yummy treats for both kids and adults, fun activities like scavenger hunts, pirate songs and sea chanties, gold (chocolate) coins and prizes, and meeting the characters—all that's wonderful, *but*—and it's a BIG but—will it even happen? What does it cost right now? The official website isn't much help. Trying to find reliable and accurate information about this delightful cruise is next to impossible. One season, I called daily for two weeks trying to book and could receive no useful information whatsoever about this event. Finally, I gave up, although the grandchildren had enjoyed it tremendously the previous May. People report having booked it months in advance, only to discover at the eleventh hour that their cruise was cancelled. Someone definitely needs to take charge and either get this experience into ship-shape or cancel it. The fireworks from the boat are beautiful to see from the water. Meeting Peter Pan at the end of the voyage is a highlight. The concept is first-rate, but the devil's in the details. You can try, but don't be too disappointed if it doesn't work out. When it does, however, it's magical.

If you have no luck booking Pirates, you might consider the **Ferrytale Fireworks—A Sparkling Dessert Cruise** instead. It departs from the Transportation and Ticket Center. You enjoy some beautiful sweet treats aboard the Disney ferry boat and then watch the Happily Ever After Fireworks over the water. Costs are currently $99 for adults and $69 for children 3-9. Reservations are required. The boat departs 50 minutes prior to the fireworks. You'll also get "Mickey Vision" glasses that enhance the viewing experience.

Fort Wilderness Resort

Artist Point—Storybook Dining at Artist Point with Snow White
DDP: One credit (T) / Cost: $$$ (TiW)
Type: American; Character Dining; Dinner
Characters: Snow White, Dopey, Grumpy, and the Queen

If you have ever visited the legendary Ahwahnee Hotel in Yosemite (recently renamed the Majestic Yosemite Hotel in a trademark dispute), you'll feel right at home here. The Craftsman-style fixtures and National Park vibe are very similar. It's rustic luxury at its best. Reservations are somewhat easier to obtain than at some of the other fine/signature hotels because it's remote, so you just might be able to get into this gorgeous restaurant if the mood strikes you, particularly if you're here during the off-season. Getting here isn't easy unless you're already staying at Fort Wilderness, however.

Dine with Snow White and some of her friends (and the not-so-friendly Queen) at this charming dinner venue. Shared appetizers are currently squash bisque, wicked shrimp cocktail, and hunter's pie. Choose one from the "core of the story" entrées: cottage seafood stew, a veggie squash, arugula, a gnocchi and Parmesan dish, Magic Mirror veal shank, royal prime rib roast, brothers Grimm roasted chicken, or Bashful's butter poached snapper. Shared desserts for the table are "poison apples" (don't worry, these are darling and yummy made with white chocolate-apple mousse), "miner's treasures" (cake, chocolate gems, buttercream icing), and a few more equally intriguing... Can you bring yourself to eat a "ganache heart" from the huntsman? There are several non-alcoholic specialty drinks and some clever cocktails that will make you sit up and take notice. The Smoking Mirror really smokes! Artist Point has an impressive wine list, and you're sure to find a vintage that will leave you feeling happily ever after. This is a newer and highly entertaining character meal at Walt Disney World.

Hoop-De-Doo Musical Revue Dinner Show

DDP: Two credits (T) / Cost: $$$-$$$$ (TiW, 9:30 p.m. show only)
Type: Country/American; Dinner Show; Dinner

There is a reason for the enduring popularity of the two Disney dinner shows (the other is the Polynesian's Spirit of Aloha)—they are outstanding. Hoop-De-Doo celebrated its forty-fifth anniversary during the summer of 2019. By then, more than twelve million guests had Hoop-De-Doo'ed, and with two or three shows a night, that was more than 40,000 performances.

Most shows are sold out. Check the seating chart online at disneyworld.disney.go.com. Section three is upstairs, and there is no elevator. The chairs in section three swivel for ease of service. You get a good view of the entire restaurant and stage. Section two is on the sides and in the back of the first floor. Section one is front and center. The difference in price between section one and section three is about $8 per adult. No need to scramble for a seat, as they are all reserved beforehand.

There is a lot of audience participation—stompin' and hollerin' and the enthusiastic wavin' of napkins. Prepay at the time you make reservations. The show's location at Pioneer

Hall is not accessible by car. You must allow plenty of time to get here. It isn't easy! From the Magic Kingdom, you can catch a boat to Fort Wilderness. (If you take the bus, tack on at least fifteen or twenty extra minutes because you'll need to switch to a shuttle bus to reach Pioneer Hall.) There are songs, family-friendly jokes, corny vaudeville-type routines, and all of it delivered with a country flavor.

Speaking of country, the meal is an all-you-care-to enjoy feast of fried chicken and barbecue pork ribs, tossed green salad, baked beans, cornbread, and strawberry shortcake, but with advance notice, special dietary requests can usually be accommodated. The vast majority of guests love the whole experience. It is highly recommended, but you may have trouble getting a reservation, so book as early as you can.

Grand Floridian Resort and Spa

Disney's Perfectly Princess Tea Party
DDP: No / Cost: !!!!
Type: British/American; English-style Tea
Frequent Characters: Aurora and Rose Petal

Held in the Grand Floridian's Garden View Tea Room, this is one of the most expensive "experiences" you can provide for your little prince or princess at Walt Disney World. (Many children will come in costume, some directly from the new satellite branch of the Bibbidi Bobbidi Boutique in the Grand Floridian itself.)

Say Mom and Dad want to treat their two daughters, ages 3–9, to tea with Aurora and Rose Petal. The cost for this family of four pretty quickly reaches $666+, not including tax, for a couple of teensy-weensy pre-made sandwiches, a pot of tea for the adults (there's a charge for extra pots of tea), and a small one of apple juice for the kids, and another couple of little nibbles like a sesame cracker and grapes. (This makes Cinderella's Royal Table at $232 at the lower end to $290 at the higher end for the same family to have a luxurious, full-service, multi-course lunch or dinner look like a terrific bargain— and at least there, you meet many princesses and get an actual meal, not a skimpy snack.)

Now, to be fair, your children do get "gifts" at the tea party, gifts that you've pre-paid for handsomely. Girls receive an 18" Princess Aurora doll with accessories, a tiara, princess bracelet, princess necklace, a fresh rose, a sticker page "Best Friend" certificate for the Aurora doll, and a princess drawstring bag. Boys receive a sword and shield, souvenir pin, Disney plush toy, and "Best Friend" certificate.

How much cash, exactly, are we talking about? All this comes at a high price. The cost for one child (ages 3–9) and one adult is $334.34; there's a charge for "one adult" because you can't just drop off your kid; at least one adult is required to attend the tea party with their child. For additional children, it's $234.08 apiece, and for additional adults it's $98.66 apiece. If the adults (that's anyone over 10) in the party should want to receive the same gifts that the children receive, you'll have to fork over an additional $136.22.

Some guests rate this tea party as an outstanding value, something their children remember fondly. Others are disappointed, even horrified, at what they received for the cost. You'll have to decide if meeting Aurora (not one of the more well-known nor beloved of the royals) and Rose Petal ("a magical rose from Aurora's garden" who has somehow come to life), having a few snacks (do you and the kids even like itty-bitty chicken curry or egg salad sandwiches?), and some "gifts" are worth this kind of serious money.

In addition to the tea and snacks, there are sing-alongs, a princess parade, and storytelling by Rose Petal who acts as the hostess for the event. It's strictly your call, and your child(ren) might just love it, but by any reckoning, this tea party is one extremely expensive little cup of apple juice.

Wonderland Tea Party

DDP: No / Cost: $49 per child (ages 4-12), plus tax
Type: American; Character Tea Party
Frequent Characters: Alice and the Mad Hatter

This is a charming little hour-long tea party is for children between ages 4–12. They will have tea, aka apple juice, decorate a cupcake with sprinkles, made a craft, and have their photos taken with Alice and the Mad Hatter. Since it lasts about an hour and adults aren't included in the festivities, you might take the opportunity to have lunch or tea yourself and simply check out the beautiful grounds and exclusive, upscale shops of the Grand Floridian during that time. Some guests are concerned that the Mad Hatter might frighten their kids. If you're one of them, you might schedule the tea party toward the end of your vacation so that children are more used to the idea of costumed characters. The characters are actually so well-trained and clever (the Mad Hatter is just hilarious) that most kids have a wonderful time and soon join in the festivities wholeheartedly. At $49, this is a good value and one that comes highly recommended.

1900 Park Fare

DDP: One credit (T) / Cost: $$$ (TiW)
Type: American; Character Buffet; Breakfast, Dinner
Frequent Characters (breakfast): Mary Poppins, Winnie the Pooh, Tigger, Alice, Mad Hatter
Frequent Characters (dinner): Cinderella, the Prince, Lady Tremaine, Anastasia, and Drizella

If you weren't able to secure a table at Cinderella Castle, here's another opportunity for you to enjoy a character meal, and one that's much easier to book. No one trains its costumed characters like Disney.

At breakfast, a "veddy Brrritish" crew of characters will cheerfully pose for pictures, sign autographs, and interact with guests at every one of the tables. Each one of them makes you feel like you have their undivided attention, and they simply could not be kinder to kids and adults of all ages. Meanwhile, you and your group will be able to sit down to a delectable buffet breakfast before heading off to the parks on the monorail that stops at the hotel. The all-you-care-to-enjoy buffet will satisfy most guests. All the non-alcoholic, non-specialty beverages are included in the price. There is a yogurt station with all the trimmings as well as a bagel station with assorted cream cheese spreads. Find plenty of scrambled eggs, bacon, sausage, pancakes, Mickey waffles, French toast, cheese blintzes, hash brown casserole, smoked salmon, and lobster eggs Benedict. Recently, we enjoyed the red velvet pancakes. Oatmeal and assorted cold cereals are available, too. Look for the delicious chilled strawberry soup and fresh fruit. This is a relatively low-key, reasonably priced way to have a wonderful meal while interacting with those delightful Disney characters.

Dinner is your chance to meet the characters from Cinderella while your party sits down to a nice buffet dinner in a beautiful restaurant. It's far easier to book this reservation than Cinderella's Royal Table or Chef Mickey's. The price is reasonable for the all-you-care-to-enjoy meal. There are more than a dozen varieties of lovely salads on display. Visit the carving station for herb-crusted prime rib and the stir-fry station. You'll find more to choose from than you could possibly imagine. Look for shrimp scampi, peel-and-eat shrimp, cheese tortellini in cream sauce, BBQ pulled pork, gumbo, red beans and rice, couscous, chicken, salmon, and the list goes on and on. Watermelon soup and fresh fruit salad are frequent features at the buffet. The children's buffet is loaded with kid-friendly fare like mac and cheese, chicken drumsticks, pasta, pizza, and sides. As usual, the buffet dessert offerings are plentiful, tasty, and intended to please most guests. You'll have the chance to interact and pose for pictures with the characters, and it is highly entertaining to see them behaving just as they would in the fairy tale. Anastasia and Drizella are vivacious, amusing, and high-spirited, especially when they try to give your young Prince a "forehead curl" and ask him to be their date at the ball. Cinderella's handsome Prince might even bestow a kiss on the hand of your own little princess...swoon... It's as much fun for the adults as it is for the kids in your party!

Polynesian Village Resort

'Ohana

DDP: One credit (T) / Cost: $$$ (TiW)
Type: Polynesian/American; Unique/Themed; Breakfast (Character) and Dinner
Frequent Characters (breakfast): Lilo, Stitch, Pluto, Mickey

The restaurant calls to mind a tropical paradise with lots of carved Tikis and sea creatures suspended overhead. Look for 'Ohana on the upper floor of the resort's main lobby. It's a gorgeous venue and a pleasure for all ages.

The Best Friends Character Breakfast is all-you-care-to-enjoy. Service here is usually (but not always) attentive, and you won't often have to wait long for refills. Juice and coffee come for the table, followed by family-style platters of scrambled eggs, bacon or sausage, Hawaiian-style ham, potatoes, and sweet pineapple/assorted breakfast breads, Mickey waffles (last season we had Stitch waffles, too), and fresh fruit. It would be pretty difficult to get it wrong, and most guests are very pleased with the 'Ohana breakfast. The characters come to every table to pose for pictures and sign autographs. They are friendly, funny, and so very accommodating. It's a delightful meal with plenty of good food and good times. Don't be late to your assigned time! You'll be sorry if you are. Who knows when you can next be seated? You want to get to the parks at a reasonably early time, not be stuck cooling your heels in the Polynesian lobby. It's on the monorail, so getting to the park is easy after you eat.

Dinner has no characters, which is too bad because they always add such fun to breakfast. Reviews are mixed at dinner, as is usual for any restaurant, but there are far more happy diners than disgruntled ones. If you are unhappy with your server or some aspect of your meal, politely alert management right away. Don't let it spoil what ought to be a wonderful experience for your party. At dinner, delicious pineapple bread and salad come out first. Chicken wings and pork dumplings are the appetizers. Skewers of chicken, steak, and spicy shrimp roasted over a tremendously huge pit are next. The steak seems to be the source of some complaints. Advise your server clearly about your preferences for doneness. Noodles and veggies are accompaniments. Rave reviews are garnered for the dessert, which is warm bread pudding à la mode with bananas and caramel sauce. Save room!

Disney's Spirit of Aloha Dinner Show

DDP: Two credits (T) / Cost: $$$$ (TiW, late show only)
Type: Polynesian/American; Dinner Show; Dinner

The Spirit of Aloha is performed in a covered but open-air theatre in Luau Cove. If it is considered too cold or too rainy for comfort, the show can be cancelled at the last minute. As with all of the dinner shows, you pay in advance for your meal.

There are three categories of seating. Check online at disney-world.disney.go.com to familiarize yourself with them. Category 3 is on the upper floor and also at the far left and right sides of the main floor. Category 2 is on the sides of the main floor and at the center of the upper floor. Category 1 is front and center of the main floor. The difference in price between an adult sitting in Category 3 vs. Category 1 is about $12. Some guests complain that posts can obscure the view, so be clear about your expectations when booking your reservations.

The lively show includes hula dancing, fire dancing, and dances from Tahiti, Hawaii, Samoa, Tonga, and New Zealand. Food is somewhat more upscale than at the Hoop-De-Doo, but you are really paying for the show, not the food. Getting here is far easier than getting to Snow White's dinner shindig over at Fort Wilderness. The Polynesian is accessible by car, bus, or monorail, and even on foot from the Transportation and Ticket Center.

Dinner includes a fresh, green salad with ginger-lime dressing, platters of pulled pork, beef ribs, roasted chicken, and a vegetable medley. Children can order entrées such as mini corn dogs and tater tots, cheese pizza, grilled fish, or grilled chicken with rice and green beans. Unlimited beverages include Coke products, coffee, lemonade, beer, and wine. There are also fruity, specialty cocktails served in souvenir carved coconuts—those cost extra. The dinner ends with pineapple-coconut guava cake with chocolate crunch.

The show is highly enjoyable, especially for children, and you'll find many families in attendance. Guests enjoy the traditional dancing, but some folks rate the show's story plot as a little "corny." The Spirit of Aloha remains an extremely popular show and the all-you-care-to-enjoy dinner is tasty and filling.

There you have it, Disney World's dinner shows and resort hotel character meals. Every one of them has something special to recommend it. You just have to decide what's the best choice for you and your family. None of them are inexpensive, but some are far more costly than others. Regardless of your choices, you're sure to enjoy your vacation if you put some time and effort into planning.

Now that we've completed our dining tour of all four theme parks, the BoardWalk, Disney Springs, the most notable of the resort hotel restaurants, the dinner shows, and the hotel character meals, it's time to let you in on a few tricks. The last chapter is filled with tried-and-true tips for getting those very difficult to obtain advanced dining reservations. Follow this advice and you'll vastly improve your chances for making magical vacation memories to last a lifetime. This is the way my family and I book our advance dining reservations, and believe me, it works! We always get the ADRs we want, and you can, too!

Getting Hard–to–Get Advanced Dining Reservations

Twelve Tremendous Tips

Tremendous Tip #1

When making ADRs on your assigned Booking Day every single minute counts! Once the available booking slots have all been filled, you're out of luck. Therefore, have two (or more) adult members in your party ready to go on two (or more) separate computers (or iPhones or iPads) at 5:45 a.m. Orlando time on the very first day you are allowed to make your advance dining reservations. You will each need separate login names and passwords, too. Become familiar with how the system works well before the booking day actually arrives. Both of you should already have your Magic Your Way reservation number, your credit card data, and all relevant information already loaded and on file so that when the clock strikes 6:00 a.m., you can begin working simultaneously on securing your dining reservations. You take half, and let your partner take the other half. You'll double your chances of success. Practice makes perfect, so practice, practice, and practice some more before your special morning arrives. That's not the time to fumble around looking for information. Read this tip again before you are ready to make your reservations.

Tremendous Tip #2

If you've booked a Magic Your Way package, you can actually make those ridiculously hard-to-get Advance Dining Reservations up to 190 days (instead of the usual 180 days) ahead of your trip, assuming you're staying in a Disney accommodation for ten days. Sometimes, you will see this "loophole" referred to as 180+10. If you're staying at the resort for seven days, then you can book dining reservations 187 days in advance, etc. That way, you can reserve Cinderella's Royal Table or a meal at Chef Mickey's at the end of your trip and get up to a ten-day jump on the rest of the public who will be madly scrambling to secure a table 180 days ahead of their trip. It is well worth remembering this!

Tremendous Tip #3

Book as many Advance Dining Reservations as you think you might possibly need. You can always cancel 24 hours ahead of time, but trying to book something "hot" at the last minute is extremely difficult if not downright impossible and frustrating. (Just be sure you don't forget to cancel the ones you don't plan to use 24 hours before they're due or you'll be charged $10 per person in your party.) As your mother probably told you, it's better to have it and not need it than to need it and not have it!

Tremendous Tip #4

Checking online and by phone 24 hours ahead of when you want to dine at a hard-to-schedule restaurant just *might* get you in. Remember that $10 per person cancellation fee if you miss the 24-hour cancellation deadline? Guests whose plans have changed at the last minute or who've decided they no longer want a reservation they made months before will be cancelling their advance dining reservations a day ahead of time to avoid paying that fee. Sometimes, getting the reservation another guest just released simply comes down to luck. Good luck!

Tremendous Tip #5

Guests who need to cancel their entire Walt Disney World package have up to forty-five days before arriving to do so without a financial penalty. You should try checking 45 days before you are due to arrive to see if anything you wanted (but didn't get) in the way of dining reservations might have opened up.

Tremendous Tip #6

As a last resort, try to book an ADR on the same day you want to dine at a particular restaurant. This is definitely a hit-or-miss strategy, mostly miss, but every once in a while, you'll get lucky and score that table at the last minute because someone else's plans unavoidably changed and they weren't able to cancel 24 hours before. While you are standing in line waiting to board an attraction, that's the perfect time to repeatedly dial and redial the restaurant you hoped to visit if you were unable to secure a reservation there earlier. Tables do occasionally open up at the last minute, for a variety of reasons. As a very last resort, try walking up to the host/hostess on duty and asking very politely for a table. Smile! It really does help. If you don't get what you want, be nice to the cast member anyway.

Tremendous Tip #7

Prioritize your picks! The most difficult dining reservations to book are those at the character meals (Cinderella's Royal Table, Chef Mickey's, 'Ohana, the Crystal Palace, etc.), the dinner shows (Hoop-De-Doo Musical Revue or the Spirit of Aloha), places to dine at Epcot with good views of the nightly fireworks show such as the Rose and Crown or La Hacienda de San Angel, the ones at the Magic Kingdom with views of Happily Ever After fireworks like the California Grill and Narcoossee's, hugely popular restaurants like Canada's Le Cellier Steakhouse, Be Our Guest at the Magic Kingdom, and Victoria & Albert's at the Grand Floridian. Decide which dining experiences are most important ones for you and your family and rank them in order.

Tremendous Tip #8

Use the "Wish List" function (again, well before your Booking Day arrives) on My Disney Experience (the special area of of the Walt Disney World website where guests are able to view and manage their reservations and vacation packages) and add the most important restaurants where you want to dine to create your own Wish List. Then, when you are ready to make your dining reservations 190 days ahead of time (or 189 if you are staying at the resort for nine days, 188 days if you are staying eight days, 187 if you're staying a week, etc.), that quick link will save you precious moments. Don't waste even a second trying to type in the restaurants/character meals/dinner shows you want during your golden window of opportunity. It will take too much time. That window snaps shut very quickly. Once it's closed, you will just have to try some of the other tips to get advance dining reservations.

Tremendous Tip #9

Type in the most important dining reservation before 6:00 a.m. on the very first day you are allowed to book. If you and another adult in the party are dividing up the critical reservations into smaller, more manageable chunks, so much the better. It will increase your chances of getting what you want. Key in your highest priority reservation at 5:45 a.m. and the website will say something like "you cannot make your reservation at this time," and that's true, but as soon as 6:00 a.m. rolls around, all you have to do is hit "submit." Suddenly, your chances of dining with Cinderella are looking a lot more rosy. If you feel you just can't work this online feature, you'll simply have to wait until 7:00 a.m. Orlando time to book by telephone at 1-800-WDW-DINE. By that time, faster fingers will have grabbed most—if not all—of the most coveted spots and times. It might be worth asking a techie friend, or maybe a friend's computer-savvy son or daughter, to walk you though the process so you'll feel confident and prepared.

Tremendous Tip #10

Book breakfast as early as possible near the most popular attractions in the parks to avoid long waits. It can save you the use of a FastPass+. This doesn't work for every park, but if you can get a jump on the rest of the guests who will be still waiting for the gates to open, so much the better. Be ready to finish your meal rapidly and head for the queues as soon as you possibly can. For example, dine at Be Our Guest at 8:00 a.m. Then, eat and immediately afterward head to the Seven Dwarfs Mine Train or Peter Pan—two of the busiest attractions in Fantasyland. Breakfast at Tusker House in the Animal Kingdom gets you out on a safari early. Breakfast at Hollywood and Vine in the Hollywood Studios at 8:00 might save a long wait at Rock 'n' Roller Coaster or the Twilight Zone Tower of Terror if you can get in and out quickly, but it's not very close to either of them (they are over on Sunset Boulevard)—and sometimes the entrance rope drops earlier than advertised at Hollywood Studios, letting guests in ahead of the announced time. In addition, guests have complained that even with 8:00 a.m. reservations, they weren't seated until as late as 8:40 AM, which entirely defeats the purpose of getting there early.

Tremendous Tip #11

A somewhat less scrupulous but nonetheless effective tip? If you're a couple, a party of two, it's a lot harder to score in-demand reservations, since most Disney restaurants have far fewer "tables for two" than they do family-sized tables for four. Therefore, if you indicate on the reservation app that you're a party of two, you're at an immediate disadvantage. If, instead, you try to book a reservation for three, Disney will open up the family-sized queue and you'll stand a better chance of getting the reservation. The unscrupulous part? When you get to the restaurant, you have to tell them at check-in that the third person in your party couldn't make it. They'll still seat you at a table for four, unless a table for two has magically popped up in the meantime. While it's probably not the best way to start your meal, it just might work for you in a pinch—especially if you're desperate.

Tremendous Tip #12

Go in person to the concierge at a deluxe resort hotel and ask for a reservation if none are available online or by phone. Cancellations are often "corralled" in the system expressly for concierge use (not for more than a few hours) before they're released into the general queue. Needless to say, be as polite and grateful as possible. The concierge is doing you a substantial favor. Remember when Grandma said you'd catch more flies with honey than with vinegar? Your attitude and demeanor do matter. Again, if you don't get what you hoped for, be nice anyway.

One final thing to clearly understand about your advance dining reservations: a table is not going to be held empty awaiting your arrival. This fact is the source of much disappointment and unhappiness on the part of guests. Your reservation only entitles you to the next available table. If people are slow to vacate, you'll be left cooling your heels. No, it's not the way most reservations work anywhere else in the country, but it's the way reservations work at Walt Disney World. There is no way around this policy, so bear it in mind. Yours should be the group that arrives several minutes earlier than your actual reservation time.

Bon appétit, buen provecho, gutten Appetit, velbekomme, selamat makan, buon apetito, smaklig måltid, and be sure to enjoy every meal while you're at Walt Disney World!

Acknowledgments

Thanks to my family for their love and support. Ron remains in our hearts and greatly missed by us all. A professorship in pediatric ocular genetics has been endowed in his name at the University of Iowa Hospitals and Clinics where Ron was an eye surgeon and professor of medicine for 22 years. While I was a Tour Guide and VIP Hostess at Disneyland, we spent many happy Friday "Date Nites" there. Daughter Elizabeth worked at Disneyland in one of the first classes of women to pilot the submarines and later at Walt Disney World on the Skyway. Liz and her brilliant husband, Amos, a former cast member on It's a Small World, met working in the College Program at Disneyland. Their daughter, Katherine, is now twelve, and son, Drew, is nine. Rob and his lovely wife, Catherine, are fond parents to William, now three, and Lucy, not quite one. We've shared a great many memorable times at Disneyland, Walt Disney World, and on the Disney Magic cruise. Maybe one day, if they are lucky, the children will become third generation cast members.

Big hugs and much appreciation are sent to very dear friends Anne, Cathy, Della, Linda, Meg, and Renee who are so important in my life, and to delightful Book Club friends Becky, Dell, Jane, Margaret, Sheral, and Wendy—who was both Chip *and* Dale at Walt Disney World. Each one of these bright, kind, and lovely ladies provide me with a never-ending source of inspiration and delight, not to mention lots of laughs!

Finally, special thanks to Bob McLain, editor of Theme Park Press. Bob is an excellent editor, a provider of good ideas, and the inexhaustible curator of all things Disney. Bob knows just about everything worth knowing about the subject, and I'm happy to say this is the ninth book he has edited for me.

Index

About the Author

Andrea McGann Keech was born in Southern California and visited Disneyland often, ever since the summer it opened in 1955. She fulfilled a life-long dream by working at the park when she became a bilingual Tour Guide and VIP Hostess during college from 1969 through 1972, experiences fondly chronicled in her first book *The Cream of the Crop: Tour Guide Tales from Disneyland's Golden Years* (Theme Park Press, 2016).

After graduating, Andrea taught students in English and Spanish in grades K-12 during her teaching career. She was a member of the National Assessment of Educational Progress Committee that established Writing Standards, 2011–2018, for students in grades 3–12. She has written for a variety of national educational journals and presented at many teaching conferences.

She lives in Iowa City with Shadow and Sunny, a pair of boisterous standard poodles. After school, she plays Mary Poppins to beloved grandchildren, Katherine and Drew, and spends as much time as possible with joyful Will and baby Lucy, her newest grandchild. For the past few years, she has begun painting under the helpful tutelage of artist Lianne Westcott and is enjoying it tremendously.

Other Disney titles for Theme Park Press are *The Indulgent Grandparent's Guide to Walt Disney World; Treasure of the Ten Tags: A Disneyland Adventure; Walt Disney World Characters 101: Your Complete Guide to Perfect Meet-and-Greets; A Mouse for All Seasons: Your Month-by-Month Guide to Walt Disney World; 50 Fun, Fabulous Foods at Disney Theme Parks;* and *The Disneyland Resort Dining Guide 2020.*

ABOUT THEME PARK PRESS

Theme Park Press publishes books primarily about the Disney company, its history, culture, films, animation, and theme parks, as well as theme parks in general.

Our authors include noted historians, animators, Imagineers, and experts in the theme park industry.

We also publish many books by first-time authors, with topics ranging from fiction to theme park guides.

And we're always looking for new talent. If you'd like to write for us, or if you're interested in the many other titles in our catalog, please visit:

www.ThemeParkPress.com

....

Theme Park Press Newsletter

Subscribe to our free email newsletter and enjoy:

- ◆ Free book downloads and giveaways
- ◆ Access to excerpts from our many books
- ◆ Announcements of forthcoming releases
- ◆ Exclusive additional content and chapters
- ◆ And more good stuff available nowhere else

To subscribe, visit www.ThemeParkPress.com, or send email to newsletter@themeparkpress.com.

50 FUN, FABULOUS FOODS AT DISNEY THEME PARKS

A Gourmand's Guide to the Magic

Andrea McGann Keech

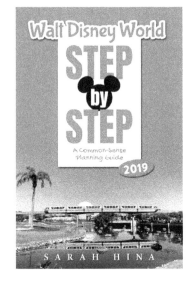

Walt Disney World STEP by STEP

A Common-Sense Planning Guide

2019

SARAH HINA

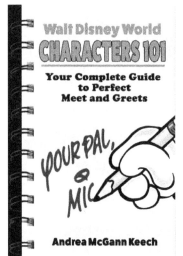

Walt Disney World CHARACTERS 101

Your Complete Guide to Perfect Meet and Greets

YOUR PAL, MIC

Andrea McGann Keech

The Unofficial Walt Disney World Drinking Companion

Christopher Schmidt

Read more about these books
and our many other titles at:

www.ThemeParkPress.com

CPSIA information can be obtained
at www.ICGtesting.com
Printed in the USA
LVHW031601060919
630200LV00010B/973/P